Urban Green

# Urban Green

## *Nature, Recreation, and the Working Class in Industrial Chicago*

Colin Fisher

The University of North Carolina Press CHAPEL HILL

Published with the assistance of the Authors Fund of the University of
North Carolina Press.

Set in Espinosa Nova by Westchester Publishing Services
Manufactured in the United States of America

The paper in this book meets the guidelines for permanence and durability
of the Committee on Production Guidelines for Book Longevity of the
Council on Library Resources. The University of North Carolina Press
has been a member of the Green Press Initiative since 2003.

Cover illustration: "Crowd of bathers on the Lake Michigan beach, ca. 1925."
U.S. National Archives & Records Administration, 535893.

Library of Congress Cataloging-in-Publication Data

Fisher, Colin (Robert Colin)
    Urban green : nature, recreation, and the working class in industrial Chicago /
Colin Fisher.
        pages cm
    Includes bibliographical references and index.
    ISBN 978-1-4696-1995-8 (pbk : alk. paper) — ISBN 978-1-4696-1996-5 (ebook)
    1. Leisure—Illinois—Chicago—History.   2. Nature—Social aspects—Illinois—Chicago—
History.   3. Parks—Social aspects—Illinois—Chicago—History.   4. Outdoor recreation—
Illinois—Chicago—History.   5. Working class—Illinois—Chicago—History.
6. Immigrants—Illinois—Chicago—History.   7. Urban ecology—Illinois—Chicago—
History.   I. Title.
    GV54.I3C546 2015
    790.109773'11—dc23
                                                                                    2014034901

A version of chapter 4 appeared in *To Love the Wind and Rain*, edited by Dianne Glove
and Mark Stoll (University of Pittsburgh Press). Used with permission.

THIS BOOK WAS DIGITALLY PRINTED.

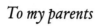

*To my parents*

# Contents

# Figures and Maps

# Acknowledgments

From outward appearance, historians cut solitary figures. We spend countless hours deep in the archives studying evidence left by the dead. When we reemerge, we spend even more time sitting alone at our desks quietly organizing data, writing, editing, and rewriting. Unlike our more collaborative colleagues in other fields, the vast majority of historians embrace the single-author model, so in the end, it is almost always one name that appears on the dust jacket. But all of this obscures the fact that good history is always the product of a rich social context. All so-called single-author books are in fact coproduced and coauthored by dozens and dozens of people behind the scenes. This book is no different.

I incurred debts even before I wrote the first word of *Urban Green*. This book would have been impossible without the aid of a number of excellent teachers, first at Lawrence University and then later at the University of California–Irvine. In particular, I want to acknowledge Dickson Bruce, Karen Carr, Paul Cohen, Nina Dayton, Frank Doeringer, Alice Fahs, Bob Moeller, Ken Pomerantz, Mark Poster, Dave Rankin, Anne Schutte, Amy Dru Stanley, Sally Stein, Tanis Thorne, Steven Topik, and Jon Wiener. As is often the case, I learned just as much from my fellow graduate students as I did from my formal classes. In particular, I would like to thank Jem Axelrod, Stan Beyer, Ian Carter, Pete Catapano, Rob Cerniglia, Brian Crawford, Mary Joyce, Kyle Julien, Doug Sackman, Raj Sampath, and Jennifer Steenshorne.

From inception to conclusion, colleagues generously listened to my sometimes-inchoate ideas, read drafts, offered constructive criticism, pointed me in new directions, and shared tips on using Chicago's rich archival resources. In particular, I want to thank: Peter Alter, Peter Baldwin, Scott Bucking, Mike Davis, Sarah Elkind, Karen Flint, Dianne Glave, David Hoyt, Bob Johnson, Matthew Klingle, Patricia Limerick, Kathryn Morse, Donald Mrozek, Dominic Pacyga, Tracy Poe, James Ralph, Mart Stewart, Margaret Storey, Jeffrey Stine, Mark Stoll, Terence Young, and Louis Warren. In addition, I would like to thank two student research assistants: Mychal Odom and Keith Albrandt.

A number of institutions also supported my work. The American Historical Association, the Smithsonian Institution, Middlebury College, and the University of San Diego all gave grants that underwrote various phases of my research and writing. I would also like to thank staff at the following archives: the Chicago Historical Society, Special Collections at the University of Chicago, the University of Illinois at Chicago, and the Harold Washington, Carter Woodson, and Sultzer branches of the Chicago Public Library system.

I also owe a debt to the University of North Carolina Press and in particular Mark Simpson-Vos for taking a bet on an unorthodox project that many cultural historians saw as too environmental and many environmental historians dismissed as too cultural. Mark, Brandon Proia, Katherine Fisher, Paul Betz, and my two peer reviewers (Andrew J. Diamond and an anonymous environmental historian) made this a much better book, and I appreciate all their labor.

Special thanks goes out to my home university, the University of San Diego. Not only has USD paid me to teach subjects that interest me and underwritten much of the research for this book, it brought me into contact with a wonderful group of supportive and stimulating scholars. Special thanks go to my colleagues in the history department (Tom Barton, Jonathan Conant, Iris Engstrand, Ali Gheissari, Michael Gonzalez, Jim Gump, Cecily Heisser, Sarah Levin-Richardson, Molly McClain, David Miller, Clara Oberle, Ken Serbin, Kathryn Statler, Andy Strathman, and Yi Sun) as well as Can Bilsel, Jonathan Bowman, Michelle Camacho, Esteban Del Rio, Halina Duraj, Kevin Guerrieri, Michelle Jacob, Alejandro Meter, Juliana Maxim, Drew Talley, Mike Williams, among many others. It's a pleasure working with you all.

This book also would never have come to completion without a circle of wonderful friends and family members who sustained me, tolerated my ups and downs, and gave me their love and support. In addition to many of the previously mentioned scholars, thanks go to John Carey and Vicki Arroyo, Gary Castaneda, Bill and Lyn Edmunds, the Lou family (Debbie, Michelle, Bob, and Mike), Karina Morales, Frank Nobiletti, Todd Olsen and Sarah Hruska, Jim and Carrie Olson, Caroline Schaumann and Bruce Wiley, Neil Soderstrom, Michael Tompkins, Richard Westberg, Kyla Winters, and Jen Boots (and Wyatt!). John, Reenie, and Steve Ruckdaeschel, Ana Bedard, and David Hoyt and Debbie Wong are not only friends, but they also kindly let me couch surf during my many Chicago research trips.

My biggest debt goes, of course, to my family: the Bay Area Fishers (Susan, Matt, Jonny, Fred, and Sep Ghadishah); the Sarffs (Jeff, Nancy, Todd, and Peter); my brother Gavin and his wife Felicia; my mother Jennifer Sarff (who not only gave me her love during this journey, but also drafted the maps within this book); my loving, generous stepmother Carol Fisher; and my father, Jonathan Fisher—former editor of *International Wildlife Magazine*, sculptor, and tireless reader of his son's many, many drafts. Thank you!

Urban Green

# Introduction

## *The Lithuanian Worker and the Lake Michigan Dunes*

> Everybody needs beauty as well as bread, places to play in
> and pray in, where Nature may heal and cheer and give strength
> to body and soul alike. This natural beauty-hunger is made
> manifest in the little window-sill gardens of the poor,
> though perhaps only a geranium slip in a broken cup.
>
> —JOHN MUIR, *The Yosemite*, 1912

On October 30, 1916, Stephen T. Mather, head of the just-created U.S. National Park Service, convened a hearing at the Chicago Federal Building on a proposal to create a new national park forty miles southeast of the city. The proposed reserve, the Sand Dunes National Park, featured massive wind-blown mounds of sand along the southern Lake Michigan shore. The Indiana dune area also included forests, marshes, oak savannas, prairies, and an extraordinarily rich diversity of plant life, so much so that the area became the outdoor laboratory of Henry Cowles, the American founder of plant ecology.[1]

Speakers at the hearing gave a number of reasons for preserving the dunes and creating a national park. Some testified that the nation's rapidly growing system of national parks underserved the Midwest, and that people there needed a signature wilderness park where they could come into direct contact with the nation's frontier past. Others explained that this unique indigenous Indiana wilderness inspired artists, musicians, and painters and served as a vital laboratory for scientists such as Cowles. Speakers also made it clear that the new national park would serve the exploding immigrant and working-class population of nearby Chicago. Contact with the dunes would restore and renew the tired industrial workers who toiled at monotonous jobs, serve as an alternative to unhealthy urban amusements, and Americanize the foreign born.[2]

T. W. Allinson of the Prairie Club (the Midwest analog of the Sierra Club and the Appalachian Trail Club) rose and spoke directly to this last issue. Chicago's poor, he told those gathered, needed not only food, shelter, and clothing but also outdoor recreation in a wilderness area such as the dunes, a place where they could "refresh the eyes and breathe pure air into the lungs" and "test disused muscles." To demonstrate the powerful effect of nature on the poor, he explained how he had taken two Lithuanian workers from Chicago out to the dunes to help build a home for sick children. After seeing Lake Michigan and the dunes, "the first thing one of those men did . . . was to drop his tools, stretch open his arms, look around and up to heaven, take a deep breath, and say, 'Just like Lithuania.'" Those in the hearing room laughed and applauded.[3]

This book does not focus on the historical experience of Mather, Allinson, members of the Prairie Club, or Anglo American nature tourists. The story of these privileged nature lovers has already been well chronicled. Instead my interest is in that unnamed Lithuanian worker and others like him: hundreds of thousands of newly arrived immigrants, their American-born children, African Americans, and industrial workers. I argue that during their scant leisure, large numbers of marginalized Chicagoans sought to escape what they saw as an artificial urban environment and come into contact with nature. Like more established Chicagoans, my subjects sought nature in rural and wild landscapes in what environmental historian William Cronon calls Chicago's recreational hinterland. But they also found nature much closer to home: at urban beaches, breakwaters, and piers along the Lake Michigan shore; along the banks of canals and polluted urban rivers; in the city's extraordinary public parks; in commercial groves, beer gardens, and cemeteries; in vacant lots and industrial yards; and even in sidewalk cracks, back alleys, and tenement rooftops. Furthermore, I argue that marginalized Chicagoans often made places they saw as green into important sites for forging community identity. While the privileged used rural and wild landscapes to imagine themselves as Americans, Chicago's rank and file made their green spaces into places to imagine themselves as Germans, Irish, Polish, and Mexican, as ethnic Americans, as Americans of African descent, as American industrial workers, and as members of a revolutionary international proletariat.[4]

One objective of this book is to contribute to scholarship in environmental history, in particular work on leisure in nature. Environmental historians have long explored this topic. It was in fact the subject of the field's first big book, Roderick Nash's *Wilderness and the American Mind* (1967).

Drawing on previous scholarship in the field of American studies (such as Henry Nash Smith's *Virgin Land*, Perry Miller's *Errand into the Wilderness*, Hans Huth's *Nature and the American*, and Leo Marx's *The Machine in the Garden*), Nash argued that wilderness was the key to unlocking American culture or identity. The heroes in Nash's account were far-thinking individuals (such as Henry David Thoreau, John Muir, and Teddy Roosevelt) who fundamentally reoriented American culture by convincing their compatriots not to fear or hate wilderness but to love it. According to Nash, these pioneering romantics were so successful at sparking recreational interest in wilderness that by the 1950s and 1960s, middle-class tourists threatened to love the wilderness to death.[5]

Starting in the 1990s, environmental historians began taking a far more critical view of recreation in nature. First, scholars documented how the creation of landscapes of leisure (such as Yellowstone National Park) often entailed the removal or eviction of Native Americans and working-class people who had long used the land for sustenance and work. Second, they showed that once established, wilderness parks and other places of seemingly uncontaminated nature often served as a "landscape of authenticity" where elite tourists naturalized or reified masculinity, national identity, and race. Lastly, historians argued that when we view nature as a mere tourist destination, as a sacred place that we only visit during our leisure, we forget the nature in our own backyard as well as our quotidian relationships with ecosystems when we eat, use water, fill up our gas tank, flush the toilet, make consumer purchases, or go to work. For these authors, fetishizing Yellowstone's seemingly pristine wilderness and making it the only nature that counts is actually a significant impediment to responsible environmentalism.[6]

In both Nash's account and in more recent revisionist scholarship on "the trouble with wilderness," the presumption is that while the privileged knew nature through leisure, the marginalized knew nature almost exclusively through work. Even urban environmental historians inspired by the environmental justice movement pay very little attention to working class or minority outdoor recreation. Their focus is fixed on how their subjects lost access to natural resources, such as estuaries and other urban food production sites, which were often transformed into middle-class recreational amenities. At the same time, these historians of urban environmental inequalities chronicle how their subjects were disproportionately exposed to environmental hazards (toxic industries, dumps, incinerators, and the effects of natural disasters) where they lived, worked, and to a much lesser extent played.[7]

The false premise that only the privileged knew nature through leisure has obscured an important history of outdoor recreation "from the bottom up." In order to tell this story well, we cannot simply chronicle environmental victimization and then document the political response to that victimization. Rather, we need to start with the marginalized themselves and stress their agency, creativity, and adaptability, even in the face of significant limitations. We will see that like well-off Americans, they too frequently viewed recreation in nature (including the wilderness) as a vital antidote to life and work in the "artificial" city. They too indulged in nature romanticism or pastoralism and made preindustrial landscapes the touchstones of distinct national, ethnic, racial, gendered, and class-based identities. To gloss the structuralist anthropologist Claude Lévi-Strauss, we know already that the poor used nature to eat, but we are only starting to grasp that that they also used nature to think. We need to pay more attention to that Lithuanian who looked past the Indiana Dunes and out onto Lake Michigan and remembered his distant Baltic homeland. We need to recognize that places such as Chicago were home to *cultures* of nature. If we do this (and a number of my colleagues already are), we can contribute to a more nuanced understanding of the relationship between marginalized people and nature over time. At the same time, we can build new bridges between environmental history and labor, ethnic, and immigration history, all fields that insist on foregrounding the historical agency of the marginalized and all fields deeply interested in the social construction of subaltern identities.[8]

Another objective of this book is to contribute to social history, a field that in contrast to environmental history has long taken immigrant, African American, and working-class leisure seriously. Starting in the 1970s, social historians began to recognize that workers' leisure was a critical but traditionally overlooked arena of working-class resistance. Initially scholars focused on vestiges of premodern European and African popular or folk culture and dismissed commercialized leisure or "mass culture" as false consciousness. But in the late 1980s and 1990s, historians such as Kathy Peiss, Lizabeth Cohen, and George Lipsitz challenged this assumption and showed that working-class women and men frequently co-opted leisure forms and venues that were not of their own making.[9]

Scholars such as Peiss, Cohen, and Lipsitz typically focused on commercialized amusements (saloons, movies, dance halls, amusement parks, professional sports, radio, and television), but some explored working-class use of public parks. None of these scholars was more influential than the late Roy Rosenzweig. In *Eight Hours for What We Will: Workers and Leisure in an Industrial City, 1870–1920* (1983) and *The Park and the People: A History of Central Park* (1992) (with Elizabeth Blackmar), Rosenzweig challenged those who saw urban parks as institutions of social control. He acknowledged top-down coercion, but he focused most of his attention on documenting the creative ways that marginalized Americans appropriated parks and put these landscapes to very different uses than landscape architects, reformers, and politicians had intended.[10]

*The Park and the People* (as well as other scholarship on urban parks and working-class leisure) has profoundly shaped my own thinking. But from the perspective of an environmental historian, one significant problem with these social histories is that they fail to account for working-class desire for nature. Rosenzweig and Blackmar argue that Anglo American park builders such as Frederick Law Olmsted viewed Central Park as a rural retreat from the artificial city, whereas average New Yorkers saw the park differently, as an extension of the city rather than its antipode. Rather than an oasis of green in the midst of an unnatural city, New Yorkers viewed their park as a public or recreational space for a wide array of working-class and ethnic sports and leisure practices. "Sadly for Olmsted," the historians argue, "most New Yorkers did not share his vision of the park as a tranquil retreat from the city."[11]

It is certainly true that Anglo Americans of Olmsted's class and rank-and-file Chicagoans fought over park space. Established Americans especially did not like boisterous picnics, athletics, concerts, and especially drinking on Sunday, the Christian Sabbath. But just because Chicagoans rejected idiosyncratic Anglo American outdoor recreational practices (such as carriage rides or quietly absorbing the pastoral, picturesque, and sublime) does not mean that the fight over parks was one that pitted nature-loving Anglo Americans such as Olmsted against amusement- or sport-loving immigrants and workers. Certainly some Chicagoans (including some elite Anglo Americans) viewed city parks as an extension of the city rather than a retreat from urban life. They merely wanted space for socializing, sports, and other leisure practices, and a plaza devoid of trees or any non-human life would suit them fine. But a surprisingly large number of people sought out not only social, recreational, or public spaces, but also urban green places where they could escape "artificial" urban environments. Furthermore, when Chicagoans had access to affordable transportation, large numbers fled to city for ethnic, working-class, and African American resorts as well as wilderness parks, such as the Cook County forest preserves and the Indiana dunes. In other words, my subjects knew nature through leisure.[12]

Late nineteenth- and early twentieth-century Chicago is an ideal laboratory for this study. During this period, the city industrialized rapidly, attracted people from throughout the United States and from around the world, and grew into one of the world's largest and most cosmopolitan cities. This diversity allows us to look at how a spectrum of migrant communities knew nature through leisure and also the ways that people of diverse origins made landscape into a site for the formation of new and unexpected urban communities. Another advantage of using Chicago as a case study is that the city's social history is very well documented. During the early twentieth century, the University of Chicago was the birthplace of American sociology, and professors and their students made the city and its inhabitants their scholarly preoccupation. At the same time, city archivists over the years have worked hard to preserve working-class and immigrant primary sources. In turn, historians of the city have used these sources to create a rich, deep, and provocative secondary literature. In these regards Chicago is distinctive, but I think it is also the case that similar conclusions about marginalized people and nature could be reached by looking at data from other U.S. and non-U.S. cities.

Although this book has a chronological arc, the chapters themselves are thematic. In chapter 1, I introduce readers to the places where my subjects often found nature. As we will see, like affluent Anglo Americans, some immigrants, ethnic Americans, African Americans, and industrial workers sought out nature in rural resorts and wilderness parks outside the physical parameters of the city. But most found nature near or even within some of the most polluted industrial neighborhoods on the planet. Subsequent chapters focus on overlapping groups within Chicago: recent immigrants, their American-born children, African Americans, and industrial workers. In each case, we follow Chicagoans out of the city and back to nature and explore how they used landscape to culturally construct Irish, German, Mexican, American ethnic, race-based, neighborhood, or working-class identities.

## CHAPTER ONE

# Where Chicagoans Found Nature

## *An Expedition with Leonard Dubkin, Urban Ranger*

> The common weeds, in spite of man's militant opposition,
> survive and flourish everywhere.... As an example of the hardy,
> well-adjusted weed, take the dandelion. Through the years man
> has fought this weed with every resource known to science, and
> he has succeeded in keeping it out of cultivated areas only with
> much effort and a great deal of expense. The dandelion grows
> everywhere, in city lawns and parks and yards, in country fields
> and meadows and swamps, on mountainsides and on the edge of
> deserts. It is probably as perfect, as well-integrated, as sensitive
> and as "intelligent" a plant as can be found anywhere in the
> world.... A single dandelion flower is to me, not for what it is
> in itself, or in competition with other, more lavish blooms, but
> for what it represents, for the vitality, the toughness, and the
> logical balance that went into its production, the most beautiful
> of all flowers.
>
> —LEONARD DUBKIN, *Enchanted Streets: The Unlikely Adventures
> of an Urban Nature Lover*, 1947

During their summer vacations, tens of thousands of turn-of-the-century
Chicagoans left their "artificial" city and traveled into what William Cronon
calls the recreational hinterland: scenic areas of Wisconsin, Illinois,
Indiana, and Michigan; and national parks, such as Yellowstone. In such
faraway places, many felt that they could escape the work, exhaustion,
illness, and artifice they associated with Chicago and come into contact
with the restorative power of nature.[1]

Marginalized Chicagoans—Germans, Irish, Poles, African Americans,
groups of working-class neighborhood youth, and trade unionists—also
made this leisure-time exodus out of the city and back to nature, especially
as transportation costs fell during the early twentieth century. As we will
see in the following chapters, Chicagoans traveled to wilderness parks, such
as the Indiana Dunes, but also to ethnic and labor resorts, such as Camp
Sokol, Illinois Turner Camp, Idlewild, Camp Pompeii, Camp Chi,

Harcerstwo Camp, and the Chicago Federation of Labor's Camp Valmar. For others, nature was even further afield, back in distant homelands: the forests of southwest Germany, a small village on the Aegean, the rich farmland of occupied Poland, the grasslands and mountains of Jalisco, a rice-growing village in Guangdong, the peaks of the Carpathians, or the dunes of Lithuania's Baltic Coast.

These destinations, though, were for the lucky few. Working-class Chicagoans typically stayed home, back in the hot, polluted city. They simply did not have the time or the money to spend a long weekend in the lakes and forests of rural Michigan or Wisconsin much less take a pleasure trip back home to a distant German, Irish, Swedish, or Mexican homeland. But this lack of means hardly implies that these Chicagoans were blind to the attractions of nature—far from it. Even though they could not afford to vacation outside the physical parameters of the city, they could and did seek out green spaces closer to home, on the urban fringe or within the city itself.[2]

In this chapter, we will survey some of these urban and peri-urban landscapes where Chicagoans found nature. We will visit six major nineteenth-century pastoral parks, dozens of smaller neighborhood athletic parks, the Lake Michigan shore, and a crescent of forest preserves that enclosed the city to the north, west, and south. We will explore commercial groves, beer gardens, and amusement parks located throughout the city as well as unexpected green spaces: vacant lots, railroad rights of way, alleys, industrial yards, wharfs, canals, the Chicago River, and even sidewalk cracks.

We need a reliable guide or "urban ranger" for this expedition, and there is none better than Leonard Dubkin. In 1907, Dubkin (who was two years old at the time) immigrated to Chicago with his Ukrainian Jewish parents. Like many other impoverished newcomers, the family moved to the slums of the Near West Side. This neighborhood was the home of Hull House, the famous "settlement" administered by Jane Addams and other native-born middle-class women who made it their mission to aid the urban poor. Although Dubkin lived in a small apartment in a densely packed urban environment completely devoid of trees (he saw his first tree when he was nine or ten years old), he developed an early interest in the natural world and hoped to become a naturalist when he grew up. As a teenager in an impoverished family, he spent most of his time going to school and working (delivering newspapers and cleaning saloons), but when he had a spare moment, he avidly read Charles Darwin, Thomas Huxley, Ernest Thompson Seton, and other famous naturalists and went on collecting trips around the city. He stuffed birds, mounted butterflies, collected rocks and fossils, and brought living snakes, turtles, snails, and crayfish back to his parent's crowded tenement. Using a public typewriter at Hull House, Dubkin wrote stories about his adventures with urban nature, which the *Chicago Daily News* published regularly on the Sunday children's page. Impressed, Jane Addams gave the boy a new typewriter as a gift. Although Dubkin never became a professional naturalist as he had hoped (he did not have the means to go to college), he did go on to write six books on nature in the city, publish numerous articles on nature for the *Chicago Daily News* and the *Chicago Tribune*, and correspond with famous naturalists, including the nature writer and ecologist Rachel Carson.[3]

Unlike the largely affluent and Anglo American members of the Prairie Club who traveled out of the city in search of original, uncontaminated Illinois, Wisconsin, or Indiana wilderness, Dubkin insisted that nature could be found within the very city that so many elite Chicagoans spurned. Whether we go to nature for knowledge, beauty, or recreation, there was no need to leave the city, he told his readers. All we have to do is open our eyes to the nature around us.

## Pastoral English Parks in Chicago

If Dubkin were to give us a tour of the places where Chicago's disadvantaged sought nature, he would probably begin by taking us to the city's great nineteenth-century pastoral parks. During the second half of the nineteenth century, Anglo American politicians, intellectuals, and physicians in cities across the nation called for the development of large urban parks, such as Manhattan's Central Park, which was opened to the public in 1857. Advocates claimed that these parks would increase surrounding property values and bring culture to unrefined frontier cities. Public parks would also further American republicanism because they gave all citizens access to restorative private park landscapes that were monopolized by aristocrats back in Europe. But foremost among the justifications for spending public money on the creation of these landscapes was health. These green oases would serve as a natural resort where one could retreat and recover from the ill effects of artificial urban life.[4]

This priority on health can clearly be seen in the writings of John Rauch, a medical doctor who was the most influential early advocate of Chicago parks. He explained in 1869 that Chicago was an "unnatural and artificial" environment where residents devote themselves single-mindedly to work, the acquisition of wealth, and the accomplishment of something "bold and novel," all of which creates an "atmosphere of excitement, more so, perhaps, than any other community in the world." One downside of such an overly stimulating and artificial environment, he wrote, was "expenditure of physical and mental force," which led to premature exhaustion, inability to work, and a host of diseases, such as apoplexy, dropsy of the brain, consumption, dyspepsia, convulsions, epilepsy, and palsy. For Rauch, the answer was not a wholesale evacuation from the unhealthy urban environment, but rather the development of large city parks where Chicago residents could temporarily escape unhealthy urban conditions.[5]

Chicago ultimately followed Rauch's advice. After opening Lincoln Park in 1865, the city began work on Humboldt, Garfield, and Douglas Parks on the West Side and Washington and Jackson Parks on the South Side (see Map 1.1). Given that park builders understood these landscapes as natural retreats from an artificial city, we might think that these nineteenth-century parks, with their rolling greensward, banks of irregular trees and shrubs, and quiet ponds, preserved the original native Illinois landscape that existed before Chicago became a city. But our guide would undoubtedly quickly disabuse us of this notion. Although Dubkin had no formal training as a naturalist, he had more than enough knowledge of native plants, animals, and topography to quickly recognize that these parks hardly preserved last vestiges of indigenous prairie wilderness.

Victorian park builders such as Frederick Law Olmsted, the dean of nineteenth-century American landscape architecture and the most influential midcentury advocate for parks, certainly believed that untamed sublime scenery had its place. Olmsted called for protecting the Yosemite Valley and Niagara Falls, and he incorporated the seemingly untamed Ramble into his design of Manhattan's Central Park. But at Yosemite, he was much more interested in the pastoral valley floor than the surrounding "cliffs of awful height." At Niagara he focused on the parklike virtues of Goat Island rather than directing attention to the overly stimulating cataracts. And in reference to urban parks, he advised in 1870 that they should not contain "very rugged ground" or "abrupt eminences." What is needed is "the beauty of the fields, the meadow, the prairie, of green pastures, and the still waters. What we want to gain is tranquility and rest to the mind. Mountains suggest effort." In an overwrought, overworked, and "nervous" nation where many still associated the wilderness with danger, terror, and toil, Olmsted—like other landscape architects of his generation—always

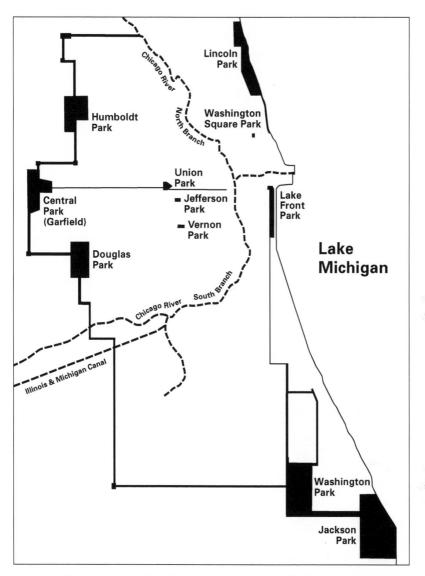

MAP 1.1 Chicago parks and parkways in 1888. Based on "Index Map of Chicago: Running South to Seventy First Street" (Chicago: Rufus Blanchard, 1888). Courtesy of the Map Collection, University of Chicago Library.

subordinated unruly sublime and picturesque scenery to the far more soothing pastoral.[6]

Landscape architects working in Chicago (including Olmsted) sometimes saw the sublime scenery of Lake Michigan as a potentially important element in urban park design. But, as historian Daniel Bluestone demonstrates, they found absolutely no value in the native prairies, marshes, forests, and dunes that sometimes still existed in reduced and simplified form in and around Chicago. Victorian park builders found the indigenous landscape exhausting and depressing, not refreshing or rejuvenating. Olmsted, for instance, described the Illinois prairie as "one of the most tiresome landscapes that I have ever met with," and he noted that "Chicago is situated in a region most unfavorable to parks and should she ever have any that are deserving the name, it will be because of persistent wisdom of administration and a scientific skill as well as art . . . such as has been no where applied to similar purpose." One of Olmsted's contemporaries, the landscape architect H. W. S. Cleveland, asked, "by what means is it possible to give to areas so utterly devoid of character an expression of natural beauty, and secure enough variety to relieve their monotony?" He answered that in Chicago, "everything must be created. Nature has not even offered a suggestion for art to develop."[7]

Instead of trying to preserve or reproduce the original "wild" landscape, Chicago landscape architects looked back East, in particular to Europe, especially England. In the early eighteenth century, English gentry began to turn away from rigid geometric gardens, such as those found at the Palace of Versailles, just outside Paris. Instead of linear walks, manicured trees and topiary, symmetrical beds, and elaborate fountains, English landlords embraced a far more informal garden composed of rolling greensward, informal groupings of trees, serpentine paths, and still ponds.[8]

Cultural critic Raymond Williams links the emergence of the informal English park to changes in agricultural production occurring throughout rural England during the eighteenth century. The quest for greater agricultural efficiency drove landlords to enclose or fence in common lands used for gardening and grazing and to evict tens of thousands of peasants, many of whom left for cities and colonies. The enclosure of common lands (as well as profits from colonial trade) meant increased profits for the landlord gentry, who symbolically expressed their newly gained wealth in the form of fashionable country estates surrounded by extensive, well-maintained landscape gardens. As the rectilinear, efficient, and productive field rigidly surrounded by stone fence or hedge became an increasingly common site throughout England, the English landscape architects of the eighteenth century abandoned level and line in favor of sweeping curves, serpentine lakes, and expanses of open meadow framed by irregular banks of trees and shrubbery. As the gentry took part in the destruction of the commons and as they benefited from market-oriented agriculture and the displacement of English cottagers, they simultaneously re-created a lost classical or medieval pastoral world for their own private use.[9]

During the nineteenth century, the informal English park captured the imagination of landscape architects working not only in England, but also in France, Germany, Australia, South Africa, India, and the United States. Olmsted, for one, noted that the medieval English deer park (whether original or reproduced by landscape architects) possessed an unrivalled therapeutic effect. It was doubtful, he wrote, whether there was any other natural scenery that was "equally soothing and refreshing, equally adapted to stimulate simple, natural, and wholesome tastes and fancies, and thus to draw the mind from absorption in the interests of an intensely artificial habit of life."[10]

In Chicago, landscape architects such as Olmsted, Cleveland, Swain Nelson, and William Le Baron Jenney transformed flat treeless prairies, wetlands, sand dunes, and other "wastes" into therapeutic parks in the English style. In Lincoln Park, Lake Michigan dunes dominated the site, and commissioners noted that "it is easy to perceive that a range of windswept sand hills is an unpromising place for a park, but hard to conceive of the immensity of the task of subduing it to verdure and beauty." The commissioners' laborers uprooted existing scrub oak, moved sand with plow and scraper, spread ten thousand loads of street sweepings on the ground, and created ponds, mounds, and ridges. They planted thousands of native and exotic trees in irregular patterns, planted grass, and applied millions of gallons of irrigated water to the sandy soil. Using pilings, oak plank, and huge blocks made of Portland cement, they also built tremendous breakwaters against Lake Michigan waves, the park's "unresting enemy." As in New York's Central Park, the commissioners even released nonnative English sparrows. As an 1896 guidebook to the park noted, "The great beauty of Lincoln Park is . . . in no wise due to original gifts of nature . . . but is, on the contrary, essentially artificial, the 'work of men's hands,' and thus is a triumph of man's skill over adverse natural conditions."[11]

On the city's West Side, landscape architects created English parks (Humboldt, Douglas, Garfield) on sites seen as even more unfavorable. One writer described the unimproved parklands as "an unbounded expanse of bleak plain, destitute of vegetation, except low . . . [vegetation] and a distant line of spindly young trees, hardly more sylvan in appearance than telegraph poles. In the foreground are stagnant pools of water and an unfenced, ungraded prairie trail. The scene is as barren, lone and desolate as could well be conceived. . . . There was upon the whole tract not a single tree of natural growth worthy of preservation." To build parks on the "bleak" indigenous landscape, the city chose William Le Baron Jenney, an engineer who, in the 1850s, had studied in Paris, where he had witnessed urban planner Baron Von Hausmann's modernization efforts, including the construction of English-style parks (such as the Bois de Boulogne in Paris) favored by Napoleon III. On Chicago's West Side, Jenny followed the Parisian model. By digging out lagoons (which helped drain the swampy site and produced raw material for the construction of hills on the prairie landscape), amending the clay soil with enormous quantities of manure from the stockyards, constructing curvilinear roads and pathways, planting thousands of native and exotic trees and shrubs, and laying "velvety green lawn which would contrast to the wild prairie in the dry of summer," he transformed the three flat, marshy, prairie sites into pastoral and picturesque parks in the English style. In such parks, Jenny wrote, "the man of business can forget the anxieties of the counting house, and rest an overworked brain. The laborer and artisan can forget his toil. The family picnic party can . . . spread their cloth and empty their baskets under the trees amid pleasing surroundings of broad lawns, shady nooks, and glimpses of lakes."[12]

Olmsted and Calvert Vaux, who together had designed New York's Central Park in the 1850s, won the commission for Jackson and Washington Parks on the South Side (see Fig. 1.1). The challenge to landscaping the site, Olmsted wrote, was how to give charm to scenery in which "flat and treeless prairie and limitless expanse of lake are such prominent characteristics." Instead of flattening the native landscape, which was the course in New York's Central Park, Olmsted and Vaux intended to make the level prairie landscape into undulating countryside. They planned to dredge out a series of lagoons along the lakeshore and create a "mere" in Washington Park, which would lower the water table and produce backfill for gentle swells of pastoral meadow. Artificial water-filled depressions, which reflected masses of banked foliage above, would also add to the illusion of hill and dale. After the fire of 1871 left the city in financial distress, Chicago hired H. W. S. Cleveland to complete Washington Park. He followed much of Olmsted and Vaux's plan, creating features such as South Open

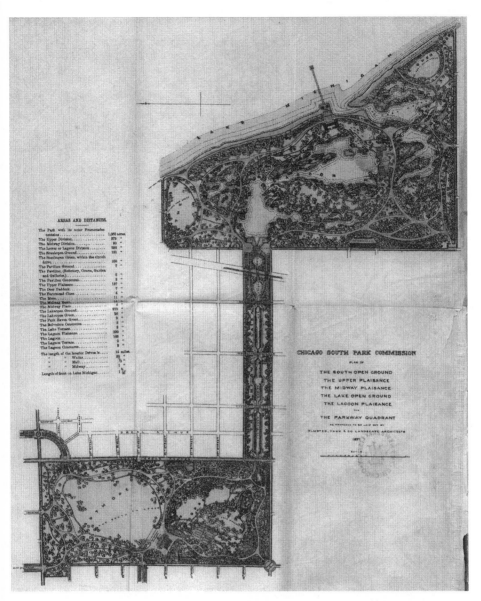

FIGURE 1.1 Olmsted and Vaux plan for what would become Washington and Jackson Parks. Olmsted, Vaux and Company, *Report Accompanying Plan for Laying Out the South Park* (Chicago, 1871). Courtesy of the Newberry Library.

Ground, a vast greensward created by thinning out native oaks and shaping tons of soil and animal waste into "pleasing slopes and graceful undulations." More expensive aspects of the Olmsted and Vaux design, such as a Midway canal connecting Washington and Jackson Parks, were abandoned.[13]

The design of Jackson Park also did not materialize as expected. The city chose the site for the 1893 Columbian Exposition and superimposed on the park a neoclassical "White City" composed of beaux arts palaces devoted to industry, arts, and the sciences. Olmsted and his firm landscaped the exposition, dredging lagoons and creating a Wooded Island bordered by riverine plants. Although he ultimately used many native plants in his Jackson Park design, Olmsted in no way hoped to replicate midwestern river scenery or reconstruct the original Lake Michigan shoreline. The canals of Venice and the lush picturesque foliage he saw in Panama inspired his design. But so too did the scenery along the Upper Thames. While recuperating from nervous exhaustion in England, he wrote his partners that "a most capital school is found on the Thames banks for the study of what we want at Chicago." The mysterious shores of the river, overgrown with gorse, hawthorn, ferns, willows, and sweetbrier, entranced him. "This is so fine and poetically suggestive," he wrote, "that though we cannot nearly approach what is to be found on the Thames, we must try to accomplish some small measure of effect in the same direction." After the fair closed and the buildings were destroyed, Jackson Park was redesigned by the Olmsted, Olmsted, & Eliot firm and reopened as a public park.[14]

In Lincoln Park, the West Parks, and the South Parks, park builders transformed indigenous dunes, marshes, prairie, oak forest, and savannah into English parks, complete with rolling greensward, irregular groupings of trees (frequently of nonnative origin), Victorian buildings, winding paths (with the occasional formal garden or plaza), and meres. In place of an indigenous prairie landscape that they found desolate and exhausting, landscape architects built salubrious English parks that they believed would best renew overworked Chicagoans.

These parks, thus, were not nearly as natural as we might at first think. But Dubkin, our urban ranger, would warn us that it is a serious mistake to dismiss Lincoln, Humboldt, Washington, or other pastoral landscapes as entirely artificial. He himself spent many hours walking through these parks, watching birds, observing squirrels, collecting insects, and watching the seasons change. He would show us that indigenous plants, insects, small mammals, and birds often recolonized these English parks and made them their own. But he would also surely tell us that nature does not have to be original or indigenous to count. Norway maples, dandelions, or the African lion in the Lincoln Park Zoo might not have existed in Chicago before Europeans arrived, but these were still living nonhuman organisms that could instruct and amaze, and many of these exotic species, such as the English sparrow, acted in unpredictable ways.

## The Wilderness of the Cook County Forest Preserves and Indiana Dunes

Although Dubkin relished finding nature within the urban core, he would also guide us just outside city limits to the Indiana Dunes and the Cook Country Forest Preserves, for these, too, were places where Chicago's marginalized sought refuge from the "artificial" city. As a youth, one of Dubkin's favorite "secret places" was the site of the future Clayton F. Smith Forest Preserve, which was a short streetcar ride from his Near West Side slum. At the end of the streetcar line, he found a marsh, a forested area, and a prairie "just like I had read in my history books." It was, he explained, "the largest space that I had ever seen in my life." Many Sundays, Dubkin explored the area. He discovered native birds such as common grackles and hermit thrushes, prairie flowers, and the tracks of small mammals, including skunk, rabbit, raccoon, opossum, and perhaps even fox. He also brought crayfish, snails, frogs, snakes, and butterflies (which he caught with a homemade net built from an old shirt and a clothes hanger) back home to his parents' tenement.[15]

The origin of the Cook County Forest Preserves dates to 1898 when the Municipal Science Club began to study the available park space in and around Chicago. Two influential members of the club (later the Special Parks Commission) were the architect Dwight Perkins and the landscape architect Jens Jensen, both of whom, along with architect Frank Lloyd Wright, considered themselves part of the newly emerged Prairie School design movement. During their spare time, both Jensen and Perkins enjoyed leaving the city behind and exploring the indigenous landscapes that still existed on the urban fringe. The two men were hardly alone in their desire for exposure to wild nature. With the close of the frontier in 1890, increasing numbers of privileged Americans approached wilderness not with fear, but with nostalgia. Instead of traveling to Europe to explore the continent's Gothic and classical past, tourists began venturing westward to newly opened national parks and reserves. In wilderness landscapes, visitors could remember America's frontier origins and turn pioneer work (hiking, camping, fishing, mountain climbing, and hunting) into play. Raw wilderness, formerly a cause of anxiety, nervousness, and exhaustion, became the place where stressed, overwrought Americans traveled to escape "artificial" life back in the city. Meanwhile, Victorian English parks, the former antipode to the city, came to look increasingly ornamental, feminine, and contrived.[16]

In the Special Parks Commission Report of 1904, Perkins, Jensen, and other members of the committee recommended that Cook County (which encompasses Chicago along with other incorporated municipalities) secure a crescent of relatively untouched natural spaces on the urban fringe to the north, west, and south of the city. Poorly written and unconstitutional legislation stalled the acquisition of proposed park areas for years, but finally in 1916 the city began purchasing land, and by 1922, the county operated more than 22,000 acres of forest preserve, including Palatine Grove, Des Plaines River Valley, Palos Hills, Salt Creek Valley, North Branch Chicago River, Beverly Hills, Thornton, Glenwood, and Elk Grove Preserves, as well as tracts at Murphy, West Hammond, Oak Forest, and Evanston. Although the nearby Indiana Dunes were not located in Cook County or even Illinois, some forest preserve boosters saw the dunes as a natural extension of the Chicago system (see Map 1.2).[17]

Although Anglo Americans clearly enjoyed playing in the wilderness, they also made it clear that the great promise of the forest preserves and dunes was that they would regenerate millions of tired, overworked industrial laborers back in Chicago. At the 1917 hearing about whether to create a Dunes National Park, Graham Taylor spoke for many of his fellow social reformers when he testified that "the situation of being divorced from God's green earth and God's open skies is abnormal," and that nowhere on the continent could one find so many people alienated from nature as in Chicago. He recalled that when he walked with flowers through the crowded Near West Side (not far from where Dubkin and his family lived), workers stood and watched, and some even pleaded for a spare lilac to give to a sick relative. Recreation in wilderness would not only expose a great cosmopolitan population to "a little of the domain that is America" and provide a healthy alternative to dissipating urban amusements (such as movies), it would regenerate industrial workers, serving as an antidote

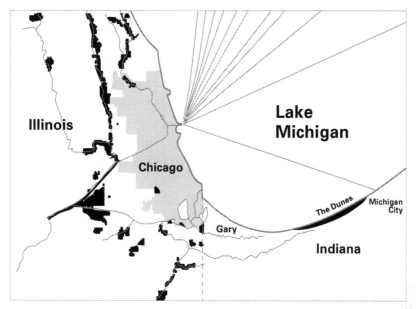

MAP 1.2 Cook County Forest Preserves, Indiana Dunes, and steamship lines leaving Chicago in the mid-1930s. Based on "The Forest Preserve District of Cook County," in Forest Preserve District of Cook County, Ill., *The Forest Preserves of Cook County* (Clohesey, 1918), 10.

to the "monotony of life" and the "stress and strain on nerve and mental stamina" that came from industrial labor in Chicago.[18]

Unlike Victorian park builders (who saw the indigenous Illinois landscape as dreary and enervating), early twentieth-century forest preserve advocates argued that the native landscape surrounding Chicago was uniquely restorative. Instead of introducing exotic species such as the English sparrow or destroying marshes, prairies, and dunes to create therapeutic English parks, Cook County tried to protect the indigenous scenery of the Chicago region as it looked at the moment when European explorers first came into contact with Native Americans. In the forest preserves, the county reconstructed and preserved "native" landscapes by eradicating exotics, destroying modern structures, stocking polluted streams with native fish, and replanting the wild parks with native plants grown in the county's own nursery. Forest preserve guidebooks urged visitors to hike old Pottawatomie trails through marshes, prairies, and primitive forests of native linden, maple, poplar, hawthorn, and oak and see wild duck, egrets, cranes, and bald eagles and encounter herds of elk and white tailed deer. Meanwhile, wilderness advocates sought to preserve the Indiana Dunes wilderness (which many saw as the most extraordinary indigenous landscape in the entire Midwest) as a national park.[19]

According to wilderness advocates, the forest preserves and the dunes would transport visitors backward in time. Cook County advertised the preserves as an "Indian paradise," as a special place where Chicago's residents, both rich and poor, could encounter the ancient ruins of Cook County's first people, the Pottawatomie. Like eighteenth-century English aristocrats who incorporated vestiges of vanished peasant life (such as a deserted village) into their parks, Cook County preserved Indian ruins and made these traces a central feature of the regenerative wilderness experience. Guides noted that the Pottawatomie had first blazed the roads and the hiking trails that now wove throughout the forest preserves, and they called attention to Indian camps, chipping stations, and Indian mounds, as well as the bluffs in the Beverly Hills where the Pottawatomie supposedly sent up smoke signals from their bonfires.[20]

Especially after touring the city's pastoral parks, we might think that the wilderness in the forest preserves and dunes was primeval. Unlike Lincoln, Humboldt, and Washington Parks, these outlying parks seemingly preserved the original landscape that existed when the first Europeans arrived in Illinois. But our guide, Leonard Dubkin, might point out that although these wilderness reserves contained far more native plant and animal species than Victorian parks back in the city, they were not as natural as they might seem. He might call attention to the work crews busy eradicating nonnative trees as well as the county nursery filled with native seedlings and saplings that crews would eventually replant in the "wilderness." He might have us examine the sewage treatment plants built to cleanse the Des Plaines and Chicago Rivers before they entered the preserves or point to efforts to restock these rivers with bluegills, crappies, black bass, and other hardy native species that could survive moderately polluted waters. He might also note that although the forest preserve managers spent considerable effort reintroducing some native species, they failed to repopulate the parks with the region's large predators: gray wolves, mountain lions, bobcats, coyotes, and black bears. Like the early twentieth-century National Park Service, the managers of the forest preserves and the dunes most likely saw the existence of large predators and tourists as incompatible, this despite these animals having once played vital roles in the ecosystems in and around Chicago. Dubkin would tell us that although the forest preserves and the dunes (like the national parks) present themselves as primeval and original, human managers gardened these landscapes, in some cases as much as the English parks back in the city.[21]

Dubkin might also be suspicious of Anglo American efforts to preserve an unchanging Indian wilderness. Before Europeans arrived, the Pottawatomie, Miami, Illinois, and other Indian groups hunted and gathered in and around Chicago (one origin for the name "Chicago" is *Chicagou*, or place of the leeks). They also grew beans, corn, and squash, and in so doing engaged in genetic engineering, discarding some strains and artificially selecting others for further propagation. Chicago-area Indians also deliberately set fires, and these fires played a crucial role in creating the distinct mosaic of forest, prairie, and savannah that Europeans encountered when they first arrived. In other words, northeastern Illinois was not an untouched wilderness before the arrival of Europeans. First Peoples had gardened the area for thousands of years.[22]

Dubkin, a Ukrainian Jewish newcomer to the United States, might also have found Anglo American fetishization of Indians peculiar. Chicago wilderness advocates noted that in the forest preserves one could find Indian ruins, but like the National Park Service personnel at Yosemite and Glacier National Parks, they went even further and tried to bring actual Indian performers into the parks. In 1920, the governor of Illinois declared September 24 "Indian Day," and Cook County organized a three-day Indian council in one of the preserves. On the 26th, a Sunday, thirty thousand automobiles clogged the forest preserve roads and one hundred and fifty thousand Chicagoans spent the day watching Indian dancing and festivities. The success of the Indian council prompted some forest preserve supporters to make plans for a permanent Indian village. Ransom Kennicott of the Forest Preserve Booster Club explained that the village would attract thousands of visitors. The county, he wrote, would plant basket willow, which would enable the forest preserve Indians to make baskets for tourists. Chicagoans, he wrote, will be "glad of the opportunity to buy the Indian baskets and beadwork for reasonable prices knowing that they are genuinely Indian-made," and he assured the club that the Indian Fellowship League, a group associated with the Chicago Historical Society, would select the "right class of Indians" for the village.[23]

Anglo Americans used the forest preserves and the dunes not only to see vestiges of a "vanishing race," but also to play Indian themselves. Just like the French aristocrat Marie Antoinette (who famously played as a peasant maid at her ersatz farmhouse situated in the midst of an informal English park), Prairie Club members wore headdresses, beads, and paint and listened to Indian stories and sang Indian songs around the campfire. They beat on Indian drums and danced the Hede-Wachi Indian dance at pow-wows and placed totem poles outside their tents. Prairie Club member Thomas W. Allinson (or Wassekigig, as he called himself) went so far as to create an Indian secret society, the tribe of Ha Ha No Mak, and took great pride in his newly adopted Indian ancestry.[24]

Members of the Prairie Club and other wilderness enthusiasts denied American Indians a dynamic, changing relationship with the natural world in the past, but they also denied these same Indians a modern present. At the forest preserve "Indian Village" and in pageants at the dunes, Indian people had to play the part of living historic relics. But early twentieth-century American Indians sometimes had urban jobs, wore ties, bobbed their hair, and drove cars. They also sometime hired lawyers (in 1914 and 1926, the Pottawatomie sued the city of Chicago in an unsuccessful effort to recover the entire Chicago lakefront). But none of these signs of Indian modernity could be permitted in the "wilderness"; hence the need of the Chicago Historical Society to select the "right class" of Indians for the forest preserves. Although Dubkin did not possess the skills of a contemporary ethnic studies scholar, he probably could not help but notice that the preservation of these supposedly primeval wilderness parks was inextricably linked to Chicago's bizarre and very unnatural racial politics.[25]

## Chicago Playgrounds: Wilderness Writ Small?

On our tour of the places where working-class Chicagoans escaped for outdoor recreation, Dubkin, our guide, would also take us to the small block-sized neighborhood athletic parks or "playgrounds" that were built in dense working-class neighborhoods during the early twentieth century. The small parks idea originated out of Hull House. In 1893, Jane Addams built the city's first playground, a tiny pocket park that Dubkin himself had surely seen on his many childhood visits to the settlement house. But even more importantly, Hull House was the site of an 1898 Municipal Science Club lecture by Jacob Riis on the value of small parks, and it was this lecture that launched the Special Parks Commission and its 1904 report that recommended not only a ring of wilderness parks, but also the creation of block-sized athletic parks in the city's densest and poorest neighborhoods. Following the release of the report, the city's various park commissions went on to build dozens of these neighborhood parks.[26]

Historians have argued that especially in contrast to romantic pastoral parks these block-sized playgrounds were artificial, modern spaces. According to these scholars, middle-class Anglo American reformers, wary of class division and urban disorder, created these playgrounds and athletic parks to socially control, rationalize, and even "Taylorize" (or scientifically manage) the bodies of working-class children and young adults. The parks, then, shared much more of a family resemblance to prisons, schools, factories, and other institutions of social control than to pastoral or wild retreats intended as therapeutic retreats from the modern urban world.[27]

Certainly the architecture of these parks might lead one to see them as sites of social control. Unlike Lincoln, Humboldt, or Washington Parks or the Cook County Forest Preserves, these "playgrounds" looked utilitarian. The block-sized Chicago parks contained sexually segregated athletic fields, an oval track, sometimes a swimming pool, a playground with swings, sandbox, teeter-totters and other equipment for young children, and a field house, inside of which were showers and lockers, indoor gymnasiums, a branch of the Chicago public library, an affordable restaurant, and an auditorium for public lectures and meetings. A wrought-iron fence generally surrounded the entire landscape. In many ways, these small parks appear a throwback to the rigid, geometric park style of seventeenth-century France. Perhaps fittingly, the South Parks Commissioners built field houses in the small parks that reflected the classical style of the 1893 Chicago Columbian Exposition White City (see Fig. 1.2).[28]

The structured activities that took place in the Chicago playgrounds also seem to suggest social control and rationalization. Professionally trained recreation leaders ran park activities, and they tried to manage the ways that children and young adults used these landscapes. The South Parks District instructed leaders to begin every day with marching to establish "obedience to authority and instant execution of orders." Later in the day, recreation workers organized group calisthenics, folk dances, games, and sports, such as swimming, track and field, baseball, volleyball, basketball, and handicrafts. The recreation experts' efforts to instill bodily efficiency through the use of stopwatch, whistle, and command look a lot like scientific manager Frederick Winslow Taylor's project of making the American industrial worker more productive.[29]

If the urban playground was in fact a modern institution of control and rationalization similar to schools, prisons, or the factory floor, a curious fact is that so many wilderness advocates heartily embraced the new urban

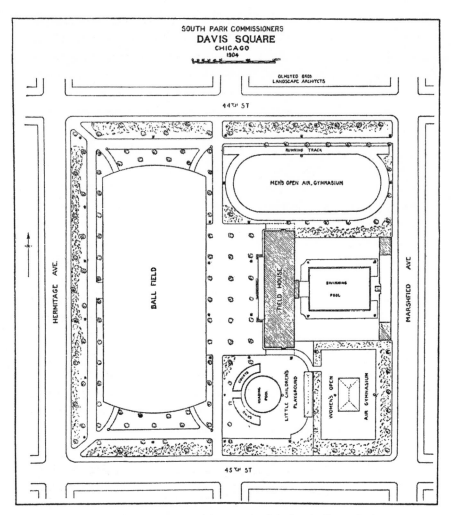

FIGURE 1.2 Plan of Davis Square Park in Back of the Yards. From Graham Romeyn Taylor, "Recreation Developments in Chicago Parks," *Annals of the American Academy of Political and Social Science* 35 (March 1910): 93.

playground movement and even played crucial roles in developing the small urban parks. Congressman and philanthropist William Kent not only gave the land that would become Muir Woods National Monument in California and shepherded passage of the 1916 Organic Act creating the National Park Service, he donated land for the Hull House playground. Landscape architect Frederick Law Olmsted Jr. (the son of Frederick Law Olmsted) not only wrote the act creating the National Park Service, but designed Chicago South Side playground landscapes. President Theodore Roosevelt (an avid outdoorsman who as president set aside millions of acres of land as national parks, forests, and preserves) was an enthusiastic supporter of the small urban park idea, served as honorary president of the Playground Association of America, and called Chicago's small athletic parks "one of the most notable civic achievements in any American city." And as we have already seen, it was precisely the same Chicago park commission and the same 1904 report that recommended the creation of an outer belt of wilderness forest preserves *and* small neighborhood parks in congested neighborhoods.[30]

At the same time, many leaders of the Progressive Era playground movement openly championed wilderness. Far from embracing the sociologist Max Weber's "iron cage," playground enthusiasts argued that "normal" play originally took place in rural and wild settings. G. Stanley Hall, the leading intellectual light of the play movement, argued that children and youth, in normal or healthy play, relived the activities of "primitive" people: they fought, fished, danced, hunted, adventured, worshipped nature, and created arts and crafts. He noted that nature "arms youth for conflict with all the resources at her command—speed, power of shoulder, biceps, back, leg, jaw—strengthens and enlarges the skull, thorax, hips, makes men aggressive and prepares woman's frame for maternity." Proper or natural play literally grew children and adolescents into healthy and robust men and women. Jane Addams, the mother of the Chicago playground movement, contrasted the stunted play life of urban children with the freedom she herself had experienced playing on the prairies and streams and in the forests and caves of frontier Illinois. Unlike the children of the Near West Side, she and her stepbrother had been "free-ranging children" who explored, played games, interacted with the natural world, and channeled "man's primitive life" by constructing an altar on which they offered dead snakes, black walnuts, and cider to the Gods.[31]

Hall, Addams, Roosevelt, and other Progressive reformers lamented that children and young adults in cities did not have access to rural and wild places where they could enjoy natural or unstructured play. Without access to natural places, youth played in city streets, converged as gangs, and found excitement and recreation in theft and vandalism. In search of excitement, the young also gravitated to places of "passive" commercialized leisure: amusement parks, dance halls, saloons, cheap theaters, or movie palaces. In such places, they enjoyed leisure that led not to moral, intellectual, and physical development and regeneration, but rather to dissipation, neurological difficulties, and fatigue.[32]

The solution was the neighborhood athletic park, which was intended to operate not as a modern site of rationalization, but rather as a highly concentrated ersatz wilderness park. Chicago's working-class neighborhoods were overcrowded with children and young adults, and despite the construction of the neighborhood parks, recreational space was extremely limited. While the free-range childhood that Addams had enjoyed on the Illinois prairie remained the ideal, the urban environment and the charge to create as many natural, healthy, preindustrial bodies as possible necessitated a different approach: tight scheduling, whistles, marching, regimented calisthenics, and organized sports on a landscape dominated by field houses, jungle gyms, perfectly oval tracks, baseball diamonds, and other delineated sports fields. As E. B. De Groot, general secretary of the Playground Association of Chicago, put it, "We must . . . rid ourselves of the notion that it is 'nature faking' to direct the play of children. . . . In the large cities the play of the children . . . is *only* free when we direct it." In other words, what looks like social control, rationalization, or scientific management was in fact an effort to best approximate the "natural" course of play in what play leaders saw as a congested and unnatural environment.[33]

It is true that Progressive Era recreation experts were never antimodernists who turned their back on industrial America. On the contrary, they viewed outdoor recreation in small parks as central to making industrial America more sustainable. They hoped that instead of enjoying commercial amusements that induced disease and fatigue, overworked youth would go to parks and participate in "active" health-giving recreation that would restore them from long hours of mechanized labor and render them more efficient and productive when they returned to the factory floor (see Fig. 1.3). Intervening into laissez-faire capitalism and ensuring that children had a chance to play and grow and that young adults got temporary breaks from tedious, specialized industrial labor would, over the long run, produce a healthier, more productive, more efficient American population. As Teddy Roosevelt explained at the Playground Association of America Conference in 1907, "A boy or girl who has a healthy body will be all the better fit for serious work."[34]

But it is important to recognize that Progressive Era advocates of working-class parks were hardly alone when they made the argument that outdoor recreation conserved labor power. Decades earlier in the 1860s, landscape architect Frederick Law Olmsted explained that one justification for large public parks is that exposure to "beautiful sylvan scenes" made

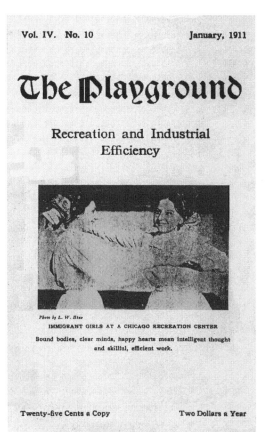

Vol. IV. No. 10        January, 1911

# The Playground

### Recreation and Industrial Efficiency

*Photo by L. W. Hine*

IMMIGRANT GIRLS AT A CHICAGO RECREATION CENTER

Sound bodies, clear minds, happy hearts mean intelligent thought and skillful, efficient work.

Twenty-five Cents a Copy       Two Dollars a Year

FIGURE 1.3 The subtitle on the cover of the *Playground* (January 1911) reflects the Progressive Era belief in the therapeutic results of recreation: healthy bodies and ultimately increased workplace efficiency.

daily labor "more methodical and regular." At exactly the same time, John Muir, the naturalist and tireless advocate for national parks, conducted some of the first time-motion studies and found that reducing hours of factory work actually increased productivity. As is well known, an industrial accident sent Muir out of the factory and into the wilderness, but he did not entirely turn his back on industrial America. Instead of taking an unequivocally antimodernist position, he noted that leisure in wilderness resulted in "more and better work." By the Progressive Era, the argument that outdoor recreation resulted in health, efficiency, and ultimately greater productivity had become one of the central justifications for preserving national parks. In other words, Chicagoans who argued that parks conserved the labor power of workers did not stand alone; rather they echoed a long-standing and quite common claim that a temporary retreat back to nature would make the chronically exhausted American more industrious over the long run. As the clockmaker Muir put it, healthy leisure would keep laborers operating at "pendulum regularity."[35]

Although Chicago's neighborhood parks seemed constricted and unnatural, park builders did try to introduce natural elements as best they could. Visitors found winding paths through small stands of trees, ball fields that doubled as meadows, and (in the larger parks) lagoons with densely planted islands. Shrubs, trees, and vines often hid ugly iron fencing and the busy industrial and residential scenes just beyond the park's borders. Visitors could find birds, insects, and sometimes fish and reptiles. At the same time, the play supervisors in the small parks tried to bring wilderness to the playground. The parks organized playground nature study and gardening instruction and showed lantern slides and films of wilderness areas. They also sponsored Boy Scouts and Campfire Girls troops and took urban children on frequent summer trips out of the slum and to Lake Michigan and to the forest preserves.[36]

Some Chicago landscape architects, such as Jens Jensen, even tried to restore Illinois "wilderness" in the heart of the city. Jensen, who is often figured as landscape architecture's Frank Lloyd Wright, rejected European influences, embraced the native scenery of the Midwest, and worked to create a "Prairie style" for park and garden design. He got his start on this project in 1888 when he boldly created an experimental "American Garden" of indigenous wildflowers and shrubs in Union Park, one of the city's oldest parks. Because no nursery carried native plants, he had to uproot wild species and transport them back to the city by wagon. During the early twentieth century, Jensen rose through the ranks and ultimately became superintendent of the West Parks District. In Garfield, Douglas, and Humboldt Parks, he ripped out foreign plants and transformed these English parks into idealized prairie landscapes. In Humboldt Park, he transformed one of William Le Baron Jenney's lagoons into a meandering Illinois river, whose source emerged from a spring above stratified limestone. In Douglas Park, he drained a shallow pond and created a broad prairie for baseball and picnics, planted thousands of native plants, and erected a prairie-style pavilion, concrete benches, and light fixtures. At Garfield Park, he built a conservatory in the shape of a midwestern haystack, inside of which he created a model midwestern river with prairie rapids, which he surrounded with ferns and other indigenous plants.[37]

At Columbus Park, located just west of the downtown Loop, not too far from Dubkin's childhood home, Jensen built stretches of prairie and reconstructed glacial ridges. On this site, he also constructed a natural-

FIGURE 1.4 Jens Jensen's Illinois swimming hole in Columbus Park, mid-1930s. Courtesy of Chicago Park District Special Collections.

looking Illinois swimming hole for the working-class children of the area (see Fig. 1.4). Using clay, cement, and Wisconsin-quarried rock, he and his crew built up the sides of the pool so they resembled the natural stratification of exposed limestone found throughout the Midwest. Ferns and grapevines came right to the water's edge, and he screened out factories and trolley cars with a small forest of native trees: elms, maples, and lindens, with an undergrowth of hawthorn, crab apple, sumac, wild plum, and cherry. "If urban children can't go to the countryside and put their clothes on a hickory limb and feel mud ooze between their toes and see willows and bullfrogs, then we must bring the country in to them," Jensen told a journalist from the *National Municipal Review*.[38]

## Commercial Parks

Our guide Dubkin would not only take us to city parks and forest preserves, but also to scores of commercial groves in and around the city. Although plans are lost or nonexistent, firsthand accounts of these private parks suggest that they sometimes possessed sylvan landscapes that rivaled an Olmsted park. But unlike parks run by the city, managers of commercial groves permitted alcohol and created spaces for distinctive ethnic and working-class outdoor recreational practices. Because of this, large numbers of working-class Chicagoans were willing to pay a small admission fee.

On Sundays during the second half of the nineteenth century, Germans made North Clark Street into a passageway out of the "dust and din" of the city and back to nature. As a reporter for the *Chicago Tribune* noted in 1877, unlike the American, who tends to stay in his house on the Sabbath, the German has no other interest but getting to nature. "Once every week there comes upon the German a hatred of pent-up rooms and houses built with hands," noted the reporter. "The old impulses of savagery come over him, and he sighs for the open air, the canopy of Heaven, and the shade of the trees. He wants to go to a park, a grove, a garden." Thousands of Germans and others went to Lincoln Park, where one could enjoy cool breezes off the lake, listen to summer concerts, row out on the artificial lake, see zoo animals, and, if need be, make beer runs to stands operating just outside park borders. Most, though, went to green places where beer was easier to come by. Many of these beer gardens were quite small, really only an urban backyard. Still, in such places, one could come into contact with trees, even if they were miserable evergreens grown in tubs and watered "not by the rains of nature, but by German waiters, who answer when one says 'Johann' or 'Franz.' "[39]

But German entrepreneurs also created much larger commercial parks. In 1879, the *Der Nord Chicago Schuetzenverein,* a shooting club comprised of former veterans of the Franco-Prussian War, opened *Schuetzen,* or Sharpshooters Park, a beautiful twenty-two acre landscape on the banks of the Chicago River. The *Illinois Staats-Zeitung* described the park as a "delightful grove" located at a place on the Chicago River where "the water is still unpolluted, and is clear as a brook" and "immense oaks, hickory trees, and elms provided ample shade, yet did not exclude the cool western breezes." One child later remembered the German park as a forest of oak and elm, blooming crabapples along the river, fields of buttercups, daisies, hepaticas, anemones, and purple violets, a boating lagoon, and a place on the river where boys swam and dove.[40]

In 1904, Wilhelm Schmidt and his son George transformed Sharpshooters Park into Riverview Amusement Park, which subsequently became one of the most popular leisure-time destinations for Chicagoans. Middle-class Anglo American reformers during the Progressive Era saw amusement parks, with their available alcohol, mechanical rides, games of chance, and illusions, as dangerous places where children and young adults might veer from nature's course. But it is a mistake to see amusement parks such as Riverside only as places of artifice. Even more popular than park rides were Riverview's picnic groves, which were situated along the banks of the Chicago River. Owners of the park understood that in addition to mechanical rides, many visitors sought escape from the city and contact with nature, and as such, the Schmidts modeled Riverview on Tivoli Gardens, a Copenhagen amusement park that devoted 75 percent of its site to green space.[41]

Although Riverview Park was the most popular commercial park in Chicago, there were many, many others. Ogden's Grove—a favorite of nineteenth-century socialists and anarchists—was, according to one fan, a place for parties under the oaks, a place of "sunshine, woodland green and woodland shade." Wright's Grove, another commercial park, was described as a "woodland garden" where visitors could drink and eat at heavy pine tables installed in "leafy glades, under the great oaks" (see Fig. 1.5). Harm's Park, a North Side picnic grove filled with stands where "the foaming stein or the succulent wiener could be dispensed," possessed one of the last remaining black walnut stands in the city. On the far South Side, another German shooting club opened a park at Palos Hills with a dancing pavilion, baseball diamond, tennis courts, bowling alleys, refreshment stands, and a small lake for boating. The forty-acre hilltop park was situated in a forest of oak and commanded stunning views of surrounding countryside.[42]

Although Germans operated most of the city's commercial groves, they had no lock on the city's park business. In the nineteenth century, the Gaelic Athletic Club owned a park at Thirty-seventh Street and Indiana Avenue, which it used to play Gaelic hurling and football, despite neighboring Anglo Americans who objected to outdoor amusements on the Christian Sabbath. In the early twentieth century, local Irish also built Gaelic Park, a picnic ground near the stockyards that contained ball fields and a dance pavilion, over which flew the Irish flag. The *Chicago Citizen*, the Irish newspaper of note, described the park as "the home of Irish sports, Irish games, Irish music, and Irish dancing." The park was where the Chicago Irish held their annual Feis, an outdoor gathering that they imagined as ancient in Irish history. Jews also had green space to call their own. In 1903, community leaders found a property with a spacious walled garden and transformed it into the Chicago Hebrew Institute (later the Jewish People's Institute). The institute hired Jens Jensen, who created a park with room for tennis, baseball, gymnastics, and track and field, but also ample space for gardening, nature study, and relaxation in nature. A writer for the *Chicago*

FIGURE 1.5 German Turner Festival in Wright's Grove, 1869.
From *Leslie's Illustrated Weekly,* August 28, 1869.

*Hebrew Institute Messenger* noted that "the entire park and garden space has been cultivated for many years, and as a result of the care bestowed upon the grounds, the grass, shrubbery, and trees, there is the impression of age never to be found in a newly-cultivated city-park or garden. Nowhere can there be found so large and so well-equipped a small park in the heart of a very thickly populated district." The Bohemian-owned Pilsen Brewing Company opened a large beer garden near Douglas Park, four miles southwest of the Loop. The six-acre wooded park, which was meant to replicate the beer gardens found in Prague, was the site of Czech harvest festivals, meetings, picnics, and athletics. Other foreign-born Chicagoans played sports, picnicked, and enjoyed nature at Olsen's Grove, Vytautas Park, Kosciusko Grove, Bonnie Brae Park, Slavia Grove, Polonia Park, and Shia-Tien Garden, to name just a few.[43]

During the late nineteenth and early twentieth centuries, immigrant Chicagoans interested in green space also sometimes visited cemeteries. Ethnic burial grounds, such as Saint Boniface, Saint Adalbert, Jewish Waldheim, Graceland, Oakwoods, Mount Carmel, Mount Olivet, Saint Casimir's

Lithuanian Cemetery, Evergreen Park, Bohemian National Cemetery, and dozens of others, were frequently well landscaped with banks of trees and shrubs, small lakes, manicured lawns, and flower beds filled with blooming annuals. On these landscapes, ethnic communities frequently continued Old World burial and memorial practices. For instance, the Greek Orthodox community constructed ancient Greek temples, and Germans built wayside shrines inside grounds protected by Gothic gates. Scandinavians erected the occasional Viking monolith, and the Chinese community built an elaborate granite shrine with embossed Chinese characters and a furnace where mourners could burn incense and messages to the dead written on rice paper. Thousands traveled to these cemeteries to remember the deceased, but observances were also frequently an occasion to escape the city, picnic, listen to music, and enjoy an afternoon in a beautiful, if somber, natural setting.[44]

## Nature in Unexpected Places

Although most Chicagoans interested in outdoor recreation ventured to the city's public and commercial parks, a considerable number (especially among the city's working-class children and young adults) found nature in more unexpected places: vacant lots, unimproved shoreline along Lake Michigan, abandoned or little-used industrial yards, forgotten sections of the polluted Chicago River, the margins along railroad tracks, and even sidewalk cracks. Our guide, the "Sidewalk Naturalist," would undoubtedly take great pleasure showing us some of his own "secret places" hidden in the interstices of Chicago's built environment.

Dubkin loved the city's many vacant lots (or "prairies" as they were known by working-class Chicago youth). These lots, he explained, could be found throughout the dense Near West Side, and when they remained undisturbed for years (as was often the case), "trees and bushes and weeds would grow high, and they would be filled with birds and snakes, insects, tree frogs, and little animals." On these lots one could find sumac, flowering weeds, and even some strays from gardens (such as morning glories, phlox, and sunflower). As a youth, Dubkin spent many hours in these lots hunting butterflies and preying mantises, observing birds, such as the invasive English sparrow, and investigating parthenogenetic or asexual reproduction of aphids.[45]

Dubkin also spent his spare time exploring the Chicago River. While delivering a dress that his mother had sewed for a client, Dubkin saw from his streetcar an expanse of open trees at California Avenue and Roscoe Street, just across the Chicago River from Riverview Amusement Park. The next Sunday he travelled to the little oasis, which he began to explore. He collected insect specimens and was overwhelmed by the "strangeness of time" when he discovered an ancient trilobite fossil and a terminal moraine left during the last ice age. He also discovered a city pumping station, and the engineer in charge invited Dubkin to watch as he cleaned the pumping station's filter, which contained, amid the algae, branches, and other detritus, live fish, frogs, a turtle, and a small snake. The "sidewalk naturalist" collected all these things, brought them back to his tenement, and used one of his mother's wash bins to re-create the river environment. Also along the river at California and Roscoe, Dubkin discovered a bat grotto, and despite the protests of his mother, he spent many evenings camping at the site and observing the behavior of bats. Later, as a young man, he would return and capture a rare albino brown bat. To Dubkin's amazement, the bat learned to fly through whirling fan blades, and the small mammal became the subject of his most popular book, *The White Lady*.[46]

While unemployed during the Great Depression, Dubkin spent many afternoons at another vernacular park: Northerly Island, a 91-acre man-made peninsula that would serve as the site for the 1933–1934 "Century of Progress" World Fair and later Meig's Field Airport. On this land, created from landfill, the unemployed reporter found rocks, little trees, and weeds, but also mammals and reptiles (rabbits, garter snakes, field mice, and even a weasel), but it was the insects (the social life of ants; the eating habits of beetles; aphid reproduction; the shape of a "stinkbug" thorax; the beauty of dragonflies and monarch butterflies) that fascinated him the most. "These strange, incredible, fantastic little beings," found in city yards, vacant lots, alleys, and sidewalk cracks, made Dubkin come to believe that "every living thing has a purpose in life, that each species was like a gear wheel that meshed with all the other species to form the vast machine of nature."[47]

Another of Dubkin's retreats was Wolf Point, the spot where the Chicago River bifurcates into north and south branches and where Indians and Europeans located the original village of Chicago. During the late 1930s, Dubkin set up an office in the Merchandise Mart, at the time the largest commercial space in the world. Curious about the destination of a flock of pigeons, he descended under the vast structure, down to where engineers had sunk the building's massive steel and concrete pilings into Chicago earth. At this site, in the midst of the concrete, brick, asphalt, and steel of the Loop and on the banks of an urban river that engineers forced to flow backwards, Dubkin discovered an urban green oasis. He found raccoons, insects, garter snakes, turtles, and also native bird species (a phoebe and a Baltimore oriole) rarely seen in downtown Chicago.[48]

Dubkin would take us to even smaller green spaces within the urban interstices. He would bring us up to the top of Loop office buildings and to the roof of his own childhood apartment building to watch migratory and resident birds, such as gulls, English sparrows, starlings, nighthawks, red-shouldered hawks, and more. He would also show us bird nests constructed within human structures, such as the steel girder drawbridges that continually opened and closed to permit ship traffic on the Chicago River. He would point to the insects and weeds that thrived in sidewalk cracks, and the chickens, horses, rabbits, ducks, and other domesticated animals that lived in working-class backyards. In the autumn, he would show us the orange and red foliage of the stunning native sumacs that thrived in alleys and along the railroad tracks that wended their way through the city. Our urban ranger might also take us down under Wacker Drive, where he once met an old small woman who spoke to and fed the enormous city rats that thrived in the built environment of the Loop. Even in one of the most artificial places on earth, Chicago's urban core, one could still find nature.[49]

Concluding his tour, Dubkin would undoubtedly revisit the central theme of all his books: that the seemingly artificial city of Chicago actually contained thousands of places where one might encounter nonhuman organic life. He would certainly concede that Grant Park in the Loop or a working-class athletic park on the South Side contained vastly less biological diversity than, say, the Indiana Dunes, but this point of comparison, he would contend, hardly made these urban parks unnatural, mere public spaces, cultural sites, or leisure spaces. These parks were also green spaces, places where one might encounter a natural world that was beautiful, instructive, unpredictable, and even awe inspiring. Perhaps Dubkin would tell us the story of Mrs. Grossetti, an Italian immigrant who lived near his childhood apartment on the Near West Side. Like many poor immigrants, she had gone years living in Chicago without ever having seen a single tree, and she had become convinced that unlike the rural countryside of Italy where she had grown up, America was a sterile country devoid of forests. But one day when walking to a distant clinic, she and her husband happened to see a single tree growing in the midst of the slum. In an emotional reaction that far surpassed the stock response of those peering into the Grand Canyon, witnessing an Alaskan salmon run, or seeing a blue whale surface off the Baja Coast, Mrs. Grossetti approached the tree, fell to her knees, and began sobbing. Only when her husband agreed to take some leaves as a memento of her encounter with nature did she agree to leave the tree.[50]

Anticipating some of the conclusions of William Cronon, Dubkin told his readers that there was no need to travel to rural Wisconsin, to Yellowstone National Park, or to the jungles of Amazonia to find nature. There was no need to leave our urban homes, for nature exists all around us. "It seems to me that people are forever traveling great distances, and journeying to strange countries, to see things that, if they only knew it, exist beside their own doorstep," Dubkin explained. "Whether one goes to nature for truth, or for beauty, for knowledge, or relaxation, these things can be found in a yard in the city as well as in a tropical jungle, for they exist in the common, simple, everyday things all about us, as well as in the rare and the exotic."[51]

When Dubkin pointed to backyard livestock, insects in office buildings, birds nesting in the iron girders of drawbridges, or rats scampering through concrete labyrinths under the Loop, he came close to deconstructing the line between nature and culture. Nature in some of his examples had so impregnated the urban built environment that it is difficult for the reader to identify where the city ends and nature begins. But despite forays to places where the city and nature hybridized, he saw cities, in the final analysis, as inherently unnatural, as artificial. The nature he found within Chicago was not part of the city, but rather a temporary escape from urban modernity.

Dubkin's understanding of urban nature as an escape is evident throughout all of his writings, but his sense of the place of urban nature can be seen most plainly when he ventured to Wolf Point in the heart of the Loop. From his spot on the Chicago River in the shadow of the Merchandise Mart, he could see factories and warehouses on the opposite bank and he could see automobile, truck, and elevated train traffic on the Lake Street Bridge. But if he focused on moving clouds against a blue sky above, the river lapping against the bank and swirling around a snag, the chirps of a cricket, and the rich carpet of grass on the riverbanks, he could leave modernity behind: "Slowly there swept through me the strange feeling that I was under some sort of spell, that some narcotic influence had entered my bloodstream and was permeating my entire being. All my ambitions, my dreams and hopes, my fears and doubts, left my mind as though they had been cleansed away, and I found myself in a peaceful state of euphoria." For Dubkin, nature was not a dynamic system with which we interact on a daily basis when we eat dinner, drink water, turn on an electrical switch, or flush our toilet. Rather it was a place separate from modern life, a place where we can temporarily escape the city and find therapy.[52]

Dubkin was a talented amateur naturalist with an understanding of the rudimentary science of ecology, and he traveled extensively throughout the city, recording what he saw in amusing, accessible, and sometimes beautiful prose. All of this makes him a unique figure and, for our purposes, an excellent guide or "urban ranger" to the city's pubic, commercial, and vernacular parks. But, as we will see in the chapters that follow, Dubkin, the sidewalk naturalist, was not *that* unique. Hundreds of thousands of immigrants, their American-born children, African Americans, and industrial workers also responded to the modern "artificial" environment of industrial Chicago by romanticizing nature. The following chapters are their stories.

## CHAPTER TWO

# Immigrants in Nature's Nation

> Sunshine, woodland green and woodland shade, the sound of
> horns! On a Sunday afternoon, what more could a German heart
> possibly wish for? ... Ha! The Germans like nothing better than
> a party under the oaks! The life our forefathers had in the woods
> still clings to us. ... I forgot that I was participating in a party
> so far away from the homeland in a foreign country. I exchanged
> many a cheerful word with many a cheerful person, was happy
> among happy people. It wasn't long however, before I was
> unfortunately called back to reality, remembered that I was a
> stranger here; oh why am I so ponderous in my attempts to
> reconcile myself with the local conditions!
>
> —"The Desplaines Hall Workers Club Picnics in Ogden's
> Grove," *Der Western*, July 22, 1869

U.S. environmental historians have largely ignored the American immigrant experience. In contrast, U.S. immigration historians have long been preoccupied with nature. This interest can clearly be seen in Oscar's Handlin's 1951 classic, *The Uprooted*, a seminal book that gave birth to the subfield of immigration history and established the centrality of immigration in America's past. Handlin argued that European peasants regarded the natural world as magical and animate, and they included the land itself in their sense of community. But migration uprooted them from the soil that had long sustained them, breaking "the ties with nature." Peasants formerly rooted in the earth now found themselves hemmed in by tall buildings and "fenced off from the realm of growing things." According to Handlin, immersion in this mechanical artificial environment resulted in dislocation and alienation. It was a world without magic, a world where rocks, streams, and trees only came back as memories "to be summoned up to rouse the curiosity and stir the wonder" of their American-born children.[1]

In the 1960s, a new generation of historians interested in immigration broke from Handlin. They found his generalizations about European peasant life overly simplistic and were troubled by the way *The Uprooted* rendered immigrants passive, socially disorganized victims of circumstance who had been yanked from the soil that had long sustained them. Inspired by the new social movements of the decade, younger scholars stressed the agency of newcomers and showed that the foreign born adapted creatively to their situation, in large part by importing or transplanting much of their social world (religion, tradition, family structure, and folk culture) into the urban industrial environment. The new botanic metaphor of transplantation in fact became the title of historian John Bodnar's influential 1987 synthesis of this new work on immigration. *The Transplanted* had eclipsed *The Uprooted*.[2]

Even as *The Transplanted* reached bookstores, historians (including Bodnar himself) yet again reconceptualized their understanding of immigrant culture. Drawing on Benedict Anderson's pathbreaking book *Imagined Communities: Reflections on the Origins and Spread of Nationalism*, literary critic Werner Sollors and a number of prominent historians argued during the 1990s that ethnic culture was hardly primordial. In other words, it was not a plant that could be uprooted from its native soil or transplanted carefully to a foreign urban environment. Rather, ethnic culture was something that was continually reinvented, articulated, and performed in the present. The group and its ethnic folk culture, then, did not grow organically out of the earth; rather immigrant leaders convinced a group of strangers that they were in fact one by pointing backward into the mist-shrouded past and identifying a common origin in the soil of a rural, preindustrial homeland.[3]

During the 1990s and early twenty-first century, interest in how the foreign born "invented ethnicity" coincided with new attention to the "transnational" dimension of migration. Scholars called attention to problems with the traditional unidirectional and "U.S.-centric" focus on how immigrants arrived, adjusted, assimilated, made room for ethnic culture, and generally contributed to American history. They showed that immigrants (or better yet, emigrants) often saw their stay in the United States as temporary, and significant numbers reversed course and returned to their original homeland. Historians also documented that while physically within the United States, immigrants maintained strong familial, social, economic, and political connections with home. Far from cutting themselves off from the past and simply cultivating American ethnic identities (German American, Irish American, or Mexican American), many of those physically within the United States imagined themselves as members of distant villages, regions, and nations. In describing these transnational cultures, migration historians turned to still other botanical metaphors: "hybridization" (the sexual reproduction of plants and animals of different species, hence the violation of boundaries assumed to be "natural" or impermeable) and "diaspora" (derived from the Greek verb most often used to describe the scattering of seeds).[4]

In this chapter, I build on this work on the invention of ethnicity and the transnational dimension of migration to undermine older American studies accounts that characterize the United States as "nature's nation," an exceptional country whose singular identity was born of a distinctive cultural relationship to nature. I also hope to challenge more recent works in U.S. environmental and cultural history that continue to portray the United States as an island somehow separate from the rest of the world. Environmental historian J. R. McNeill is absolutely right that far too much U.S. historical scholarship "looks rather like some American TV weather maps, where everything, including advancing thunderstorms and high pressure cells, stops at the border."[5]

As we will see, new arrivals in Chicago eagerly sought out nature, which they found in outlying wilderness areas but also in the heart of the city. Once through the gates of parks, immigrants sometimes used landscape to remember (and even vicariously visit) preindustrial rural homelands and to imagine subaltern ethnic, village, regional, and national identities.

## The Urban Industrial Environment

During the second half of the nineteenth century and the first decades of the twentieth, political oppression, colonialism, warfare, racism, and natural disasters pushed millions of Europeans, Chinese, and Mexicans out of their homelands. Economics, though, played the most significant role in prompting migration. New transportation networks gave small landowners, peasants, and craftspeople access to new markets, but these same networks also exposed them to fierce competition. Larger farms with state-of-the-art technology in fertile regions (including Chicago's far-reaching and extraordinarily productive hinterland) outcompeted small producers. At the same time, cheap manufactured goods from cities drove many village clockmakers, weavers, tailors, and other artisans out of business. Unable to make a living, millions migrated to cities, which were hungry for cheap, unskilled industrial labor. Chicago was one such destination.[6]

Once in Chicago, former farmers and craftspeople from the European, Asian, and Mexican countryside found themselves suddenly living in some of the grimmest industrial neighborhoods on the planet. Nearby packinghouses, rail yards, steel mills, brickyards, and manufacturing plants released irritating and toxic pollutants and noxious odors over adjoining homes while dirty coal from the furnaces that heated and powered the city blocked the sun, choked lungs, and blanketed everything in black soot. Many lived in dilapidated, dangerous, and congested wooden-frame houses situated on a monotonous flat grid of dirty, trash-filled streets and alleys. In 1905, the science fiction writer H. G. Wells, reporting from an observation car of the Pennsylvania Limited Express as it left the city, captured the scene: "Chicago burns bituminous coal, it has a reek that outdoes London, and right and left of the line rise vast chimneys, huge blackened grain-elevators, flame-crowned furnaces and gauntly ugly and filthy factory buildings, monstrous mounds of refuse, desolate, empty lots littered with rusty cans, old iron, and indescribable filth. Interspersed with these are groups of dirty, disreputable, insanitary-looking wooden houses." Although Wells acknowledged the occasional "gallant struggle of some spindly tree," he noted that in Chicago the original prairie had been obliterated by a smoky, industrial "nineteenth-century nightmare."[7]

The best known of the city's many bleak immigrant neighborhoods was Back of the Yards, the setting for *The Jungle* (1906), Upton Sinclair's famous muckraking exposé of the meatpacking industry. The Union Stockyards was the world's greatest animal-killing machine. Each day thousands of hogs and cattle, fattened up off prairie grasses and corn, walked off railroad cars and into the efficient, industrial maw of the meatpacking industry. Out the other end came steak, hairbrushes, bacon, fertilizer, canned meat, glue, and lard. To transform animals into commodities, the meatpackers needed cheap labor, and wages attracted waves of immigrants: Germans and Irish first, then eastern Europeans (Czechs, Poles, and Lithuanians, such as Jurgis Rudkus, the protagonist in *The Jungle*), and finally Mexicans and African Americans.[8]

Immigrants in Back of the Yards depended on the meatpackers for their livelihoods, but they also directly suffered the industry's considerable environmental impact. Back of the Yards was notorious for being smelt before being seen. According to Sinclair, the neighborhood had a "strange, fetid odor . . . a ghastly odor, like all the dead things of the universe." Even in the early twentieth century, streets remained unpaved and lacked basic sewer service. As a result, residents encountered mud and large puddles of fetid water. Flies bred prolifically at the fertilizer plants, in the stinking heaps of trash, and from decaying animal skins drying in "hair fields." Meanwhile, roving packs of rats gorged in the meat warehouses.[9]

Besides the stockyards and subsidiary industries (such as glue making), other environmental hazards boxed in the neighborhood. Loud, smoke-spewing freight trains ran on tracks that ringed the area. A local alderman ran a brickyard and a series of large open-air dumps. Trash from throughout the city came to the neighborhood, and it was not uncommon to see women and children scavenging for wood, scrap metal, old mattresses, clothes, and food. Meatpackers dumped some of their industrial waste into an adjoining pit that continuously smoldered. They also transformed a blind, stagnant tributary of the Chicago River that ran along the northern edge of the neighborhood into "Bubbly Creek," a giant open sewer. Sinclair noted that Bubbly Creek got its strange name because once dumped into the slimy depths, all the organic waste and chemicals from the stockyards underwent all sorts of strange transformations. "It is constantly in motion, as if huge fish were feeding in it, or giant leviathans disported themselves in its depths," the novelist and labor-rights advocate wrote. "Bubbles of carbonic acid gas will rise to the surface and burst, and make rings two or three feet wide."[10]

Immigrants not only found themselves living in polluted and seemingly artificial urban neighborhoods, they also often worked long hours in dangerous industrial environments. There they did increasingly specialized, repetitive work at a pace imposed not by available daylight, weather, or seasons, but by managers and machines. Many newcomers (such as the fictional Jurgis) had slaughtered animals back in rural Europe or Mexico, but they were completely unprepared for the "disassembly lines" at Armour and other plants. Here pigs and cattle moved along lines of workers, each of whom was responsible for one small task: killing, attaching a chain to the leg and sending the animal down the line, slicing off its head, draining blood, removing hide, scraping bristles, loosening entrails and spilling guts, removing hoofs, slicing, boiling, cleaning, packaging, and a thousand other small tasks. Although the gruesome work on packinghouse disassembly lines was distinctive, labor at other Chicago companies (U.S. Steel, International Harvester, the Pullman Palace Car Company, the Illinois Central Railroad, and Hart, Schaffner & Marx) was just as specialized and monotonous.[11]

Like elite Anglo Americans, immigrants found some relief from the stress of urban industrial life during their leisure. In working-class neighborhoods, such as Back of the Yards, there were plenty of options. After a long day slaughtering pigs, making steel, or sewing garments, large numbers of the foreign born retreated to their homes or to churches, synagogues, the halls of mutual aid societies, or gymnasia of national athletic organizations. There, during their scant leisure, they spent time with their families and compatriots. Newcomers also sometimes passed their spare time in places where leisure was more commercialized. If you threw a rock in Back of the Yards or nearly any other Chicago immigrant neighborhood, you stood a good chance of hitting a saloon. In these warm places, hundreds of thousands of men found beer, whiskey, food, and companionship. Large numbers of Chicagoans also passed their spare time going to ethnic theaters, dance halls, spectator sports venues, nickelodeons, department stores, and movie palaces. All of them, at a cost, provided contact with the magic distressingly absent from everyday life.[12]

## Recreation in the Outdoors

The foreign born certainly found catharsis by indulging in commercialized indoor amusements, but like their Anglo American counterparts, many also sought relief from the industrial urban environment by getting outdoors. Hundreds of thousands of immigrants made extensive use of Victorian pastoral parks, neighborhood athletic "playgrounds," and the outlying forest preserves.

Take Lincoln Park on Independence Day, 1892. The *Chicago Tribune* estimated that 20,000 people came out to enjoy themselves and that park goers made up a veritable "congress of nations." The reporter spotted "Mongolians" (Chinese from nearby Clark Street), Greeks, Persians, Poles, Swedes, Russians, Jews, Italians, Germans, Irish, French, and Arabs as well as African Americans. These immigrants came to Lincoln Park to socialize, listen to music, and to play sports for sure, but as the reporter made clear, the chief attraction was escaping the city and enjoying nature. The journalist explained that those from neighborhoods where "grass and sunlight and flowers are unknown" spent their day in the park looking at the lions, tigers, monkeys, buffalo, elk, and prairie dogs confined behind bars at the Lincoln Park Zoo. Others gathered under the trees, took boats out on the park lagoon, strolled along the parks' winding pathways, or picnicked on the grass. Meanwhile, children, "pale and bleached like vegetables growing in the dark," waded in the water and played on the lawn. The *Tribune* reported that while each was "free to select his mode of pleasure," everyone in the park was there "to enjoy the sunshine and the refreshing breezes from the lake." The journalist reported similarly diverse crowds in Garfield, Jackson, and Douglas Parks, as well as along the Lake Front. In fact, wrote the journalist, "every public green and common in the city was crowded with happy human beings enjoying the day in the open air and the warm sunshine."[13]

Despite the scene in Lincoln Park, immigrant use of parks was hard won. Conflict emerged almost as soon as large numbers of Germans and Irish immigrants arrived in the city during the late 1840s and early 1850s. The Europeans brought to America the so-called Continental Sunday, the practice of enjoying amusements on the Christian Sabbath following church. For Germans, in particular, this meant retreating to parks and beer gardens, where they listened to music, danced, enjoyed athletics such as gymnastics, drank beer, picnicked with family members, and enjoyed sunshine and fresh air under shade trees.[14]

Established Chicagoans found the Continental Sunday galling. It is true that by the mid-nineteenth century, many old-stock Americans such as Reverend Henry Ward Beecher had abandoned their parents' and grandparents' suspicions regarding all leisure. Instead of spending the entire Sabbath indoors in religious observance, the native born in Victorian Chicago had begun venturing outdoors after church, and they could be seen strolling in their own private gardens or in Lake Front Park, Chicago's answer to New York's Battery. Nevertheless, one could only enjoy nature quietly and contemplatively in a way befitting "the Lord's Day." Sports, music, loud picnics, and especially drinking were beyond the pale.[15]

Shocking Sabbath desecration in Irish saloons and German beer gardens resulted in action at the polls. In 1855, anti-immigrant nativists and temperance advocates elected a more conservative slate of candidates to the city council and mayor's office. Levi Boone, the new mayor (and nephew of noted frontiersman Daniel Boone), barred immigrants from city jobs, hiked liquor license fees, and began enforcing the city's 1845 Sunday closing law, which stipulated fines for those who dispensed alcohol or who disturbed "the peace and good order of society by labor (works of necessity and charity excepted) or by any amusement on Sunday." At the same time, the city began to make rules about how to properly use its few public parks. Chicago's political rulers outlawed playing "ball, cricket, or at any other game or play whatever." In later years, the city went on to ban walking on the grass (unless clearly posted), fishing, bathing, the playing of musical instruments, drinking alcohol, boisterous language, and gambling.[16]

German and Irish immigrants did not sit quietly as the "Puritans" curtailed their leisure activities. Sundays were workers' one day off in what was an intense American workweek, and the foreign born meant to defend what little freedom they had. The first scheduled trial of a violator of the Sunday law prompted hundreds of armed immigrants to gather at Washington Square (one of the city's first public parks) for a march on the courthouse. As the protesters approached, the mayor raised a drawbridge over the Chicago River and the police fired on the crowd gathered on the other side. This was the so-called Lager Beer Riot, a conflict about beer and saloons for sure, but also importantly a struggle over how to enjoy oneself in green spaces on Sundays.[17]

The Lager Beer Riot inaugurated decades of tension between Americans and Europeans over leisure. Boone's policies and the heavy-handed tactics of the police prompted Germans and Irish to form the first of the city's many interethnic political coalitions. Together, the two immigrant groups voted Boone out of office and reversed his draconian approach to amusements on Sunday. But following the Great Chicago Fire of 1871 (which killed hundreds and incinerated a huge swath of the city), city conservatives regrouped. Worried that the fire had been divine retribution for urban sin, they pushed a reluctant mayor to once again enforce the law against alcohol and amusement on Sunday. In response, immigrants rallied anew, forming the interethnic People's Party, which made the case that no individual or class could prescribe "how and which manner Sunday or any other day shall be enjoyed by a free people in a free Republic." One of the founders of the People's Party, A. C. Hesing, asked his followers what harm there was in going to Lincoln Park on Sunday after "working hard in a dirty, dusty shop all the week." What was so wrong with taking your family to "breathe a little of the fresh air the Lord . . . made?" What was the harm, he asked, in listening to the same music in parks that the Sabbatarians listen to in their churches? And what was so terrible about refreshing oneself with a little lager or wine? "You are a pack of slaves if you suffer laws that prohibit this." As they had in the 1850s, immigrant politicians during the mid 1870s again rolled back enforcement of the Sunday closing law.[18]

Tension between immigrants and native-born Americans over appropriate use of park space can also be seen during the opening of Humboldt Park during the summer of 1877. A largely Anglo American contingent of about 500 city officials and private citizens officially dedicated the park on Saturday July 14. In typical fashion, they rode in their carriages, rented rowboats, strolled the paths, and admired the park scenery. The next day, Sunday, 20,000 largely immigrant residents arrived for the informal opening. German Turnverein gymnastics groups, Danish and Swedish singing societies, and Irish soldiers carrying American and Irish flags paraded to the island of green. And once on the ground, the Turners set up gymnastics equipment and gave exhibitions, immigrant luminaries gave speeches in German and Swedish, and bands played European and American standards. Meanwhile, participants ate from enormous picnic baskets and made one-mile runs to the park edge to refill their steins, much to the great offense of some Anglo American observers.[19]

While conservatives bemoaned such "Sabbath desecration," immigrants lampooned the house- and church-bound Americans. An example of such satire is an 1883 article in the *Chicagoer Arbeiter-Zeitung*. The writer of the piece admitted that Anglo Americans had in fact invented the picnic, but he explained that the original picnic was largely an indoor affair devoid of dancing and drink and where participants indulged in hymns, Biblical verses, and pious activities. Those Americans who ventured outside the house "bore themselves as though they were being sentenced to death in criminal court instead of relaxing and having fun out-of-doors." It was the German societies, claimed the author, that made the American picnic an outdoor excursion where "families, far from the four walls of their lodgings, can get away from the toil, problems and strains of day-to-day life" and where participants can "hang up the day-to-day mask of constraint and depression and . . . thoroughly enjoy that untranslatable something: Gemütlichkeit." Puritans angered by so much fun in the outdoors promised divine retribution, and this has come, joked the author, in the occasional rain shower that bedevils the modern picnic.[20]

While the conservatives seethed, the immigrants ultimately won the war over how to use park space. Not only did park goers bend and even break rules, immigrant communities used their ever-increasing political power to press for change. They demanded Sunday concerts in the parks, the opening of grassy areas to picnics and sports, and the construction of athletic facilities, such as baseball diamonds, tennis courts, swimming pools, and outdoor gymnasia. In 1905, the city even quietly eliminated the ban on playing sports in parks on the Sabbath. Visitors from out of town noted that Chicago's large pastoral parks seemed more open than comparable parks in Boston and New York. For instance, Amos J. Cummings, a U.S. congressman from New York, observed in 1893 that while children in New York go to parks to learn how to read (from "Stay Off the Grass" signs), the people in Chicago spread out on the grass. "The people own their property in Chicago."[21]

It is true that when the foreign born went to urban parks, they often enjoyed outdoor recreational practices that many Anglo Americans found odd or troubling. Not only did they stroll along park paths, picnic, and enjoy scenery, sunshine, and fresh air, they also often played ethnic sports, listened to music, gathered in large boisterous groups, and drank alcohol. But these cultural differences are not grounds for concluding that Americans saw parks as natural spaces where one could escape from the industrial city, whereas immigrants viewed these same parks as mere recreational, social, or public spaces, as an extension of the city rather than a rural resort. Social historians of sports and leisure have typically divorced immigrant recreational practices from their environmental context, and doing so obscures the fact that leisure practices were frequently not ends in and of themselves, but rather vehicles through which immigrants enjoyed the outdoors. On this point, a writer for the newspaper *Illinois Staats-Zeitung* is instructive. The German, he wrote, is "interested in music and dancing as well as in beer and wine. But all this gives him but partial satisfaction if there is no sylvan environment. . . . To relax in the green, shady forests,—that is the German's ideal diversion."[22]

During the early twentieth century, immigrants not only tried to escape the industrial city by venturing into urban green spaces such as Lincoln Park, they also made recreational forays farther afield, outside city limits. By the mid-1920s, over 7.5 million people visited the Cook County Forest Preserves annually (in contrast the national parks saw only 1.7 million visitors in 1925). Not only did ethnic politicians (including the future mayor Anton Cermak) play significant roles in running and expanding the preserves, but representatives of nearly every one of Chicago's ethnic groups could be seen enjoying the "wilderness."[23]

If during a summer Sunday in the 1920s or 1930s we were to canoe the Chicago or Des Plaines Rivers or hike the old Pottawatomie trails through the forests and across the prairies of the Cook County Forest Preserves, we would see tens of thousands of immigrants. We would come across German, Italian, Slovene, Greek, and Polish campers, hikers, swimmers, and boaters. Perhaps we might also see a member of a Danish, Polish, German, Ukrainian, or Bohemian recreational fishing and hunting club casting into a lake, pond, or semipolluted river (see Fig. 2.1). Or we might meet Czeslawa Kowalewski, a Polish émigré who loved to pick flowers, berries, and mushrooms. "I always enjoy woods," the Polish woman told an interviewer. "I like Easter because it was close to spring and going out in the

FIGURE 2.1 "Gut Heil!, or "Good Health!," the traditional greeting of German Turners, such as those here at Turner Camp in Cary, Ill. Courtesy of the Lake County (Ill.) Discovery Museum, Curt Teich Postcard Archives.

woods, picking flowers, picking things like that. . . . I love to pick those things [mushrooms], berries, anything. That's for me, I don't know why, I love woods."[24]

Perhaps in a quiet grove along the river bank we might see hard at work Hugo Von Hofsten, a Swedish painter who made it his mission to preach through his art "the gospel of nature's beauty—a gospel which modern man, in his hurry, is apt to overlook and forget." Hofsten painted not only the landscape of rural Sweden, but he also made it his mission to introduce Chicagoans to the extraordinary beauty that they have at the edge of their great industrial city. He was not alone in his quest to visually reproduce landscapes around Chicago. He was joined by fellow Swedish painters Charles Hallberg, Birger Sandzén, and Leon Lundmark, the Dutch artist Tunis Ponsen, the Jewish Romanian modernist Emil Armin, and the artists in the Czech Umelecky Klub, who frequently ventured with their easels out to the dunes and nearby "primeval forests."[25]

Walking through the wilderness, we might see immigrants, such as our urban ranger Leonard Dubkin, eagerly absorbed in nature study. We might encounter the German physician and birder Carl Helmuth, who not only amassed an extraordinary collection of stuffed birds, but wrote and illustrated a guide to avian life in North America that, at least according to the

*Illinois Staats-Zeitung*, rivaled the *Birds of America*, written by John James Audubon (yet another immigrant to the United States). We might see August Sala, a Bohemian glassworker of modest means who rode to the outskirts of the city and collected butterflies and other insects, which he mounted in dozens of display cases. So impressive was the collection that it found a new home in the Field Museum of Natural History following Sala's death.[26]

In the wilderness, we would come across groups of children from immigrant schools botanizing, birding, and capturing insects. The Chicago Hebrew Institute (later the Jewish People's Institute) had its own natural history museum with over three thousand specimens and conducted nature study classes, with talks on flora and fauna and "trips to sunken gardens, flower exhibitions, and forest preserves." At the Resurrection Sisters' Academy for Polish girls, "walks in the meadows, fields, and nearby woods [the school was next to a forest preserve] are not only healthy but supply material for natural studies, which, when properly directed, teach love of nature."[27]

Perhaps in the woods, we might even see Jens Jensen, the dean of the Prairie School style of landscape architecture. During the 1890s, Jensen took his family on weekend excursions to seemingly untouched places just outside of Chicago. In these areas where local rail lines ended, Jensen spent years collecting plant specimens and carefully studying the landscape, which, despite his fame as a fierce defender of the indigenous Midwest, reminded him of his own native Denmark. Exposure to "wild" places just outside the city played a formative role in the development of Jensen's unique style of landscape architecture, as could be seen in Columbus Park and in his many garden commissions throughout the Midwest. Additionally, it was his fear that these landscapes on the urban fringe were quickly disappearing that prompted him to play the leading role in the preservation of the Cook County Forest Preserves and the Indiana Dunes.[28]

More than anything else, though, we would encounter foreign-born picnickers in the woods, on the prairies, and along the rivers of the forest preserves. Charles G. Sauers, general superintendent of the preserves, described the scene: "Each nationality has its own distinctive characteristic in the conduct of its picnics, in the choice of their location, in their amusements and costumes. Indeed on a single Sunday, one might pass from one grove to the next and easily imagine that he was traveling in Europe." Hiking through the wilderness, supposedly that most American of spaces, we might see picnics of the Polish National Alliance, Italian American

Citizens Club, Persian Hebrew Congregation, Aloysius Parish, Vizoko Litovzk Aid Society, Tatran Slovak Union, American Sokol, Sarah Kamensky Ladies Aid, Spartaco Lavagnini Club, St. Vladimir Ukrainian Orthodox Church, Eleventh Ward Jugo-Slavian Croatian American Club, Independent Sisters of Odessa, Circolo di Culture e Divertmento, Russian-American Citizens' Association, Temple Sholom Men's Club, Circle of Serbian Sisters, Slovenian National Benefit Society, Michael Flynn Boosters, the Mexican Methodist Church, and many, many more. We would perhaps see women in native garb serving succulent roasted lamb at a Greek picnic, a Polish nationalist chronicling sacrifices made in the defense of mother Poland, a priest giving a Croatian high mass, synagogue congregants singing Jewish folk songs, or Mexican couples dancing to the music of the Marcias and Garcia Orchestra. Perhaps in the woods we might even see the Hungarians portrayed by Carl Sandburg in his famous poem "Happiness":

> I asked the professors who teach the meaning of life to tell me what
>      is happiness.
> And I went to famous executives who boss the work of thousands
>      of men.
> They all shook their heads and gave me a smile as though I was
>      trying to fool with them.
> And then one Sunday afternoon I wandered out along the Desplaines
>      river
> And I saw a crowd of Hungarians under the trees with their women
>      and children and a keg of beer and an accordion.[29]

Especially after the arrival of cheaper train and steamship tickets and, later, the affordable automobile, the foreign born went even farther afield. While Anglo Americans travelled to Lake Geneva and other exclusive resort areas in the Wisconsin Lake Country, middle- and upper-class immigrants escaped to their own ethnic vacation destinations. Jews, for instance, made the town of South Haven, Michigan, into what historian Irving Cutler describes as a miniature (although flat) borscht belt. Czech families vacationed at the Vavra Resort and Lubuse Inn at Union Pier, Michigan, while Italians from Cicero visited Tosi's Restaurant and Resort in Stevensville, Michigan. Norwegians retreated to Scandia Beach in the woods of northern Wisconsin and the Norge Ski Club, which boasted an enormous fabricated ski jump built on top of Illinois prairie. Chicago Swedes started a camp and resort settlement at Bethany Beach, Michigan, as well as a summer colony called Skansen (after the famous living history museum) in Wisconsin that had the feel of a real Swedish village, complete with cottages painted bright red. Bosnians, meanwhile, traveled to the Dilich farm on the Wisconsin-Illinois border. Here, according to historian Samira Puskar, visitors would boat, picnic, roast lamb, and "get away from the bustle of the city and enjoy little reminders of the natural scenery of homeland Bosnia."[30]

According to oral histories collected by Elaine Thomopoulos, Greeks would take steamers or automobiles to southwest Michigan. Once there, they canned vegetables and fruit and dined on freshly slaughtered lamb. One of Thomopoulos's subjects, Adrienne Georgandas, explained that the food tasted better "because we were always outside. You know? It was that outside living that we liked so much, and I experienced the same kind of thing when I lived in Greece, the outdoor living. I like it so much better than everyone being closed in here." They also played the mandolin and the lyre, danced ancient Greek circle dances around the campfire, explored, swam in Lake Michigan, played cards, went on long walks in the countryside, stargazed, watched the sunset over Lake Michigan, and formed friendships and romantic attachments. According to Thomopoulos, in little resort communities throughout Michigan, vacationers from Chicago recreated "the idyllic rural Greek-village type of life left behind in Greece."[31]

During their often-scarce leisure, large numbers of immigrants eagerly escaped to urban parks, wilderness areas, and rural resorts. We might thing that the foreign born simply followed well-off Anglo Americans out of the city and back to nature. We might think that figures such as Olmsted taught newcomers to "appreciate" nature and that nature romanticism or pastoralism simply trickled down from above. But evidence from Chicago suggests a different story. At least on Sunday, it was the immigrants who taught overworked and overly pious sons and daughters of "nature's nation" how to get out of their homes, offices, and churches and enjoy and appreciate nature. As a writer for the Swedish paper *Svenska Nyheter* noted, the Anglo American considered it an "unforgivable sin" to spend Sunday with "God-created nature, in the cool forest and sunny meadows under a blue sky, far from dusty streets and crowded dwellings and far from dry sermons in stuffy churches." Instead of caving, Germans, Irish, and other immigrants fought for the right to enjoy parks on Sunday. Ultimately they won the culture war and taught conservative Americans to appreciate the outdoors. As Carl Sandburg understood, the foreign born showed the Americans who bossed thousands of men that if they wanted happiness, all it took was a Sunday afternoon picnic under the trees along the Des Plaines River with family, an accordion, and a keg of beer.[32]

## Cultivating Memories of Home

One Anglo American reaction to modernity was to flee into an Anglo Saxon past, and many undoubtedly found this by visiting one of Olmsted's English parks or, better yet, by crossing the pond on vacation and visiting the pastoral parklike scenery and Gothic ruins of the mother country. Others responded to growing urban heterogeneity by retreating during their leisure into pastoral New England, the villages of which many imagined as the seed of the future nation. Especially in the early twentieth century, Americans discovered that a therapeutic answer to modern urban life was a vacation in a national park or other wilderness area where they could "See America." Preserved in these places were vestiges of the original frontier wilderness that supposedly gave rise to a distinctive nation. As one publicist put it, past the park gates, visitors entered into the "National Museum of Original America, depository of unique unmodified irreplaceable examples of the vast wilderness which our forefathers conquered." After a day of transforming Indian and pioneer labor of fishing, camping, hiking, and outdoor cooking into play, established middle- and upper-class tourists converged around the campfire. Despite the fact that their automobile license plates showed that they came from New York, Tennessee, California, and Texas, tourists in the national park wilderness imagined themselves as citizens of a coherent, long-standing American community rooted in native soil.[33]

Although the relationship between landscape, memory, and Anglo American identity has been well documented by historians, immigrant nature romanticism or pastoralism has received little attention. As we have seen, the foreign born ventured to parks to picnic, camp, play sports, and enjoy fresh air and sunshine. But they also went to these landscapes of leisure in and around Chicago to remember the past. Think of the Lithuanian with whom this book began and how upon first seeing the Indiana Dunes he dropped his tools, stretched, inhaled, and recalled the Coronian Spit on the Baltic back in his homeland. Or think of the German worker with whom this chapter began. Once off the city streets and within Ogden's Grove, he found himself in an environment of "sunshine, woodland green and woodland shade." Industrial Chicago faded away, and he was magically transported back to his homeland. Under the green trees, he drank beer and ate coffeecake and noted that all the picnic tables and benches were filled with German workers and their families and friends. He heard all the dialects of his homeland, as well as the sound of "horn, flute, and fiddle ... through the woods," which brought dancers from throughout the grove and soon "all of Germany was dancing together." "The Germans," he explained, "like nothing better than a party under the oaks! The life our forefathers had in the woods still clings to us." So powerful was the illusion of travel that he "forgot that I was participating in a party so far away from the homeland in a foreign country." As we will see, that Lithuanian at the Indiana Dunes or that German in the urban forest of Ogden's Grove were hardly alone. Large numbers of immigrants responded to the fragmenting effects of urban modernity and their sense of displacement and homesickness by using Chicago urban and wilderness parks to remember distant villages, regions, and nations.[34]

Although Anglo Americans often viewed immigrants as representatives of nations (or races), many newcomers to industrial Chicago arrived without strong allegiances to abstract father and motherlands. Many countries, such as Germany and Italy, were quite new, and peasants were often relatively untouched by nationalism. Once in Chicago, newcomers often continued to understand their identity in very local terms. They reserved their fealty not for Austro-Hungary, Greece, or Russia but rather for their home villages. Italians, for instance, adhered to *campanilismo*, or loyalty only to that area over which one could hear the bell from the village church. Meanwhile, the frame of reference for many Eastern Europeans was the *okolica*, or surrounding countryside. The village or town also figured as a powerful marker of identity for many Mexicans and Chinese.[35]

Immigrants made green spaces an important site for remembrance of distant villages. Despite the legacy of Old World persecution, Jewish *landsmanshaften* (or hometown) organizations often met in Douglas Park where they played mandolin music, danced the *hora*, and rekindled memories of Eastern European *shtetls*. Many Polish villages had their own societies, and throughout the summer many of these clubs met for picnics, sometimes in the wilderness of the forest preserves. In parks and picnic groves but most often at the Desplaines River Resort, migrants from Klepa, Tripoli, Messia, Arachamites, and other Greek villages roasted a lamb, drank wine, joined in circle dances, reminisced, and, at least for an afternoon, converged again as a village.[36]

In a number of American cities, Italians re-created village *festas*, which included processions of uniformed members of various societies who escorted patron saints (often updated Catholic versions of ancient place–based gods common throughout the Mediterranean world). In Chicago, Italians frequently traveled to the countryside outside the city to remember their saints. "The secluded location permitted these homesick immigrants to enjoy the illusion that they were reenacting this pageant under their native skies," notes historian Rudolph Vecoli. One participant described a Chicago *festa* this way: "there in the midst of these Italians, with almost no Americans, it seemed to be truly a village in southern Italy." The most important such gathering was the *Festa Della Madonna*, held annually in the suburb of Melrose Park on the Sunday closest to July 16. After the procession, participants gathered at the nearby Stefano Farm (which was transformed into a picnic ground) for Old World culinary specialties, Italian sports such as bocce, games of chance, and fireworks.[37]

Chicagoans also gathered in parks to remember regions that they had left behind. Norwegians formed *bygdelag*, or old-home societies, devoted to remembering the customs, traditions, and landscapes of regions within Norway. Immigrants from the area in and around Bergen, Norway, for instance, remembered their homeland (located on the coast of the Norwegian Sea) by taking regular excursions on Lake Michigan. Germans organized a number of *Heimat* (homeland) organizations, such as the Rheinischer Verein, Saarländer Verein, the Schwabenverein, and the Eifelverein, a group which dedicated itself to "preserving the love and honor of our Heimat, the familiar Eifel mountains, here in the far West, far from the homeland." At picnics and outings, migrants remembered the region, and these homeland sentiments, according to historian Thomas Lekan, "maintained the contours of an imagined local community spanning the Atlantic."[38]

During the late nineteenth and early twentieth centuries, the largest such regional gathering was the Cannstatter Volksfest, which began in 1878. Each August, thousands of Swabians (from southwest Germany) and other Germans marched to Ogden's Grove and later Brand's and Sharpshooters Park. They came with floats that carried allegorical figures, including a rock meant to represent the homeland; Emperor Frederick Barbarossa in his final resting place within the Kyffhäuser, an actual mountain in the Harz range; and the four seasons, spring ("Flora"), summer (a cart full of hay); autumn ("Bacchus" in a golden wine cart); and winter (a spinning room and hunting party). The centerpiece of every festival was a thirty- to fifty-foot column, decked out in fruits, vegetables, and grains, which represented the harvest. For participants, many of whom dressed in the distinctive garb of home villages, the fest was an opportunity to eat regional delicacies, to drink lager, and sample Neckar wine, which the King of Württemberg sent to Chicago each year from his private cellar. Organizers of the Cannstatter folk fest went so far as to painstakingly reconstruct southwestern Germany within Chicago rural retreats. One year, they built the entrance and towers of Stuttgart Castle; another year, they recreated the sixteenth-century town of Ulm, complete with a *Bürgermeister* who greeted members of the audience as if they were long-lost friends. Visitors enjoyed *tableaux-vivant* of scenes from Johann Wolfgang von Goethe's *Faust* and Friedrich von Schiller's *Wallenstein* as well as shadow pictures and stereopticon slides of towers, villages, castles, the Black Forest, and the Neckar River. For participants, the Volksfest offered an opportunity to vicariously travel home. As one writer for the *Abendpost* put it, "a Suabian could not forgive himself to neglect this great fest. It reminds him, more than anything else, of his beautiful homeland."[39]

Only after arriving in Chicago did many of the foreign born learn that they were in fact "Germans," "Italians," or "Mexicans." Immigrants quickly discovered that native-born Americans frequently defined the United States in exclusive Anglo American terms and grouped newly arrived "foreigners" into different (and often inferior) races and nations. Bosses, journalists, and politicians saw no difference between Sicilians and those from Basilicata, Campania, or even northern Italy and sometimes identified everyone collectively as "wops" or "dagos." In such a hostile environment, extending one's sense of community beyond those who could hear the village bell had obvious advantages. Furthermore, America was not an island. Foreign-born intellectuals also drew on currents of romantic nationalism circulating in the homeland, and, as historian Kathleen Neils Conzen and her colleagues put it, appropriated and reworked "preexisting communal solidarities, cultural attributes, and historical memories." At the same time, natural disasters, invasions, colonization and oppression, and national triumphs sometimes powerfully shaped identity formation. In Chicago, for instance, continued foreign occupations played hugely important roles in the continual reinvention of Irish and Polish identities. Lastly, leaders carefully modulated the cultural construction of nationalism to the internal dynamics of migrant communities, which were often divided by region, religion, class, generation, languages, politics, gender, neighborhood, and more. Because the American context, the situation in the homeland, and the political

FIGURE 2.2 "Crowds Standing on a Field at Humboldt Park during a
Norwegian Celebration Day on May 17, 1925," DN-0079051, *Chicago Daily News*
Negatives Collection, Chicago History Museum.

dynamics within the community were always shifting, the work of community leaders was ongoing and never complete.[40]

Immigrant nationalists imagined the nation in political speeches, at indoor events in society halls, and at parades through city streets. Ethnic radio
and a vibrant immigrant press also projected origins and helped forge a
sense of identity. But for our purposes, what is most interesting is that immigrants frequently used green spaces in and around Chicago to invoke
common roots and invent nationalism. At precisely the same moment that
millions of middle-class Anglo Americans ventured into the national parks
and other wilderness areas in search of contact with the true and original
America, the foreign born entered into urban and peri-urban green spaces
and rural and wild landscapes of nature's nation and remembered Ireland,
Germany, Sweden, Czechoslovakia, and Mexico (see Fig. 2.2 and Fig. 2.3).

Every year in mid-August, thousands of Irish Chicagoans traveled to
parks and celebrated Our Lady Day in Harvest, otherwise known as the
Feast of the Assumption. The holiday marked the Virgin Mary's ascent into
heaven and the beginning of the fall harvest as well as the Prince of Ul-

FIGURE 2.3 Japanese Americans at a 1928 Picnic. Courtesy of the
Chicago Japanese American Historical Society.

ster's routing of the English at Yellow Ford in 1598, the victory of Red Hugh
O'Donnell in the Battle of Curlew Pass in 1599, and the joint French and
Irish victory at Castlebar in 1798. Our Lady Day in Harvest also probably
contained vestiges of the ancient Celtic Festival of Lughnasa, an August
harvest celebration devoted to the Sun God Lugh and the Earth Goddess
Tailtiu, who supposedly sacrificed her life preparing the Irish fields for
agriculture. Under the trees at Brand's and other Chicago parks, participants picnicked, listened to Irish musicians, watched jigs and step dancing,
and participated in Irish sports, such as Gaelic hurling. Speakers, meanwhile,
invoked the landscape of Eire, reminded listeners of the historic struggle
of the Irish people against English colonialism, and urged listeners to re-
dedicate themselves to the ongoing quest to free their nation from the
English yoke.[41]

Immigrants from Germany also used Chicago landscapes to imagine the
nation. The Cannstatter Folkfest ultimately became a national German
festival, but even before that, Germans sometimes used green space to imagine the nation. Such patriotism was especially evident in 1871, at the end
of the Franco-Prussian War. To celebrate victory over the French and the

unification of Germany, 30,000 Germans marched from the Loop to Wright's Grove in a parade that stretched ten miles in length. The parade (which featured floats of German oak and evergreen forests and the Rhine River as well as reenactors playing Hermann and his wife Thusnelda, skin- and fur-clad German tribesmen, heralds, pages, archers, crusaders, and no- table German writers, poets, musicians, and scientists) depicted the his- tory of Germany, in effect rendering the new nation ancient. Germans then gathered in Wright's Grove (a leafy private picnic ground on the North Side). They watched gymnastics, danced, sang, picnicked, drank Bismarck-, Moltke-, and Wilhelm-brand beer, and listened to the orchestra play "Die Wacht am Rhein" and "Nun danket alle Gott." They also heard patriotic speeches from immigrant leaders, such as Franz Arnold, who congratu- lated those gathered in the park for coming together in the land of their adoption to recognize the land of their birth. He told the history of ani- mosity between Latin and German races, narrated German achievements, and noted how German civilization had spread, including now to North America. He noted that Prussians, Badenese, Swabians, and Bavarians had united as one to throw off the invader. We celebrate, he told the crowd, the reunification of Germany after five hundred years, the reconquest of two provinces, and the "deliverance of the Rhine, our symbolic stream."[42]

On the Sunday closest to the summer solstice, tens of thousands of Swedes massed in various Chicago parks to celebrate *midsommar*, a thousand- year-old Viking fertility rite. At Columbus, Elliott, Alton, Riverside and Good Templar Parks, Scandinavians, often wearing regional clothing, raised a fifty-foot maypole and built huts representing the different provinces of Sweden, all of which they covered in green boughs. Swedes danced around the maypole, elected a *midsommarbrud* (or Queen of Midsummer) and drank the old Swedish honey beer *mjod*. They watched pageants, par- ticipated in Swedish sports and games, and sang Swedish folk songs, such as *Du gamla, Du fria*, which evoked the mountains, sun, sky, and meadows of the northern home. "We have again celebrated Midsummer here and we have once more gone back in our thoughts to old Sweden, with its clear blue skies, under which young and old danced around the Maypole," noted one participant in 1899. "We Chicago Swedes have faithfully preserved the customs of our forefathers, even if the Midsummer sun is shining over us thousands of miles from the land of the Midsummer sun."[43]

Bohemians in Chicago celebrated *Posvíceni*. In Pilsen Park, visitors, many dressed in peasant clothing or in the uniforms of various societies, con- sumed pretzels, sausage, cucumbers, and gingerbread, and drank beer from the nearby brewery. They watched folk dances and circus acts, and listened to tunes from a Czech village band. According to the Bohemian newspaper *Denní Hlasatel*, the organizing committee of the Czech harvest festival Posvícení did everything possible to reconstruct Czech conditions in Pilsen Park. The committee did "its utmost to incorporate in the event everything colorful, interesting, and indigenous in our old-time Czechoslovak Posvícení, combining it with outstanding features of old-fashioned pilgrimages, processions, and various other rites in the life of our forebears. All these patterns will be followed as closely as practicable under new conditions in a new homeland." Another writer for *Denní Hlasatel* explained that everyone who attends Posvícení "will re-live and re-experience all the joys of Czech pilgrimages, such as he always looked forward to in his youth."[44]

After the start of World War I, Bohemians used Pilsen Park to organize resistance to Hapsburg Rule and to fight for a free Czechoslovakia. As historian Dominic Pacyga demonstrates, the very idea of Czech independence originated, in part, from this Bohemian park on Chicago's South Side. After the end of World War I, the new Czech nation recognized Chicago's contribution to the liberation effort by sending to Pilsen Park an urn which contained sacred soil from Říp Mountain (an extinct volcano where Praotec Čech supposedly led the first Slavs and gave birth to the new nation), Velehrad (the thirteenth-century site of the first Cistercian Monastery), and Devín (an eighth-century Slavic castle atop a rock formation located at the confluence of the Danube and Moravia Rivers). The National Alliance of Bohemian Catholics urged all to go to the park to see the soil, "for by viewing the urn with its sacred contents—the soil from places infinitely dear to us—we are to remember the land of our birth and bear in mind that we are a transatlantic branch of the brave and now liberated Czechoslovak nation."[45]

Mexicans, meanwhile, rented and appropriated Pilsen Park, using the Czech park to remember their own distant homeland. As was the case with many other immigrant groups, it was in Chicago that people from different villages from disparate regions (such as Jalisco and Michoacán) began to think of themselves as members of a nation. During the 1920s and 1930s, Mexican Independence Day fiestas in the Czech park is where much of this imaginative work took place. At these nationalist celebrations, organizers erected an altar to the fatherland, showed heroes of the revolution, gave speeches on "the duties of the citizen and how to preserve the citizenship of our country," and remembered the land of the Aztecs.[46]

Immigrants might be from Sicily, Bergen, Swabia, County Cork, or Jalisco, but nationalists in Chicago reminded them that they were in fact Italian, Norwegian, German, Irish, and Mexican. Even more, they urged compatriots to sacrifice for their homeland and even to defend it with their lives. The large number of young Chicagoans eager to give their lives for Greece, Ireland, Poland, Czechoslovakia, or Ukraine is a testament to the power of such appeals. It is also important to note that although Chicago's foreign born imagined themselves as Greek, Polish, Irish, Mexican, and Chinese, many simultaneously used green space to articulate new ethnic-American identities. When Anglo Americans talked about America's English roots and its racially Anglo Saxon character, ethnic leaders often responded with what historian Orm Øverland calls "home-making myths." In these counter myths, immigrants showed their unique contribution to America and thereby tried to establish a place for their group within an exclusive nation. Chicago Italians loudly proclaimed that Christopher Columbus founded the nation; Norwegians across town disagreed and pointed to Leif Eriksson. The Poles meanwhile celebrated Tadeusz Kosciusko and Casimir Pulaski, both heroes of the American Revolution. In speeches and in the press, others remembered ethnic sacrifices on Civil War battlefields or the work of subduing Indian frontiers, cultivating the country, and building up cities.[47]

The foreign born often saw no contradiction in having allegiances to two nations. Charles Schurz, the noted German revolutionary, Civil War general, journalist, and secretary of the interior, described the relationship between the immigrant and the Old World nation as that between a son and a mother, but the relationship between the immigrant and America as that between a man and a new wife. Marrying a new wife hardly meant forsaking one's mother and other descendants. Using highly gendered language that positioned the citizen of both nations as inherently male, Shurz explained: "He who does not keep his mother in true remembrance is not able to love his young bride truly; he who does not honor the old fatherland is not worthy of the new one."[48]

Physical ruins of this earlier world when immigrants used urban green spaces to look backward and imagine ethnicity can still be found in Chicago's parks. In "nature's nation," one can still visit Humboldt, Amundsen, Dvorak (or Svatopluk Čech), Kosciusko, Chopin, and Pulaski Parks. One can also still see many of the monuments that immigrants raised to ethnic heroes. So many statues were erected in Chicago parks that sculptor Lorado Taft complained in 1921 that instead of "themes harmonious with sylvan beauty," we find in the Chicago parks "a petrified congress of nations, a sculptural card-index of the peoples represented in Chicago's mighty melting pot." In Lincoln Park there are statues of philosopher and playwright Friedrich von Schiller, musician Ludwig van Beethoven, the Swedish naturalist Carolus Linnaeus, and poet and novelist Johann Wolfgang von Goethe, Italian nationalist Giuseppe Garibaldi, and the Danish writer of fairy tales Hans Christian Andersen. At Humboldt Park, one finds monuments to Alexander von Humboldt, the writer Fritz Reuter, the Polish patriot and American Revolutionary War hero Tadeusz Kosciusko, and the Viking explorer Leif Erikkson. Garfield Park is home to a statue in the memory of the Scottish romantic poet Robert Burns; in Douglas Park, there is a memorial to Czech journalist, poet, politician, and nationalist Karel Havlíček; and in Grant Park, Italians installed a replica of explorer Christopher Columbus's anchor and, later, a statue of the man himself.[49]

Just as the immense rock carvings at Mount Rushmore in South Dakota are windows into the cultural construction of an early twentieth-century hegemonic version of American identity, the ethnic monuments in Chicago's public parks are a lens on the ways that the turn-of-the-century foreign born used landscape to remember the past and forge community. But Mount Rushmore and other monuments to official memory are maintained by the federal government and visited by millions of people, whereas the ethnic monuments in Chicago parks are hidden and deteriorating. They are crumbling ruins of a forgotten world when immigrants appropriated landscape in "nature's nation" and used those green spaces to remember home and imagine subaltern identities (see Fig. 2.4).[50]

Like privileged native-born Americans, newcomers to Chicago often viewed work and life in industrial Chicago as artificial. One response was to seek out green space during leisure. They travelled to the Cook County Forest Preserves, the Indiana Dunes, Starved Rock State Park, and ethnic resorts in Michigan and Wisconsin. Those unable to leave the city sought out oases of green closer to home: large nineteenth-century pastoral parks, the Lake Michigan shore, small neighborhood parks, cemeteries, and even vacant lots. Although some visitors undoubtedly saw urban parks as an extension of the city, there is abundant evidence that many foreign born, like their Anglo American counterparts, sought during their leisure to escape the modern urban environment and get "back to nature." Germans and Irish picnicked, listened to music, played sports, and drank in the outdoors. Italian women, meanwhile, danced the *tarantella* in the wilderness of the

FIGURE 2.4 Unveiling of Monument to Johann Wolfgang von Goethe on June 13, 1914, in Lincoln Park. Later that summer, World War I began, and in 1918, vandals painted the Goethe statue yellow, a color traditionally associated with traitors. DN-0062958, *Chicago Daily News* Negatives Collection, Chicago History Museum.

Cook County Forest Preserves; Czechs ventured to Indiana to camp like Gypsies just as they had in the Old Country; Mexicans took their after-dinner *paseos* in nearby parks; Russians and other eastern Europeans went on mushroom hunts; the Chinese gardened and went to Lake Michigan to fly kites; and Sandburg's Hungarians enjoyed a Sunday picnic and keg of beer on the banks of the Des Plaines River.

Although immigrants sometimes fought with Anglo Americans over when and how to use parks, it was not the case that the battle pitched nature lovers versus immigrants interested only in public, social, or recreation space. Nor was it the case that Americans such as Olmsted taught the "foreigners" to enjoy nature. At least on Sundays, it was in fact the immigrants who showed the native born the folly of spending a beautiful Sunday afternoon cooped up in their homes and churches rather than outdoors in the sunshine and fresh air.

Even more, the foreign born used landscape to make meaning and imagine community. While Anglo Americans traveled to national parks, the forest preserves, and the Indiana Dunes to remember the frontier experience that supposedly bound them together as a cohesive community, the foreign born in Chicago ventured to wilderness parks and rural resorts as well as urban parks with the express purpose of remembering a common  preindustrial past and imagining diasporic community in the present. Our subjects entered into Chicago green spaces not to "See America First," but to remember villages such as Arachamites, regions like Bavaria and Sicily, and even nations, such as Ireland, Mexico, and Czechoslovakia.

Keenly aware of the bonds that newcomers maintained and reforged with old homelands, Progressive reformers focused their attention on the American-born children of immigrants. Intent on naturalizing children to the United States, reformers spent a great deal of effort trying to bring ethnic children into contact with nature. As we will see, tens of thousands of ethnic children and young adults eagerly flocked to green spaces, but the experience hardly assimilated them into the Anglo American middle class. On the contrary, many of these young people used natural spaces to forge ethnic working-class neighborhood identities that reformers saw as dangerous and even pathological.

## CHAPTER THREE

# Turf

## *Working-Class Ethnic Youth and Green Space*

> Studs Lonigan walked north along Indiana Avenue. His cap was
> on crooked, a cigarette hung from the corner of his mouth, and
> his hands were jammed into the pockets of his long jeans . . . .
> Warm sun sifted dozily through an April wind, making him
> feel good. He liked spring and summer. There were things in
> winter that were all right—ice skating, plopping derbies with
> snowballs—but spring and summer, that was the ticket. Soon
> now, there would be long afternoons ahead, at the beach and
> over at Washington Park, where they would all drowse in the
> shade, gassing, telling jokes, goofing the punks, flirting with the
> chickens and nursemaids, fooling around and having swell times.
> Like last summer, only this one was going to be even better.
>
> —JAMES T. FARRELL, *The Young Manhood of Studs Lonigan*, 1934

Studs Lonigan, the young Irish American protagonist of James T. Farrell's
*Studs Lonigan* trilogy, spends his leisure in a variety of South Side locations. He and his friends in the Fifty-eighth Street Gang visit Bathcellar's
Billard Parlor and Barber Shop, the Palm Theater (where Studs saw Char-
lie Chaplin, Fatty Arbuckle, and Mary Pickford), and Joseph's Ice Cream
Parlor. The gang gathers around the fireplug in front of the drug store on
the corner of Fifty-eighth Street and Prairie. And once the boys are older,
they visit speakeasies such as the Cannonball Inn, jazz clubs such as the
Sunrise Café in the Black Belt, various brothels or "can houses," and interethnic dance halls, such as Midway Gardens, the Trianon, the Bourbon
Palace.[1]

At the same time, Studs and the Fifty-eighth Street gang also regularly
venture to green spaces. As a boy, Studs and his friends play in vacant lots
or "prairies," such as the one at Fifty-eighth Street and Indiana, where
they dig trenches and recreate the battles of World War I. Throughout
the summer, they also go to the beaches that served as an urban-wild interface between South Side neighborhoods and Chicago's great inland
sea. Here is where Studs, as an adolescent, floats, looks up at clouds, and

feels all of his problems disappear, a sensation which prompts him to consider "swimming out into the nothingness." But for Studs, no place was more important than Washington Park, the 372-acre pastoral landscape designed by Frederick Law Olmsted and Calvert Vaux just after the Civil War. He and his friends boat on park lagoons, sit on the grass, and play baseball at park diamonds, which figured as a life-giving escape from the harsh city streets in much of Farrell's fiction. In other words, the young men might smoke cigarettes, wear their caps crooked, brawl, and harass women, but they still view the park not as an extension of the city so much as a green escape from their urban problems. It is a place to relax and enjoy sunshine, fresh air, grass, shade trees, and Lake Michigan.[2]

In addition, for Studs, Washington Park serves as a homeland of sorts. In the mental geography of foreign-born parents, the *shtetl*, the Sicilian village, the *Heimat*, or the imagined national landscape of Greece or Poland were the touchstones of identity. We can see nostalgic yearning for a distant homeland in Stud's Irish-born father, Patrick. The trilogy begins with Patrick singing "Where the River Shannon Flows" (a popular song of the day that evoked nostalgia for the landscape of Ireland and a girl left behind). Patrick dreams of returning to Ireland for a second honeymoon with his wife, reuniting with lost relatives, kissing the blarney stone, and touring the Lakes of Killarney. At the novel's close, Patrick is a broken man. He has lost his son Studs to pneumonia, and after blacks start moving into the neighborhood, he has sold his house at a loss. He drives his old Ford back through time, to his former homes and finally to the Bridgeport Irish slum where he had grown up. Ultimately, he ends up in a speakeasy where he drinks whiskey, longs to hear the River Shannon, revels in Irish pride, and drunkenly toasts "the dear old sod."[3]

Studs, in contrast, longs nostalgically for Washington Park. The park is the site of his adolescent romantic encounter with Lucy Scanlon, his first love. On a beautiful summer afternoon, he and Lucy walk across the wooden bridge to a forested island in the midst of the park lagoon. They climb into the branches of an old oak, look out at the water, feel the cool breeze, listen to the sound of birds, hold hands and kiss. Despite his profound love for Lucy, Studs drives her away, and throughout the rest of the trilogy, he nostalgically revisits the magical afternoon in the park. After his family joins the "white flight" out of the Washington Park neighborhood to the ethnically mixed but racially segregated suburb of South Shore, a displaced Studs returns to the park. Mirroring his own father's drive backward through time and his drunken toast to the "dear old sod," an inebriated Studs spends a night stumbling through a pitch-black Washington Park while the wind blows through dead leaves and denuded trees. "It had used to be his park. He almost felt as if his memories were in it, walking about like ghosts." Despite his efforts to find the magical oak tree where he and Lucy had once sat together looking out at the park lagoon, he cannot locate it.[4]

The *Studs Lonigan* trilogy is obviously a work of fiction. But, Farrell, who was influenced by the urban sociology pioneered at the University of Chicago, portrays the world of Irish ethnic youth in rich, even obsessive, detail. The places and the larger historical events (such as the 1919 race riot) are all real, and many of the characters are based on people that Farrell knew intimately. As we will see, the importance that Studs and his friends gave to vacant lots, city parks, and urban beaches was hardly unusual. Throughout Chicago, city-born ethnic youth eagerly sought out green space, and in some cases they made these places their "turf."[5]

## Progressive Reformers and the Problem of Immigrant Youth

During the first decades of the twentieth century, relations between immigrant leaders and Anglo American reformers were often strained. But the two groups shared one thing in common: they worried about kids like Studs Lonigan who gathered in informal, unsupervised groups, or "gangs," at street corners, pool halls, movie theaters, and dance clubs. Both held that such urban leisure would lead to physical, mental, and moral degeneration as well as the disintegration of community.

As we saw in chapter 1, urban reformers, such as Jane Addams, believed that children and adolescents developed best in rural and even wild environments where they could develop physically, mentally, and morally to their full potential. The problem was that in cities, children who spent their day in school and young adults who worked long hours at specialized tasks in factories had no natural spaces where they could engage in wholesome, life-giving play or recreation. So they satisfied their biological urges by going to motion picture theaters and other places of "passive" commercialized leisure (which led to muscular and neurological problems) or by engaging in vandalism, petty theft, or tramping (all of which led inevitably to greater criminality). As Jane Addams noted in *The Spirit of Youth and the City Streets*, the "'Looping the loop' amid shrieks of simulated terror or dancing in disorderly saloon halls, are perhaps the natural reactions to a day spent in noisy factories and in trolley cars whirling through the distracting streets," but such urban excitements led to loss of sound physique, eye problems, mental disorders, dissipation, and ultimately unnecessary waste of vital energy. Unhealthy commercialized leisure "uses up strength and does not create it."[6]

As we also saw, Chicago reformers and sociologists worried that "passive" commercialized leisure (or "wreckreation") not only destroyed the health of the individual but also fragmented community. In rural environments, a village, tied together by ancient folkways and anchored to the land, played together as an "organic" face-to-face community. On village greens, community members in search of adventure came out to enjoy games, sports, and folk dances that had been handed down since time immemorial. But migration to an artificial urban environment such as Chicago severed these connections to soil and tradition. In particular, American-born children in search of stimulation could leave their family and ethnic group behind and venture to amusement parks, movie theaters, and dance halls where they met other adolescents from other parts of the city. At these commercialized leisure venues, ethnic youth joined not a "primary" community, but an anonymous and often mixed crowd where the only commonality was a shared interest in a given sensation. In such places, "the individual's status is determined to a considerable degree by conventional signs—by fashion and 'front,' " wrote the sociologist Robert Park. "The art of life is largely reduced to skating on thin surfaces and a scrupulous study of style and manners." For Chicago School sociologists and reformers, the ultimate result of exposure to such environments was decadence and personal and social disorganization.[7]

The principle tool to combat the dangerous deracination and inorganic disorganization of the "crowd" gathered at the movie theater or the dance hall was the neighborhood playground or athletic park. Supervised outdoor recreation on these landscapes would not only build natural bodies but also introduce children growing up in artificial environments to the ancient games, dances, customs, traditions, and folk culture enjoyed in American villages. Park staff introduced ethnic youth not only to American traditional values (democracy, fair play, and respect for the law) but also to American symbols (such as the flag), national holidays, and American and midwestern history. Staff taught park goers old English and American folk and barn dances as well as Anglo American games, such as "Looby Loo," "Round and Round the Valley," and of course baseball. According to Florence Warren Brown and Neva L. Boyd, both from the Recreation Department of the Chicago School of Civics and Philanthropy, games of the "mother country," brought to America by early colonists, would tie Americans of diverse origins together as one people. "These simple old games," they wrote, "melt away both national and social differences and help the children to find that common bond, the expression of world-old emotions and social relations."[8]

It would be inaccurate, though, to say that Chicago park "play experts" only introduced ethnic youth to Anglo American games, folk dances, and cultural traditions. Play leaders also hoped that children and adolescents would learn the wholesome cultural traditions once enjoyed by their parents back in European villages. For instance, at the 1907, 1908, and 1909 play festivals held in Chicago parks, recreation leaders asked ethnic youth to play old English and American children's games, pledge allegiance to the flag of the United States, and dress as American Indians. But they also had American children of Russian, German, Swiss, Bohemian, Danish, Lithuanian, Jewish, and Irish descent dress in European peasant garb and play the games and perform the folk dances of European villages. Jane Addams noted that those who attended the first play festival in the newly created Ogden Park will never forget the long summer day of children playing games and sports and "the evening light made gay by the bright colored garments of Italians, Lithuanians, Norwegians, and a dozen other nationalities, reproducing the old dances and festivals for the pleasure of the more stolid Americans." Muckracking journalist Ida Tarbell noted that the immigrants "bring here a wealth of peculiar handicrafts, customs, songs, dances, folk lore, all hallowed by traditions." The Chicago play festival tells the immigrant to perpetuate the past: "your dances in costume preserve in a way the spirit of your race. Do not forget them or neglect them. Cultivate them and once a year let us share your pleasure in them."[9]

Anglo American recreation advocates encouraged the performance of ethnic folk culture in Chicago public parks because, undoubtedly, they hoped to attract and involve immigrant communities in outdoor recreation programs. A strict diet of Anglo American folk culture stood little chance of success in Chicago's working-class neighborhoods. Even more, reformers such as Addams and Tarbell worried that because New England Puritans had so effectively repressed an otherwise rich Elizabethan play tradition in favor of work and indoor prayer, there simply were few "American" games, sports, dances, and outdoor holidays to impart. Confronted with their own impoverished Puritan heritage and desperate to counter the lure of Chicago's exciting commercial and mechanized amusements, Addams and Tarbell turned to continental European folk culture.[10]

In so far as reformers encouraged young Irish, Swedish, and Greek Americans to retain the ancient folk traditions of their parents, they made Chicago parks into multicultural spaces rather than simply Anglo American landscapes. But while reformers tolerated and even encouraged the replication of European peasant culture, they had no patience for public manifestations of Old World nationalism or the speaking of languages other than English by children. They did not conceive Chicago parks and forest preserves as international or transnational spaces, but rather as intrinsically American places where immigrant children offered up ethnic folk culture to enrich the culturally impoverished United States, their new homeland. Of course, asking migrants and their children to decouple ethnic folk culture from nationalism was much easier said than done. As Amalie Hofer, one of the founders of the Playground Association of Chicago and an immigrant herself, noted, the immigrant was unwilling to publicly share ethnic culture "unless it is raised to something on the level of poetry and patriotism."[11]

But Addam's and Tarbell's acceptance of ethnic (rather than national) culture proved short lived. The outbreak of World War I in August 1914 stoked nationalist passions among Chicago Irish, Germans, Poles, Czechs, and Ukrainians, among others. Meanwhile, the descent of Europe into barbaric trench warfare shocked many native-born Anglo Americans, many of whom had grown up viewing Europe as the seat of civilization. The chaos and violence in Europe and the growing possibility of American intervention fueled American nationalism. This trend was manifest in calls for "100 percent Americanism," a resurgent anti-immigrant nativism, a drive to rapidly Americanize existing immigrants, tourist campaigns to "See America First," and patriotic celebrations of America's distinctive history and culture.[12]

In such a context, the celebration of Scandinavian, Italian, and Slavic peasant culture in neighborhood parks was replaced with often heavy-handed efforts at Americanization. During Fourth of July celebrations (which had traditionally been a largely laissez-faire event), city leaders asked immigrants to come to the city parks and sing patriotic songs, form into giant American flags, participate in "melting pot" pageants (in which the foreign born were ritualistically transformed into citizens), and to demonstrate to Americans (including federal agents who promised in 1918 to show up with motion picture cameras) that "the melting pot was seething, boiling, and welding vigorously and loudly." During the rest of the year, local businessmen and the Young Men's Christian Association transformed the city's small neighborhood parks into "educational and Americanization centers" where an estimated one million Chicagoans received instruction in American law, citizenship, and history. As historian David Glassberg notes, during the war, play advocates moved away from imparting an Elizabethan English play heritage and celebrating the folk traditions found elsewhere in Europe. Instead they turned to the frontier as the font of national culture.[13]

In the minds of reformers, parks were sites where the deracinated children of the foreign born learned about American history, culture, and games, but they were also places that would literally naturalize ethnic youth to American soil. In Jens Jensen's Columbus Park (which was designed and largely built during the course of World War I), working-class children and young children could play on an island of indigenous prairie in the heart of industrial Chicago. They might swim in an ersatz midwestern swimming hole banked in stratified limestone, take part in outdoor Indian pageantry at the "player's hill," or gather around the council ring, which harkened back to Native American council fires. Of course Jensen's park was unique, and recreation experts recognized the limitations of encountering the real America in the small more formal parks that were built in working-class neighborhoods during the Progressive Era. So they compensated, not only by showing children lanternslides of the national parks, but also by organizing trips out of the city. In camps underwritten by the city's various charities or in the forest preserves and dunes, the children of the foreign born could leave the city and "see America." They could hike, swim, camp, and perhaps gather around the campfire under the stars and imagine themselves as citizens of a coherent, long-standing American community rooted in the soil.[14]

## Emigrants, Ethnic Youth, and Outdoor Recreation

Like Anglo American reformers, immigrant community leaders, journalists, parents, and clergy worried about the effects of the "artificial" urban environment on children and young adults. Some argued that because of polluted urban conditions, long hours working at mechanized jobs, and especially dissipating American leisure practices, Chicago-born youth lacked the same physique and health of those raised back in the rural countryside of the homeland. And like reformers such as Jane Addams, community leaders worried that life in the artificial city resulted in alienation, lack of connection to soil, and fragmentation of community. But instead of trying to naturalize ethnic youth to the American national community, immigrant leaders focused on preventing "denationalization" and keeping children within the cultural, linguistic, and nationalistic fold.[15]

Much of the effort to keep American-born children true to culture, religion, and nation took place indoors. Groups organized language classes, religious instruction, lectures, clubs, and built gymnasiums. But outdoor recreation and wilderness programs in Chicago green spaces were also vital to such efforts at community building. In developing these outdoor recreation programs, Chicago immigrants did not blindly emulate the Anglo American middle class; rather they largely drew on developments in their own homelands. The foreign origins of outdoor recreation programs on U.S. soil may surprise some readers, since we have long been taught that Americans have had a unique or exceptional relationship with nature. The idea that nature is "*the* American theme" has blinded us to the fact that other nations also had similarly "obsessive" relationships with nature. Romantic attachment to land (including wilderness) and the development of back to nature youth organizations were an international phenomena that had far more to do with urbanization than the unique expression of American culture or civilization. To fully understand immigrant and working-class nature tourism, we need to move beyond problematic accounts that paint America as an island called nature's nation and return to the homelands of the foreign born.[16]

When it came to outdoor recreation, Germans in Chicago drew on a youth-based gymnastics program called *Turnen* that was created by the German nationalist Friedrich Ludwig Jahn following the Napoleonic invasion of Prussia in 1811. Jahn believed that his physical culture program (which he imagined as the physical regime of early German tribesmen) would not only physically and morally restore unhealthy and undisciplined German young men, but transform feudal German states into a united republic and help drive the French out of the Fatherland.[17]

Contact with nature figured prominently in Jahn's scheme. He and his followers dressed in loose linens meant to evoke the simple garb of peasants, and he held that gymnastics should be performed outdoors at special athletic grounds "where woods alternate with open fields, where groves, bushes, shrubs, thickets, and open spaces are all encountered." At the Hasenheide (or rabbit field) just outside of Berlin, Jahn built the first such park, which he described as a *Tie*, or an outdoor meeting site of the ancient German peoples. There students practiced on horizontal bars, climbed trees, and played games beneath the evergreens and in the fields. Besides events at the park or *Turnplatz,* Jahn also advocated ascetic hiking (what he called a *Turnfahrt*). He and his followers took day outings and multi-week treks through the German forests, fields, and mountains, often singing patriotic songs and taking note of the nation's natural wonders.[18]

During the mid-nineteenth century, the importance that Jahn originally gave to contact with nature faded as movement leaders established halls for indoor gymnastics and made exercise more regimented. But with increased urbanization in the late nineteenth century, German gymnasts revived Jahn's original emphasis on recreation outdoors. Members of *Turnvereine* increasingly exercised in the fresh air, and some even invented their own outdoor sports, such as handball (which many Germans hoped would compete favorably with a recent and popular English import: football, or soccer). At the same time, gymnasts began to leave the city and hike and camp in the German countryside. Some Turners formed new organizations, such as the *Wandervogel* (or wandering bird), whose members trekked into Germany's mountains and forests, learned basic woodcraft, sang folk songs, and embraced Germany's Teutonic tribal roots. As historian George Mosse notes, for both the Turners and for the German youth in Wandervogel organizations, rambling linked the "eternal German landscape to the eternal spirit of the nation."[19]

Eastern European nations followed suit. In Czechoslovakia, the art historian Miroslav Tyrš appropriated the *Turnen* program and put it into the service of Czech nationalism. For Tyrš, *Sokol* (or Falcon) units would strengthen the body and the nation, resulting, ultimately, in freedom from the Austro-Hungarian Empire. Polish nationalists, intent on freeing their nation from Russian, German, and Austro-Hungarian rule, also developed their own version of the Falcons, the motto of which was "a salute to the fatherland, talons to the enemy." Slovenes, Croats, Bulgarians, Ukrainians, Serbians, and Russians appropriated the Czech Sokol as well. The Scandinavian nations, Italy, and Greece also formed their own nationalistic gymnastics programs. Jews, increasingly excluded from participation in Central and Eastern Europe athletic societies, developed a program of physical culture, which they frequently tied to Zionism.[20]

As in Germany, contact with wilderness became an increasingly important component of gymnastic and other youth programs by the end of the nineteenth century. In occupied Czechoslovakia, Sokol members engaged principally in gymnastics (which often took place indoors in urban gymnasiums), but they also hiked through the countryside (bringing their nationalistic message to isolated peasant villages, much to the alarm of Austro-Hungarian officials) and visited iconic national landscapes, such as the top of Říp Mountain, the legendary spot where Czech history began. The 1890s saw increased interest not only in outdoor gymnastics training and outdoor sports (in particular soccer) but wilderness hiking, camping, and visits to mountain hostels.[21]

The new importance placed on contact with nature also influenced gymnastics instructors in occupied Poland. In Galicia (the birthplace of the Polish Sokol), gymnastics teachers took their young charges on hikes and canoe trips and introduced them to sites of national memory as well as striking Polish landscapes, such as the Tatra, Pieniny, and Gorgany ranges in the Carpathian Mountains. Similarly, Hungarian teachers began to introduce students to the historic places and natural beauty of their homeland, bringing them to tourist spots just outside cities (such as the Buda Hills and the Danube Bend near Budapest) and to more distant destinations, such as Transylvania and the Carpathian Mountains in the north and east, which were imagined as intrinsically Hungarian landscapes. At the same time, youth educators, including some gymnastic instructors, appropriated the English Boy Scout and Girl Scout movement and put it into the service of Slavic nationalisms. Instead of cultivating Indian lore, some Slavic troops romanticized a premodern European peasant world. They mastered "national" folk dances, wore peasant scarves, and erected totems in their camps to ancient Slavic gods, such as Svetovid, the lord of war and the harvest.[22]

The *fin de siècle* creators of muscular Judaism also linked contact with nature to personal and national regeneration. Advocates of Zionist gymnastics, such as the noted physician and author Max Nordau, argued that the Jews of Palestine had once been strong, but anti-Semitism and cramped urban life in European ghettos had alienated the Jew from nature and led to physical decline. Following the German example, Jewish gymnastics advocates organized youth organizations devoted to bringing children and young adults out of the city and into contact with the larger natural world. Advocates of outdoor Jewish life, such as the Zionist Theobald Scholem, argued that exercise inside the gymnasium was only a substitute for recreation in nature and that "in the forests and fields, in rain or in sun, the Jew will get to know what he has lost for millennia, namely love of mother earth." Jews also developed the *Blau Weiss* (their own version of the Wandervogel) and Zionist boy scouting.[23]

The Irish also moved outdoors. Partially in response to the growing popularity of English football, Michael Cusack, a devout Irish nationalist, formed the Gaelic Athletic Association (GAA) in 1884. He argued that English colonialism and the potato famine had driven the Irish indoors, away from their "their trysting places at the cross-roads and the hurling fields," and that the revival of national sports, such as hurling and Gaelic football, would restore physical, racial, and national vitality. The GAA also served as the foundation for the Irish Boy Scouts (*Fianna Eireann*), formed in 1909 by Countess Constance Markiewicz. The paramilitary organization sought to prevent boyhood decadence (attributed primarily to smoking, dime novels, loafing, and Anglicization) by introducing them to Irish history and culture, Gaelic sports, military training, as well as camping and mountain hikes.[24]

In the late nineteenth century, Swedes and Norwegians also discovered their own "national" outdoor sports, especially skiing, but also hiking, rowing, sailing, and skating. For both nations, this renaissance in native sport coincided with a new appreciation for northern wilderness landscapes. Nationalists in both Sweden and Norway imagined their homelands as nature's nation and pointed to the mountains, rivers, and forests as the font of national rejuvenation. Recreation in such landscapes would generate a love of country, but they also would physically strengthen the bodies of urban youth.[25]

Once in Chicago, immigrants transplanted Old World athletic organizations. In 1852, Germans, fleeing the failed revolution of 1848, established the city's first *Turnverein*. In 1866, Bohemians organized Chicago's first Sokol. A year later, Chicago Swedes started the *Nordsidans Skandinaviska Turnerforening*. Poles created their first Falcon unit in 1887. At the same time, the Chicago Irish formed a local Gaelic Athletic Club and began to play old Irish sports, such as hurling. The 1890s and the first decade of the twentieth century saw the formation of the Norwegian-American Gymnastic Union out of a number of independent Turner groups as well as the emergence of a Slovak Sokol, the Ukrainian Athletic Association (or *Sich*), the Greek Olympic Athletic Club, and an Italo-American National Union sports program.[26]

Athletic organizations, such as the Turnverein (or Turners), had long used Chicago green spaces. Exhibitions of gymnastics and the playing of sports were often an important component of the harvest festivals and national holidays discussed in chapter 2. But especially with the advent of more convenient and less expensive transportation, national groups made increasing use of Chicago's hinterland for rural and wilderness recreation (see Figs. 3.1 and 3.2). In the twentieth century, some Sokol gymnasiums

FIGURE 3.1 "Open Air Gymnasium, Turner Camp, Cary, Ill." Courtesy of the Lake County (Ill.) Discovery Museum, Curt Teich Postcard Archives.

FIGURE 3.2 "A Hike, Turner Camp, Cary, Ill." Courtesy of the Lake County (Ill.) Discovery Museum, Curt Teich Postcard Archives.

simply shut down for the summer. One member reported that instead of indoor exercises "we have picnics, hikes, trips out in the country on large trucks." Gymnastics instructors at the Jewish People's Institute led approximately six outings per week to the forest preserves, the Indiana Dunes, Starved Rock State Park, and other destinations. The Falcons also took advantage of the "wild" places in and around Chicago. One Falcon member, Lillian Cwik, remembered that her nest (as Falcon units were called) routinely rented trucks and travelled to the woods on the outskirts of the city for "drillings and outings and campings." By 1928, a writer for *Dziennik Chicagoski* could boast that the Polish Falcons not only fostered strength, health, national discipline, patriotism, fluency in the Polish language, familiarity with Polish heroes (such as Bolesław the Great, King John Sobieski, Kosciusko, Pulaski, and Chopin), but also "the appreciation of nature by the study of nature, trees, birds, and flowers."[27]

As back in distant homelands, nationalists in Chicago addressed youth problems by forming scout troops. Poles drew explicitly on the Polish scouting movement (or *harcerstwo*), which the leader of Polish scouting, Andrzej Małkowski, defined as scouting plus independence. Various Polish institutions (the Polish Roman Catholic Union, the Society of King John Sobieski III, St. Hedwig Parish, etc.) established troops, and the Polish newspaper *Narod Polski* urged every Polish mother to raise her son a scout. The newspaper explained that "a scout is able to tell where is north and where is south, where is east and where is west even if he found himself in a dense forest. A scout is able to tie a knot that holds well. He is able to swim across a river. He is able to pitch a tent and is able to mend his torn trousers. He is able to tell you which fruits or seeds are poisonous. He is able to distinguish nut-bearing trees from a considerable distance. . . . In the forest he can recognize different birds by their feathers and by their sound. He walks through a forest with such certainty as though he had to be drawn back from it by someone with a thread." Małkowski saw the Chicago troops as a vital component of the Polish scouting movement, and in 1916 he planned to come to Chicago and take all the city's Polish scouts on "an outing and camping expedition." The Chicago Jewish community also formed its own Boy Scout and Girl Scout troops (as well as scouting analogs, such as the Volunteers of Zion, the Herzl Scouts, and the Rothschild Guards). The city's Bohemian troop was led by a Czech soldier and met at Dvorak Park. German St. Augustine's and Immaculate Conception churches sponsored troops. So too did the Greek Athenian Hall, the Hungarian Verhovay Fraternal Society, the Ukrainian Catholic Youth League, the Italian

FIGURE 3.3 Chinese American Boy Scouts, 1920s. Courtesy of the Chinatown Museum Federation / Chinese-American Museum of Chicago.

Garibaldi Institute, and the Chinese Consolidated Benevolent Association (see Fig. 3.3).[28]

Getting children and young adults out of the city was of paramount importance, so Turners, Czech Sokols, Polish Falcons, and other youth organizations also established their own camps within a one-day steamer or train ride from Chicago. In 1904, the Bohemians opened Camp Sokol in southwestern Michigan (see Fig. 3.4). At the camp, which was located in rolling countryside not far from the Lake Michigan shore, members engaged in rigorous gymnastics under the trees, pitched tents in the open meadows, hiked, and swam in the lake. Polish scouts retreated to Harcerstwo Camp in Tinley Park. In 1914, the German Turners established the Illinois Turner Camp on the banks of the Fox River, just northwest of the city. Here Chicagoans practiced on exercise equipment under the trees, but they also slept in tents, took hikes through the rolling countryside, and swam, boated, and fished in the river. As one Turner explained, the camp, "situated along the high rolling banks of the Fox River . . . dotted with the bivouacs of the Turners, is really an ideal spot, only an hour from the sultry hub-bub of the bustling city. . . . Nature is good to us in furnishing the surroundings in which to exercise and maintain our bodies."[29]

At the same time, Jews established reform, orthodox, labor, and Zionist camps in Wisconsin, Indiana, Illinois, and Michigan. At these camps, boys and girls enjoyed outdoor sports, nature study, and arts and crafts. S. Kirson

FIGURE 3.4 Camp Sokol, New Buffalo, Michigan, mid-1920s.
Courtesy of the American Sokol Organization.

Weinberg, a student of sociologist Ernest Burgess (and a future sociologist herself), noted that Camp Chi "veritably brings the girl back to nature, to a free, unhampered but disciplined life. This is the distinct quality of the camp; it affords the city girl an opportunity to escape the cramped spaceless, smoke-stained air of the city, to breathe air in its purity. . . . The nature study class gives the girl a chance to be interested in the flowers, trees, and appreciate them intelligently. The athletics give a girl a chance to limber up unused muscles. Its benefits are obvious." But unlike at Anglo American camps, campers at Camp Chi and other Jewish camps observed the Jewish Sabbath; ate kosher food; learned Jewish history; sang Jewish folk songs; became better acquainted with their own religious, cultural, and national heritage; and followed current events in Palestine.[30]

Although many immigrant leaders saw great value in leading children and young adults out of the city and to parks and forest preserves, they believed that such trips could not compare with making contact with the soil of the original homeland. Only such a trip would fully instill patriotism and a willingness to defend the nation against foreign aggressors. Greek youth have never "seen the beautiful setting sun of Greece, nor have they inhaled its spicy mountain air. They have not watched the blue ocean waves nor have they seen our unbelievably blue sky," lamented a writer for the newspaper *Saloniki*. "How can they be expected to show their love and sacrifice themselves for a country that is unfamiliar to them?"[31]

A trip to the German Rhine, Říp Mountain, the shores of the Baltic, the Polish Tatras, or the northern Swedish forests was an expensive proposition, so nationalists tried to bring the American born back home through theater, music, lanternslides, moving pictures, and outdoor national festivals. But surprisingly large numbers of immigrant communities did execute successful youth excursions back to homelands. The intention was to strengthen the patriotism of Chicago children by exposing them to the culture, historic sites, and natural landscape of the old father or motherland. According to a writer for the newspaper *Zgoda*, "the contact of a foreign born Polish child with the holy land of its ancestors brings about in its soul a miraculous transformation." He noted that "like that mythical Greek, Antheus, who by only touching the earth was regaining his strength in mortal combat, so also the emigrant child, by visiting Poland, by beholding her ancient memorials and monuments of fame, and by breathing the air of the million-people Polish center, inhales and imbibes into itself that miraculous national power, which will remain in the child and some day will develop into something immortal."[32]

Like most Anglo American park builders and recreation experts, immigrant directors of outdoor recreation programs focused most of their attention on boys and young men. The great fear for everyone was male decadence, and only males were envisioned as future citizens and physical defenders of the nation. At the same time, nationalists shared Anglo American sexist views that girls and women should not exert themselves and that physical competition was unfeminine. "One seldom hears, among the Lithuanians, that exercise is as necessary for women as it is for men," complained one writer for *Lietuva* in 1914. "A girl, they believe should be concerned only with getting married; and, once she is married, her sole duty is housekeeping. Tradition places the life of women in this narrow a frame." Some conservative Poles went so far as to blast the idea of female athletics and outdoor recreation. One editorial writer for *Dziennik Chicagoski*, for instance, warned in 1896 against "modernized girl turners." He noted that Polish pagan women during the time of the Romans began with dancing, then engaged in gymnastics, and soon wore armor and learned to use the pike. The "terrible Amazon" in "her pursuit of publicity and emancipation . . . played with tame lions and tigers."[33]

Despite patriarchal views regarding female recreation, immigrant women, like their Anglo American sisters, used outdoor sports and nature excursions to challenge circumscribed lives that relegated them strictly to the home. By the late 1880s, German women and girls had created a niche in the city's *Turnverein*. By 1893, Czech American Sokol women, unlike their sisters back in the Old Country, successfully pushed the National Sokol Union of the United States to become more inclusive and change its mission to "the spiritual and physical development of young people, women, and men." Polish women had to wait longer, but they ultimately fought their way into Falcon units despite continued criticism from men who believed that women should not be outdoors, but rather at home, cooking, cleaning, and raising children.[34]

## Studs Lonigan in Nature's Nation

In developing outdoor recreation programs, both Anglo American reformers and immigrant leaders targeted a newly emerged ethnic youth culture that was neither European nor Anglo American, a culture with its own distinctive street language, music, fashion, gender roles, invented traditions, heroes, and meaningful places. To both reformers and immigrant parents, the street culture of the teens and twenties was unnatural, implicitly oppositional, and monstrous, a social world born not of history, tradition, and soil, but directly of the urban slum.[35]

Historian Liz Cohen argues that mass culture played a crucial role in the development of this "second-generation ethnic, working-class culture." During the teens and twenties, young people, sometimes of diverse background, frequently gathered together and mixed at amusement parks, dance halls, and movie theaters, and it was in these places that young people created this new hybrid culture. She also argues that this Jazz Age youth culture enabled workers who had historically divided along lines of nationality, ethnicity, and race to successfully organize themselves into the Congress of Industrial Organizations (CIO) during the 1930s and early 1940s.[36]

Although sociologists and their graduate students followed groups of working-class youth to places of commercialized amusement, they just as often trailed young people to urban green spaces: forest preserve and Indiana Dunes wilderness parks, Lake Michigan beaches, neighborhood parks, vacant lots, and other spots hidden within the interstices of Chicago's built environment. Therefore, to understand the development of interethnic working-class youth culture, we need to look not only at amusement parks, dance halls, and movie theaters, but also green spaces. We need to pay close attention to Studs Lonigan and his friends in Washington Park.

Our best window on Jazz Age working-class youth culture comes from the scholarship of University of Chicago sociologists and their graduate and undergraduate students, but it is important to use these primary sources with caution. Sociologists typically viewed any gathering of unsupervised young urban people as a "gang," which they saw as a symptom of urban social disorganization. Not only did they have a very expansive definition of what counted as a gang, they were also ever attentive to signs of male juvenile delinquency, a preoccupation that biased their collection of data, interpretations, and conclusions.

Of all the sociologists who studied Chicago youth in parks, none gives us as detailed a picture as Frederick Thrasher, author of *The Gang: A Study of 1,313 Gangs in Chicago* (1927). In this classic work on juvenile delinquency, Thrasher argued that a gang typically starts as an informal group of boys who live in the same neighborhood and enjoy the same pursuits. Initially, there is no leadership, group identity, or sense of territory. But as the gang comes into conflict with community members and other neighborhood gangs, the boys become more aware of themselves as a group. Natural leaders emerge, rules are codified, and traditions and rituals established. At the same time, the group establishes a strong connection to local territory. Eventually as the boys grow into young men, the gang or social athletic club (SAC) cements ties with local merchants and ethnic politicians, charges dues, rents official headquarters, and organizes uniformed athletic teams. They also sometimes become criminal organizations.[37]

Thrasher noted that although gang members enjoyed sensational newspapers, amusement parks, vaudeville, burlesque, gambling, arcades, circuses, and especially films, they also liked green spaces. He described how boys looking for adventure left their urban slums and ventured to the Lake Front, the Chicago River, abandoned lots, and other islands of nature within the city. "The wastelands and prairies adjacent to the city's numerous canals and slips, along the various branches and forks of the Chicago River, and near the unimproved portion of the lake front make ideal 'camp grounds,'" he noted. "Good hiding places for games are found here and boating, wading, and swimming even in polluted waters attract the gang boys." The urban boys viewed piles of earth along the Sanitary and Ship Canal as a mountain retreat and made vacant lots into the "prairies of the Golden West."[38]

Gang members also escaped the city entirely and "vacationed" in rural and wild areas on the urban fringe. Thrasher noted that a significant percentage of the so-called "tramps" riding freight cars and living in hobo camps or "jungles" outside the city were males under the age of twenty-one, and unlike the homeless and unemployed who had no other choice but to camp permanently in the jungles, many of the young were on a sort of holiday. Gang boys, he explained, often scraped together money for tents, hunting knives, and "frontier paraphernalia" and often went "*en masse* for overnight hikes or camping expeditions to Fox Lake, the Des Plaines River, and the various forest preserves adjoining the city," where they seemingly escaped from all social control. Another group of youth studied by Thrasher camped along the overgrown banks of the Illinois and Michigan Canal, the 1848 waterway built to connect the Chicago and Mississippi Rivers. Frequently, gang boys stole money and vehicles to facilitate their trips "back to nature." One group was able to spend a vacation "swimming, fishing, and tramping in the woods" at Fox Lake by pilfering money from a cash register and stealing a Ford. The Woodstreeters traveled to the forest preserves, where they "borrowed" a boat and stripped nearby orchards clean of apples and pears, which they transported back to the city in potato sacks. Thrasher also found three boys and a girl who stole cars and retreated to the forest preserves, where they had lived in an army tent for weeks.[39]

Thrasher and other sociologists reported that sometimes young working-class Chicagoans went even farther afield. One of the informants of Anthony Sorrentino (a sociology student and future community activist) reported that he and his friends hoped to escape to the mountains of the West and become cowboys, where they would raise cattle and sheep and fight Indians. Stanley, the Polish American subject of sociologist Clifford Shaw's *The Jack-Roller*, explained that "nothing appeals to my imagination any stronger than an evening in the 'jungle' [or hobo camp]—after a good supper, to lean back and smoke and tell stories of adventure and be free, out in the open spaces." He and a coworker at the ink and glue factory where he worked ultimately left, via boxcar, for "beautiful California, the land of eternal spring time." One neighborhood gang, the V-A-Cs, decided they would see the world and rode freight trains within a 1,000-mile radius of the city. Most Chicagoans, though, lacked time, money, or gumption for such boxcar odysseys. As M. A. Rachwalski, a member of several athletic clubs, remembered in an oral history, it was difficult to escape the city. He and his friends did not have access to convenient transportation, such as cars, "so we're more confined here. We're confined to our parks."[40]

Rachwalski's lament should not blind us to the importance that Chicago youth invested in their local neighborhood park. As we have seen, park builders viewed athletic parks as spaces that would naturalize ethnic youth to Anglo American tradition, history, and soil. But neighborhood young people viewed these landscapes quite differently. Almost as soon as the city opened public parks and playgrounds, local youth appropriated them. To the dismay of staff, parks typically became a place for the production and reproduction of working-class ethnic youth culture. In green spaces, youth played baseball, swam, fished, socialized, and enjoyed grass and trees and cool breezes. They also smoked cigarettes, gambled, drank, hid stolen property, flirted, kissed, and had sex. As Thrasher and others conceded, city youth viewed parks and other green spaces not as places where they would be naturalized to a middle-class Anglo American version of American culture, but rather as places where they could temporarily escape the authority of parents, police, teachers, and employers and enjoy their own pastimes.[41]

Gangs and SACs also made parks and vacant lots into their turf, viewing them as homelands of sorts and protecting them with the same intense passion that their parents reserved for defending distant nations. Most often neighborhood youth and park staff reached a tense accommodation, but sometimes gangs used violence to conquer a park. Just a few months after the 1905 opening of Mark White Square (one of the ten small South Side parks that served as a national model of park design), local youths assaulted a police officer and took control, transforming the park into what the *Chicago Tribune* called a nightly scene of "lawlessness and thuggery." Similarly, two weeks after the opening of a North Side playground, local adolescents claimed the space as their own, and when police tried to take the park back, they were met with a barrage of wood, stones, and tacks. At Fulton Playground, there was, according to one observer, "a general attitude of revolt against all authority which makes discipline hard to secure." At Raster Playground, an Italian "gang, led by two or three 'tough' fellows, creates trouble by opposing the instructor at every turn—their favorite form of recreation!"[42]

Once secure, gangs and SACs defended their parks from outsiders. Most gangs were ethnically homogenous, and preexisting national or racial hostility fueled rivalry and fights. Just after World War I, reports of vicious anti-Jewish pogroms on the one hand, and stories of Jewish collusion with Russian Bolsheviks and Ukrainians on the other, inflamed tensions between Chicago Jews and Poles. During the summer of 1919, gangs of Polish and Jewish youth skirmished in Douglas Park. After thirty Polish youth attacked a group of Jewish baseball players with bricks and rotten fruit, the news quickly circulated through the Jewish community, and fifty Jews (including high school students, amateur prizefighters, and denizens of the local pool halls and lunchrooms) raced to the park to "Wallop the Polock."

"Usually the Jewish boys involved were not personally acquainted with their enemies," one observer of the conflicts in Douglas Park explained. "It was enough that they were Poles, and vice versa. It was a matter of racial, cultural, and religious solidarity."[43]

Similarly, sociologist Harvey Warren Zorbaugh noted that on the Near North Side, "the play parks were the scenes of many a 'battle' when the Irish boys would attempt to run out the Italian, and alley garbage cans were stripped of their covers which served as shields in these encounters." Italian and Swedish youth also brawled, including one melee where one hundred boys fought with knives, blackjacks, bricks, and air rifles. One Italian American remembered that in the late 1890s, boys of his neighborhood faced "stoning brigades" and "fierce shock troops of young hooligans" when they tried to go play in Vernon Park.[44]

Ethnic defensiveness can certainly be seen in *Studs Lonigan*. The Fifty-eighth Street Gang is Irish American, as were many other gangs and SACs on Chicago South Side. Studs and his friends consider themselves patriotic white Americans, but they look beyond the boundaries of their neighborhood and see a threatening world inhabited by "Polacks," "Dagos," "Hunkies," "Kikes," "Bohunks," "Huns," as well as "Niggers," and they avoid certain beaches because they associate them with Jews, Poles, Hungarians, or African Americans. At the same time, Studs and his friends defend their turf, Washington Park, from outsiders.[45]

Despite the intensity of rivalries between Irish, Jewish, Polish, Italian, and Swedish gangs, it would be a serious mistake to see 1920s Chicago youth culture in simple national or ethnic terms. As the sociologist Frederick Thrasher first noted in *The Gang*, neighborhood identity often trumped allegiance to ethnicity. Insular neighborhoods produced ethnically homogenous gangs and SACs, but ethnically heterogeneous areas (and there were many in Chicago) could and often did give birth to mixed groups of youth. For instance, the Wizard Arrows Social Athletic Club contained Germans, Italians, Irish, Poles, Jews, and Greeks. The Wigwams gang was made up of Polish and Irish youth. A member of the SSP Group explained that the gang counted Jews, Irish, Protestants, Swedes, Germans, Christian Scientists, and a janitor's son as members. Jews and Italians belonged to Itschkie's Black Hand Society whereas Poles and Greeks made up the Kluck Klan. According to Thrasher, 39.9 percent of gangs were multiethnic, although he was quick to point out that this mixing did not amount to genuine Americanization. "Assimilation to the gang and its activities does not mean genuine Americanization," he wrote, "for gang activities usually are symptoms of immigrant disorganization and are demoralizing in the long run."[46]

Such "white" interethnic mixing even permeates Studs's insular Fifty-eighth Street Gang. Although he reminds Andy Le Gare (whose father is French) and Davy Cohen (who is uncomfortably Jewish) of their outsider status, he ultimately befriends them. Cracks in ethnic insularity can also be seen in a Washington Park football game between the Fifty-eighth Street Cardinals and the Monitors, led by the extraordinarily talented "Jewboy Schwartz." Literary critic Daniel Shiffman notes that although the Cardinals brawl with the Jewish Monitors during halftime (sending Schwartz to the hospital), it is also the case that playing center for the Cardinals was Nate Klein, "the crazy Hebe."[47]

The trumping of ethnicity by neighborhood could be seen also at Gaelic Park, as well as other commercial groves and parks run by social athletic clubs. Gaelic Park on the South Side had long been a favored destination for Chicago's Irish. It was a place where the community could escape the industrial city for a moment and enjoy sun and fresh air, traditional Irish dances, picnics, and hurling matches between teams such as the Shamrocks and the Clan-na-Gaels. The park was also sometimes the site of the annual Feis, an outdoor assembly that dated back to ancient times when Tara was the capital of a free Ireland. In the twentieth century, the Feis became a moment to remember the Irish past and celebrate Celtic language, poetry, and culture. It was an occasion to enjoy Irish sports, folk dancing, and storytelling, but also to renew commitments to the nation.[48]

During the 1920s, the Irish Hamburg Athletic Club (which had played an active role in the 1919 race riot and also had future Mayor Richard J. Daley as a member) began to manage the park. On Sundays, Irish outdoor festivities continued to attract countrymen from throughout the city. But on Saturdays the American-born Irish youth took over. Club members, whom sociologist Paul Cressey described as types you would see in a poolroom or cigar shop, smoked cigarettes, spoke in slang, and emulated Hollywood stars, such as Rudolph Valentino, the sheik. Instead of dancing jigs and quadrilles to the sound of fiddle and accordion, the Hamburgers and their dates danced fox-trots and other "American Dances" outdoors under the stars to the strains of jazz.[49]

The club maintained a tight perimeter and was suspicious of outsiders. But outsiders were not necessarily non-Irish. The club in fact admitted a few trusted German and Polish American young men into their circle. At the same time, their bitter rivals were not German, Polish, or Lithuanian, but rather an Irish-dominated SAC from the adjoining neighborhood of Canaryville. It was these young Irish toughs from a hostile neighborhood that were most likely the scoundrels that broke into Gaelic Park and burned down the Hamburg's outdoor dance pavilion.[50]

Boys and young men dominated the world of Chicago gangs and SACs. As historian Andrew Diamond shows, young men in gangs and SACs publically performed working-class masculinity, largely though fashion (think of Studs Lonigan's crooked cap, cigarette, and jeans in the opening passage of this chapter), baseball prowess, bravado, sexual conquest, and street fighting. But it is a serious mistake to think that girls and young women were entirely absent from the scene. Young females may have received little attention from University of Chicago sociologists, but they could be seen in every park. They too wanted to escape the urban environment and enjoy fresh air and sunshine and outdoor sports. [51]

Just like boys, girls formed gangs. According to a 1927 Chicago School Board survey, all-girl gangs made up 9 percent of the 226 gangs that frequented Chicago parks. As girls grew up and became young women, they socialized more with boys. Amusement parks, dance halls, and movie theaters were places where teenagers mixed in a heterosocial environment, but so too were urban parks and forest preserves. Women not only attended SAC outings, they most likely played a substantial role in organizing and executing them. They too worked long hours in factories doing monotonous, repetitive work, and like young men, they too wanted to enjoy the outdoors in a social setting. For example, young Lithuanian, Polish, and Bohemian young women flocked to Hamburg SAC social activities in Gaelic Park. According to one sociologist, most of them welcomed the outdoor dances as a reprieve from long hours of work in the nearby stockyards. He went on to note that the young women dressed in fashion that "rivals the rainbow" and mystified their Irish American dates by speaking in Polish. These were the younger Jazz Age sisters of the assertive young women that Jane Addams described in 1908. "As these overworked girls stream along the street, the rest of us only see the self-conscious walk, the giggling speech, the preposterous clothing," noted the founder of Hull House. "And yet, through the huge hat, with its wilderness of bedraggled feathers, the girl announces to the world that she is here. She demands attention to the fact of her existence, she states that she is ready to live, to take her place in the world."[52]

Although the sons and daughters of European immigrants sometimes forged an ethnically mixed world, this hybridity rarely extended across the color line. Their world was almost exclusively white. According to Thrasher, only 2.8 percent of gangs and SACs included African Americans. The low rate of racial mixing reflected the fact that during the 1920s, there were many ethnically mixed Chicago neighborhoods, but very few racially mixed ones. The city was already remarkably segregated. As such, groups of African Americans largely played together. Similarly, Chinese youth kept to themselves, sometimes associating with Tongs. Mexicans, facing hostility especially from Polish youth, formed their own gangs and SACs, such as the Mayas, Yaquis, Southern Arrows, Aztecas, and Incas.[53]

But segregation in housing does not entirely explain the racial politics of 1920s Chicago youth culture. Although it is true that neighborhood demographics played a significant role in determining gang and SAC composition, it is also the case that the children of European immigrants appropriated Anglo American views of race. Studs and his gang see ethnic outsiders as racial threats, but such prejudice pales in comparison to that aimed at African Americans, a group the Irish see as an ever-expanding existential threat. Although Studs and his friends dance to jazz and frequent African American clubs on State Street in the nearby black ghetto, they are simultaneously terrified that blacks are moving into their Washington Park neighborhood, buying up and renting homes, strolling on the sidewalks, showing up for mass at St. Patrick's newly built church, and entering into Washington Park, their green oasis. Studs and his friends seethe that blacks are ruining "their" park. "Niggers didn't have a right in a white man's park," Studs thinks to himself. "And the sooner they were taught that they didn't, the better off they'd be."[54]

Although the children of European immigrants could join young African Americans and imagine themselves as a class (an option repeatedly proposed by some union leaders as well as the "reds" who gave speeches in Washington Park during the 1930s), the vast majority opted to open the door only to ethnic mixing and drew a hard line in the sand when it came to color. In fact, European American youth gangs such as the Hamburgs and Ragen's Colts (whose motto was "Hit Me and You Hit

Two Thousand") played key roles in antiblack violence that triggered and perpetuated the vicious 1919 race riot.

The riot, which was sparked when a man threw a rock and drowned a black boy whose raft had drifted into the waters just off the "white beach," divided the city along racial lines. Even for European Americans not directly involved, the perception of a common threat further eroded ethnic distinction and played an important role in the further solidification of a white American identity among Chicago's Europeans. On the other side of the color line, the race riot prompted many African Americans to give up the dream of assimilation and to reimagine blackness. As we will see in chapter 4, African Americans made urban green spaces and rural and wild landscapes critical sites for the rearticulation of identity.[55]

## CHAPTER FOUR

# The Negro Speaks of Rivers
## Nature and Leisure in the Black Metropolis

> For sheer physical beauty—for sheen of water and golden air, for
> nobleness of tree and flower of shrub, for shining river and song
> of bird and the low, moving whisper of sun, moon, and star, it is
> the beautifulest [sic] stretch I have seen for twenty years; and
> then to that add fellowship . . . all sons and great—grandchildren
> of Ethiopia, all with the wide leisure of rest and play—can you
> imagine a more marvelous thing than Idlewild?
>
> —w. e. b. du bois, "Hopkinsville, Chicago, and Idlewild,"
> *Crisis*, 1921

In his weekly "Keep Healthy" column for the *Chicago Defender* (the black
paper of note for Chicago and much of the nation), health editor Dr. Wilberforce Williams frequently urged his African American readers to venture
to the countryside surrounding Chicago and also to the city's parks and
beaches. For Dr. Williams, these landscapes were not just mere public
spaces. They were places where one could escape exhausting work, pollution, and overly stimulating amusements in the seemingly artificial city
and retreat back to nature. Take the family for a ten-cent trolley ride out
to the woods and fields at the city limit, he urged his readers in August
1913. Such an all-day excursion "under sun and sky" may wear you out, but
a day spent breathing "clean, fresh country air" in "close communication
with birds and trees and flowers" will help you sleep. "Besides, for the little
ones, a day amid such surroundings is worth a whole week in school in the
new and instructive lessons they will get from the greatest of all teachers,
Nature." For poor blacks unable to pay the trolley fare, Williams prescribed
nearby urban parks, which he described as "beautiful bits of God's country brought right into the city for the benefit of those who dwell in sections
were air, sun and elbow room are hard to get."[1]

Large numbers of black Chicagoans took Dr. William's prescription.
While the "talented tenth" ventured into Chicago's recreational hinterland, those with limited resources passed their scarce leisure in urban green
spaces within or not far from Chicago's congested South Side ghetto. But

especially after Chicago's black population exploded during World War I, white gangs—the real-life equivalents of Studs Lonigan's group in Washington Park—made it increasingly difficult for blacks to get to parks and beaches. Ultimately, white efforts to limit black access to green space would play a significant role in the devastating 1919 race riot, the most violent and destructive incident of civil unrest in Chicago history.

In response to the riot, African American leaders during the Jazz Age turned their backs on the rest of the city and worked on building a self-sufficient and modern Black Metropolis, a city within a city. At the same time, blacks secured greater control of urban, rural, and wild green spaces where they could temporarily retreat from urban life. In their islands of green, African Americans picnicked, fished, swam, and enjoyed trees, fresh air, and sunshine. At the same time, they often used these landscapes to remember the past and imagine themselves as a community. While Germans, Irish, Poles, and others used Chicago green spaces to recall the preindustrial landscapes of rural Europe, black Chicagoans imagined the race by remembering African soil.

## Black Chicago

Although Chicago's first non-Indian permanent resident was of African descent (the Haitian fur trader Jean Baptiste Point DuSable), few blacks followed, largely because Illinois prohibited all black migration into the state until the Civil War. But after the war and especially after the collapse of Reconstruction in 1877, Chicago's black community grew rapidly. By 1890, the city was home to a community of 14,271. There were black professionals, businessmen, and pastors, but the majority of African Americans earned their living in the domestic service industry as cooks, porters, washerwomen, servants, and waiters. And while the community's center of gravity was on the South Side, just south of the downtown Loop, African Americans were dispersed throughout the city and often lived near the homes of their affluent white employers. In others words, although Chicago in the 1880s was hardly immune from antiblack racism, such racism did not manifest itself in the form of intense spatial segregation.[2]

During the 1870s and 1880s, African Americans seem to have encountered little or no opposition when they used public parks and commercial groves. They regularly retreated to places such as Oswald's Garden (Fifty-second Street and Halsted) that would be entirely off limits in later years. And sometimes blacks and Europeans mixed. Take an 1888 picnic of the

Knights of Pythias, an event attended by black Knights and their families but also by Germans and Scandinavians. The mixed-race crowd played baseball, drank beer, visited under the shade trees, and danced to a German band (although the Europeans excelled at waltzes while the African American dancers favored the schottische—a step that in later years would be associated with ragtime). According to the *Chicago Tribune*, "it was a large, good-humored, parti-colored crowd, resembling at a distance a huge dish of ice-cream, vanilla and chocolate mixed."[3]

During the 1890s, as black southerners migrated in ever greater numbers, whites began to draw the color line, and African Americans found themselves increasingly concentrated into ghettos. By far the largest was the so-called Black Belt, a narrow strip just a few blocks wide that ran along State Street from Twelfth to Fifty-seventh Streets (see Map 4.1). Black professionals lived in the Black Belt, often in well-appointed middle-class brick homes with lawns, trees, and flowerbeds, but the area also contained some of the worst slums in the city. Like their white neighbors in Back of the Yards, poor African Americans had to contend with unpleasant and sometimes dangerous environmental conditions (piles of rotting garbage, smoke and other air pollutants, noise, rats, flies, roaches, overfull backyard latrines). But unlike their European neighbors who could conceivably decamp for bucolic suburbs, African Americans were an increasingly captive population. Landlords took advantage of this, refusing to make needed repairs and charging blacks higher rents than whites in comparable properties. In addition, police pushed the city's thriving sex industry into the Black Belt, much to the consternation of African American preachers, professionals, and middle-class reformers, among others.[4]

Black migration from the rural South to the urban North increased dramatically in 1914 with the onset of World War I. War orders to city factories streamed in at precisely the moment that the flow of cheap immigrant labor from Europe dried up. In addition, when America entered the war in 1917, thousands of industrial workers living in Chicago left to fight in the miserable trenches of Europe. Desperate, employers turned to populations they had previously spurned: women, Mexican Americans, and African Americans. Throughout the rural South, stories of high-paying jobs and new lives in the "promised land" lured tens of thousands of blacks northward. They were also pushed out of the South by acts of racist violence, a crushing cycle of debt and poverty, poor schools, inequality in courts, disenfranchisement, soil exhaustion, falling cotton prices, and natural disasters, such as the devastating Mississippi flood of 1915 and the

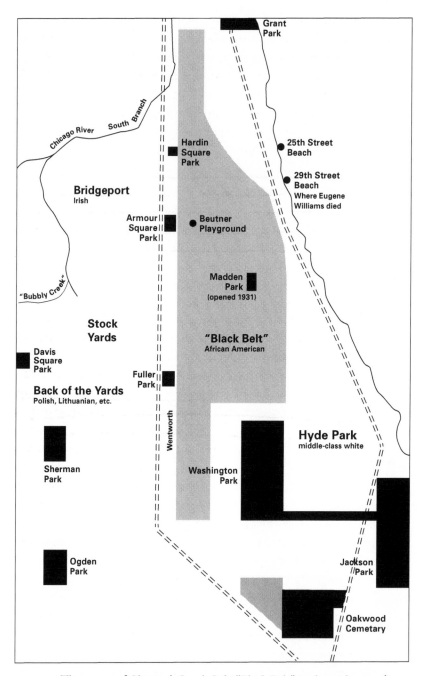

MAP 4.1 The extent of Chicago's South Side "Black Belt" in the mid-1920s (in grey) with nearby parks and beaches. Based on "Distribution of Negro Population in 1920" and "Recreation Facilities," Chicago Commission on Race Relations, *The Negro in Chicago* (Chicago: University of Chicago Press, 1922), 110, 272.

arrival of the cotton-hungry boll weevil. By 1920, the black population of Chicago had ballooned to 109,458, and African Americans made up more than 4 percent of Chicago's total population.[5]

Upon arrival, rural migrants tried to adjust to urban life in the North as best they could. In the rural South, blacks frequently worked long hours cultivating and picking cotton and engaging in other agricultural work, but nature played a significant role in dictating the pace of labor. The season of the year, weather, and the rising and the setting of the sun all structured work in the fields. But in the packinghouses, steel mills, garment factories, steam laundries, and tanneries of Chicago, rural southerners found themselves in new, alienating, and seemingly artificial environments where they did mechanized, specialized, monotonous work, the pace of which was set by machines and management. To make matters even worse, blacks frequently had to deal with hostile white coworkers and racist foremen and found themselves relegated to the worst industrial jobs.[6]

Leisure afforded some escape from long hours of alienating industrial labor in Chicago's packinghouses, steel mills, sweatshops, and laundries. Like Europeans, Mexicans, and Asians and their city-born children, many African Americans enjoyed their leisure indoors. Many went to church, enjoyed club life, or visited with friends at home, but large numbers also indulged in indoor commercialized amusements. Despite the warnings of black preachers (some of whom shared Anglo American conservatives' suspicion of all leisure outside of church) and black reformers such as Ida B. Wells (who, like white reformers, hoped to provide healthy alternatives to urban "wreckreation"), thousands went in search of cheap amusement. In the 1890s and early twentieth century, some visited establishments in the nearby levee "vice" district. By the war, the action was on the Stroll, a section of State Street known throughout Chicago for its vibrant nightlife. Attractions included jazz clubs, vaudeville performances, movie theaters, pool halls, saloons, ice cream parlors, policy outlets for illegal gambling, and even a small black-owned amusement park. Langston Hughes, author of the 1921 poem "The Negro Speaks of Rivers," noted that on the Stroll one could find "excitement from noon to noon. Midnight was like day. The street was full of workers and gamblers, prostitutes and pimps, church folks and sinners."[7]

At the same time, thousands of African Americans found escape from the smoke, trash-filled alleys, and congestion of the ghettos and long hours of monotonous industrial work in urban green spaces. In Washington Park, in tiny bits of green in the Black Belt, and along the Lake Michigan shore, they picnicked, fished, swam, boated, played baseball, lounged on the grass or the sand, and enjoyed fresh air and sunshine. Work and urban life, the *Defender* editorialized, make the individual into an "automaton, performing his duties in a methodical, perfunctory manner amid the smoke grim[e] and roar of city life." In nature, the editorial continued, the individual can find renewal and a new life and realize that he is but an insignificant atom in the universe. "It is spring and to those who are not financially able to answer the call of the wild, the parks afford at least a breathing space, a place to dream."[8]

## Drawing the Color Line across Nature

Although whites had started confining blacks in the 1890s, they redoubled their efforts during the teens. The sudden arrival of so many rural southerners on the South Side led to far greater density. Extension of the narrow Black Belt southward toward Washington Park alleviated some pressure, but the expansion was hardly fast enough for established African Americans, who often saw the poor southerners as an embarrassing blight on the community. But when affluent blacks tried to move out of the ghetto, European Americans responded with racially restrictive covenants and exploding dynamite bombs.[9]

At the same time, whites increasingly drew the color line across parks, playgrounds, and Lake Michigan beaches. As we saw in chapter 3, gang attacks on ethnic and racial outsiders were hardly unusual. Poles fought with Greeks, Italians, Mexicans, and Jews. Lithuanians and Jews also scuffled. Germans and Hungarians brawled with Italians. Syrians and Assyrian Persians came into conflict. But Irish and interethnic attacks on blacks in green spaces were marked by unusual intensity as well as the targeting of children, women, families, old people and other civilians usually exempt in gang rumbles.[10]

The Chicago Commission on Race Relations, which was organized to study the underlying causes of the devastating 1919 race riot, reported racial tension in Beutner Playground as early as 1903 when a young black man had been run out of the park. But with the onset of the Great Black Migration during the teens, conflict became pervasive and very dangerous. In 1913, a gang of white boys attacked nineteen black boys and a YMCA official as they left Armour Square Park, and the black children had to flee into nearby saloons and houses until police rescued them a half hour later. In 1915, white youths attacked a group led by a black priest from St. Thomas

Episcopal Church which had come to Armour Square to play basketball. At Ogden Park, white gangs routinely attacked black visitors. During one such encounter in 1914, a white youth with brass knuckles hit a black park director. White gangs also frequently attacked blacks in Washington Park, especially at the baseball diamonds and boathouse. In June 1918, the *Chicago Defender* reported that for the last two weeks, a "gang of white hoodlums, a modern Ku-Klux-Klan" had ambushed black visitors, regardless of age or sex. Fifty of these "white rodents" had attacked a couple in the park, beating the boy nearly unconscious and then throwing his girlfriend in the lagoon. The gang then gave chase to two girls, ages fourteen and sixteen, who were "almost outraged, right under the shining arc lights of the boathouse."[11]

Blacks also faced intimidation and violence on the Lake Michigan shore. "Even the waters of Lake Michigan are not available to colored children," reported the Juvenile Protective Association in 1913, noting that a little boy's efforts to enter the water at Thirty-ninth Street Beach had resulted in mob action by white bathers and a riot call. Starting in 1913, projectile-throwing white gangs made it impossible for the black YMCA to escort children to the lake. At the Jackson Park Beach, a white crowd dunked and nearly drowned a black boy whom they accused of "polluting the water." During the summer of 1918, the *Defender* reported that "a gang of white ruffians" was patrolling the shore between Twenty-ninth and Thirty-third Streets, trying to "prevent Race people from bathing in the lake."[12]

Although white gangs had tried to foreclose black access to green space since the onset of World War I, their efforts increased dramatically during the spring and summer of 1919. Gangs stepped up their attacks in Washington Park, and brawls at the baseball diamonds and the boathouse became a weekly occurrence. At Carter Playground, a fight between a white child and a black child turned into a mini race riot, as spectators divided along racial lines and fought in the adjoining street. Just two weeks before the race riot, the *Defender*, in an editorial entitled "Ruffianism in the Parks," complained that "young savages" had been attacking black people of all ages and that "no citizen of color, even when accompanied by women members of his family, is safe." The paper urged judges and park officials to enforce the law and protect blacks. "The attention of the park boards," the *Defender* concluded, "has been repeatedly called to this situation, and the blame for whatever happens under their jurisdiction rests with them alone."[13]

The ferocity of gang attacks certainly made the African American experience distinct, but black segregation was also exceptional because city officials, park directors, park police, and lifeguards played a significant role in blocking full black access. Before 1908, the white park director at Beutner Playground, at the behest of the surrounding community, "showed by his actions to the colored people that they were not fully accepted." A similar pattern appears to have occurred at Armour Square, Fuller Park, and Hardin Square, all of which had very low black attendance despite close proximity to black neighborhoods. White lifeguards also limited black use of Lake Michigan. When a crowd of whites assaulted a black boy at the Jackson Park Beach, the white lifeguard on duty reacted by joining the mob. Two black aldermen investigating racism along the Lake Michigan shore in 1918 reported that white lifeguards "were largely responsible for the assaults on Race people seeking the privileges of bathing there." The aldermen also blamed the lifeguards for encouraging gang violence against blacks. White police officers also turned black children away from parks and beaches and failed to protect black visitors. According to one report, when a white gang tried to attack two girls in Washington Park, a white park policeman at the scene simply looked on.[14]

When black community members complained about such injustices, the city responded by creating separate (and frequently inferior) parks for blacks. After whites pushed blacks out of Beutner Playground, the Special Parks Commission recommended that the city sell the park and use the proceeds to build a brand new park in the Black Belt (see Fig. 4.1). Ultimately, city officials opted for a cheaper solution. They simply pushed whites out of Beutner, presumably to the vastly superior Armour Square Park two blocks away. According to the Chicago Commission on Race Relations, the park district then hired a black park director for Beutner and instructed him to "turn over the playground particularly to Negroes" and "to give them more use of the facilities than whites." In similar fashion, the city hired black lifeguards at the unattractive Twenty-fifth Street Beach, which they informally designated as a black beach. The creation of exclusive black parks and beaches ought not to be seen as an example of "discrimination in favor of the Negroes," as the Chicago Commission on Race Relations put it in 1922. Rather, city officials undoubtedly hoped that the creation of a few black parks and beaches would serve as a device to limit black encroachment on "white" outdoor recreational amenities and defuse the city's mounting racial tension over limited park space.[15]

Many nonprofit recreation organizations discriminated against blacks, as well. In 1910, the Cook County Baseball League expelled black teams. In 1913, the YMCA set up a separate "colored branch," and the YWCA fol-

FIGURE 4.1 Forlorn Beutner Playground with sickly tree. Until the appropriation of Washington Park and the opening of Madden Park in 1931, Beutner Playground, with its inferior equipment and landscaping, served as the biggest green space in black Chicago. Reprinted from the Chicago Commission on Race Relations, *The Negro in Chicago* (Chicago: University of Chicago Press, 1922), 286.

lowed two years later. White ethnic Chicagoans could form their own ethnic Boy Scout troops (such as the Italian Garibaldi Troop or the Polish Boy Scouts), but they also could freely join more ethnically mixed troops if they desired. However, African Americans, Mexican Americans, and "Oriental Boys" appear to have been barred from white troops. Even the Prairie Club, the Midwest's answer to the Sierra Club, drew the color line, announcing baldly in the city's *Social Service Directory* that its wilderness activities were "open to white people of any nationality or creed."[16]

While African American leaders often complained in the press and demanded a response from the city, southerners and young people sometimes fought for equal rights to parks and beaches with their fists. Despite signs posted near Washington Park warning blacks that they would be run out of the neighborhood on July 4, 1919, African Americans picnicked there and at other parks on Independence Day, but they carried weapons in their picnic baskets along with their food.[17]

FIGURE 4.2 The scene at the Twenty-ninth Street Beach just after Eugene Williams's drowning. Reprinted from the Chicago Commission on Race Relations, *The Negro in Chicago* (Chicago: University of Chicago Press, 1922), iii.

Tension over access to parks and Lake Michigan beaches would ultimately explode in Chicago's worst racial altercation, the 1919 race riot. On July 27, a sweltering hot Sunday, thousands of working-class Chicagoans escaped the sweltering city for the cool waters of Lake Michigan. Joining the exodus were four African American boys. To get to Chicago's wild inland sea, the unsupervised adolescents jumped on the back of a produce truck and ran through Irish gang territory, where they had previously been attacked by rock-throwing whites. They did not go to an official city beach, but rather trespassed onto a lakeside industrial area they called "Hot and Cold" because of the temperature of the affluent coming from an ice company and the Keeley Brewery. The informally segregated "black beach" at Twenty-fifth Street lay just to the north. Directly south was Twenty-ninth Street Beach, a lakeside swimming area that working-class whites claimed for themselves. At Hot and Cold, the boys boarded a raft that they had probably constructed out of stolen railroad ties from the Illinois Central Railroad, whose tracks ran along the Lake Michigan shore. After unmooring their raft, the four, including fourteen-year-old Eugene Williams, pushed off into the vast lake, beginning what would become one of most ill-fated outdoor excursions in American history.[18]

While Eugene Williams and his friends pushed off into Lake Michigan on their raft, a group of young African American men and women attempted to use the "white" beach at Twenty-ninth Street. Those on the beach responded with rocks and taunts. But the blacks regrouped and responded in kind, at least until white reinforcements arrived. Meanwhile, Eugene Williams and his friends swam and dove around their raft, entirely unaware of the chaos on the white beach. As they drifted south, a white man on a jetty spotted them and began throwing rocks and bricks, one of which hit Williams in the head. When Williams slipped beneath the surface of the water, his horrified friends raced back to the black beach at Twenty-fifth Street, where they alerted a black lifeguard and police officer. After a futile rescue effort, the black officer took the boys to the white beach to look for the rock thrower. An altercation ensued, and the race riot was on (see Fig. 4.2).[19]

Over the next four days, white street gangs attacked African Americans at home, work, and on the street, sometimes shooting at them from moving vehicles. Blacks (some of whom were returning World War I veterans) fought back and returned fire. As attacks spread beyond the South Side to the West Side and into the Loop, Mayor Thompson finally allowed the governor to deploy state militia regiments. That plus the arrival of a cooling summer rainstorm brought the conflict largely to an end. Four days of rioting had left 38 dead, 537 injured, and 1,000 homeless.[20]

## Nature and the Jazz Age Black Metropolis

During the 1920s, the memory of the race riot certainly frightened some African Americans away from parks and especially beaches. In his autobiographical history of black Chicago, African American businessman and writer Dempsey Travis blamed the race riot for his never having learned how to swim as a child. He recalled that "the tragedy forever affected my parents' attitude toward Lake Michigan. . . . To Dad and Mama, the blue lake always had a tinge of red from the blood of that young black boy." But despite the viciousness of the riot and continuing acts of racist violence and official segregation, African Americans continued to seek out nature.[21]

Before the war, blacks left the city and ventured into rural and wild Illinois, Wisconsin, Indiana, and Michigan. Nineteenth-century Chicago was home to at least two black sportsmen's clubs, the Buckner-Dewey Fishing Club and the Newport Hunting and Fishing Club. Little evidence remains of these clubs, although we do know that at the 1885 annual meeting of the later, members dined on wild turkey, roast venison, prairie chicken, braised rabbit with cream sauce, and stewed bear with jelly. After a desert of ice cream, the club's leadership (composed of black Chicago's male elite, including F. L. Barnett, the husband of Ida B. Wells) gave talks on hunting, fishing, camp life, ammunition, and fear. Before World War I, Chicago's affluent blacks also vacationed at resorts, the most popular of which was the West Michigan Resort. There, far from the city, visitors could enjoy a whole variety of outdoor recreational opportunities and spend the night in tents and cabins near the Lake Michigan shore. A *Defender* writer described beautiful scenery and country life, a place run with the "sole purpose of giving a breathing spot to our people." One "Race girl" at the resort reported that the golden quality of the autumn light, the yellow of the beeches, the Indian orange of the sassafras, the fiery sumac, the glittering lake, and the bird song left her "rioting in sentiment." Another Chicago visitor to the Michigan resort asked: "Why am I so enthusiastic over this place? Here I am transported to Arcadia, to a forest of Arden, bounded by a vast expanse of blue water. Over me is the sky, rich with golden clouds and a streamer of sunlight. Great trees everywhere protect me from the worries of life."[22]

Despite Indiana gas stations that posted "we cater to white trade" signs, segregated resorts and state parks (such as the Indiana Dunes), and racist wilderness organizations (such as the Prairie Club), increasing numbers ventured out of the city and to the country. As the Associated Negro Press reported in 1925, "There are many who love hunting, rowing, hiking, and the call of the great outdoors. All of this is conducive to better health conditions, and there is hope that thousands in the congested cities may more and more become interested in God's great outdoors."[23]

After the riot, the most popular destination for black Chicagoans was the resort community of Idlewild, located in rural western Michigan. Chicago's African American elite built the Black Metropolis back on Chicago's dense South Side, but while on vacation, they retreated to Idlewild, the "Black Eden" (see Fig. 4.3). The resort boasted a clubhouse, a dancing pavilion, numerous cottages, a church, and excellent bands, but the main attraction for many visitors was the outdoors: abundant wildlife, pine forests, wild flowers and berries, hiking and riding trails, and a sandy beach on a crystal-clear lake filled with fish. Every summer, visitors stayed in cottages or pitched tents and spent their days swimming in the lake, hiking through the forested countryside, fishing, and canoeing. With its birdlife, wildflow-

FIGURE 4.3 Beach at African American resort of Idlewild in western Michigan. Courtesy of the Archives of Michigan.

ers, rabbits, porcupines, deer, and majestic forests of pine and oak, Idlewild, noted one advertisement, was the perfect place for the camera-toting nature lover. "Nature hikes and picnics coupled with study of wildlife peculiar to our location are perfect ways in which you can forget the hustle and bustle of the city." The sociologist and civil rights leader W. E. B. Du Bois was so taken with the place that he purchased an oak-covered lakeside lot, which he jokingly called "Bois du Bois." "For sheer physical beauty, for sheen of water and golden air, for nobleness of tree and shrub, for shining river and song of bird and low, moving whisper of sun, moon and star," he wrote, "can you imagine a more marvelous thing than Idlewild?"[24]

It was not just Chicago's black elite that left the city and took hikes in the wilderness. After the riot, African American organizations continued to spend scarce resources transporting urban children "back to nature." Large black churches not only organized outings for parishioners, but sponsored Boy Scout and Girl Scout troops, which traveled to the forest preserves and to the dunes. "Hike along out to the dunes once in a while," urged the writer of the *Defender's* "Boy Scout News Column." "Nothing surpasses a hike to the dunes any day. Now that the leaves are falling and nature is coloring up a little. Nothing will give you more of a thrill than an overnight hike to the dunes." The black YMCA and YWCA also took black children to the country—to Sturgeon Bay, Wisconsin, for cherry picking; to Hammond, Indiana, for "pure country air, swimming, wienie roasts, and hikes"; and to Camp Wabash, the black YMCA's forty-acre camp located near Benton Harbor, Michigan. Here, poor black children who might otherwise spend the entire summer in the city could "swim in the warm, crystal lake water, fish, go canoeing and boating, make overnight hikes, go hunting, and [do] many other things which you cannot do in the city."[25]

Back in Chicago, official racial restriction of parks and beaches remained in place, despite the 1922 report on race relations that held segregation in recreation to be a major factor in the 1919 riot. According to the director of Fuller Park, "separate parks and playgrounds for colored people are advisable . . . not because one group is any better than the other, but because they are different. Human nature will have to be remodeled before racial antipathy is overcome." The director of Armour Square told interviewers from the Chicago Race Riot Commission that her park had traditionally been reserved for whites and that the city should build blacks their own park and field house so they would not use Armour Square. At Hardin Square, Officer Daniel Callahan, the white officer who failed to arrest the rock thrower at the Twenty-ninth Street Beach, explained that you "can't make the two colors mix" and that if "a Negro should say one word back to me or should say a word to a white woman" a group of young men from the district would fight shoulder to shoulder with him and that they would make a "complete clean up this time."[26]

At the same time, swimming at one of the "white" Lake Michigan beaches would certainly result in trouble. When, for instance, African Americans tried to use the Thirty-eighth Street Beach, park police and local gangs intervened. As one African American playground director pointedly put it, "They rock you if you go in." Blacks also encountered resistance when they tried to use beaches at Jackson Park. In the mid-1930s, Spencer Castle, the editor of the *Hyde Park Gazette*, called for official segregation of the lakefront, and Republican Joseph M. Artman promised his constituents that if elected alderman he would maintain Jackson Park Beach "for WHITE PEOPLE." During the summer of 1933, a mysterious fence appeared on the sand, which many blacks saw as a subtle effort by the park district to separate the races. When a group of white communist students from the University of Chicago invited some blacks to the white side of the fence, the park police arrested the group. The police explained that they had acted to break up an effort to "mix niggers and whites" and "prevent a race riot." One policewoman later testified that she was driven to act because the group "was singing songs and looked threatening."[27]

Despite continued segregation and violence, black Chicagoans continued to demand equal access. Although the *Defender* urged readers not to drink alcohol, play instruments, dance suggestively, be vulgar, or wear inappropriate attire on city beaches or in parks, the paper did make it perfectly clear that African Americans paid taxes and thus had a right to the entire Lake Michigan shoreline and all the city parks.[28]

The *Defender* noted bitterly that while African American taxpayers subsidized park space elsewhere in the city, tired black workers had no place to "sit in the sunshine and rest and breathe the clean fresh air, as nature meant them to do." The situation, the *Defender* continued, forced black men, women, and children to use the filthy and polluted streets for their recreation. Maxwell Bond, a black playground supervisor, noted that despite some playgrounds filled with "moving, playing colored life," African Americans lacked adequate opportunities for restorative recreation. "The remaining masses," he lamented, "are left to frequent pool rooms and other questionable places of warmth and immorality." In 1927, the Chicago Health Survey confirmed what most blacks already knew: in Chicago's predominantly black wards, there were 8,059.9 people per park acre compared to 507.4 people per park acre in the city as a whole.[29]

African American leaders had long demanded that the city set aside park space in the Black Belt, but after the war the community became much more insistent. The fearless civil rights advocate and journalist Ida B. Wells led the fight, urging that the city build a large recreation park in the heart of the Black Metropolis. Although it took years of pressure, the city did begin to buy land in the late 1920s, and finally in 1931 African Americans got Madden Park, a city-block sized island of green. In the early 1930s, black volunteers played an active role in weeding, building architectural additions, and planting trees and grass. Finally, with the help of federal Works Progress Administration funding, the park was expanded and equipped with a modern field house, additional ball fields, tennis courts, a swimming pool, and improved landscaping, including additional grass, flowers, shrubs, and two hundred elm trees.[30]

Most important of all, African Americans increasingly laid claim to Washington Park—372 acres of rolling greensward, irregular groves of trees, winding paths, and lagoons for boating designed in the English style by the landscape architects Frederick Law Olmsted and Calvert Vaux. After the 1919 riot, Irish Americans, such as the fictional Lonigan family, fled the vicinity around Washington Park for the suburban Bungalow Belt,

FIGURE 4.4 In *The Picnic* (1936), African American painter Archibald J. Motley captured a common scene in the green spaces of black Chicago. Collection of Valerie Gerrard Brown and Mara Motley, M.D., courtesy of the Chicago History Museum.

including South Shore. As blacks moved into formerly Irish neighborhoods, they began to make greater claim to Washington Park, the former "turf" of Studs Lonigan and the Fifty-eighth Street gang. Especially by the late 1920s and 1930s, Chicago's "Black Metropolis" incorporated much of Washington Park, which both African Americans and whites began calling Booker T. Washington Park. But it would be more accurate to say that the Black Metropolis acquired its therapeutic antipode, a vast green oasis where African Americans could escape the stress of urban modernity. To this "two-square-mile plot of green," reported the black sociologists St. Clair Drake and Horace Cayton, "Bronzeville's teeming thousands swarm, lounging on the grass, frolicking in the Black's Belt's one large swimming pool, fishing and rowing in the lagoon, playing softball, tennis, or baseball." Here, noted the scholars, was the "playground of the South Side" (see Fig. 4.4).[31]

"I've Known Rivers"

A number of historians have argued that the 1919 race riot played a key role in eroding intra-European national distinction and forging a hybrid white American working-class culture. Less explored by scholars is that the riot also prompted African Americans (old settlers and southerners alike) to rearticulate and reimagine their own racial identity.[32]

After the Civil War, most elite black Chicagoans, or "Afro-Saxons" as historian Christopher Reed calls them, challenged antiblack racism by adopting Anglo American cultural norms, advocating racial uplift, and demanding full equality. Indicative of this assimilationist position was the black response to Colored American Day at the 1893 Columbian Exposition. While Germans, Irish, Norwegians, Poles, and Bohemians (among other Europeans) used their allotted national days at the fair to proudly remember their respective homelands and to imagine ethnicity (most often in national terms), the vast majority of African Americans boycotted the separate day, choosing instead to go on a park picnic. Despite the boycott of Colored American Day, the great civil rights advocate Frederick Douglass entered the White City and took the stage. He explained to those in attendance that although blacks had been blocked by the fair administration from showing their contributions to American civilization, these contributions were great, especially so since they were made in the face of racist violence and persecution. To demonstrate African American progress, he pointed to the West Africans exhibited at the "Dahomey Village," which was located on the Midway, the amusement district that adjoined the White City. "Look at the progress the Negro has made in thirty years," Douglass told the crowd. "We have come up out of Dahomey unto this. Measure the Negro. But not by the standard of the splendid civilization of the Caucasian. Bend down and measure him—measure him from the depths out of which he has risen."[33]

Starting in the 1890s, as white racism became more manifest and African Americans found themselves increasingly contained in the ghetto, new Chicago leadership questioned the goal of assimilation. By the time of the 1919 riot, during which angry white mobs cut Chicago blacks off from the rest of the city and forced them to fend almost entirely for themselves, the older integrationist position had lost all credibility. In its place came a focus on economic independence, the development of black institutions, and the building of the Black Metropolis, a city within a city.[34]

At the same time, African American cultural leaders championed "race pride" and began looking back for origins. In articulating a common identity for a heterogeneous, divided urban population, these leaders could look to the rural South as a common origin. But the legacy of slavery and the ongoing horror of lynching made southern nostalgia or pastoralism problematic to say the least. There could never be a southern black Garden of Eden, for the soil was mixed with sweat from uncompensated toil, blood, and tears—and from the trees hung the victims of lynch mobs. For most African Americans, the rural South was still too violent, terrifying, and alienating to serve as a suitable object of nostalgia. But this does not mean that black intellectuals and everyday Chicagoans turned away from the land and embraced anti-pastoral or anti-environmental thinking. U.S. environmental historians, ecocritics, and American studies scholars interested in landscape need to go further in recognizing that the African American environmental imagination—like that of Chicago Germans, Poles, Jews, Mexicans, and others—often extended far beyond the physical boundaries of the United States. Yes, "the race" had come to the Chicago from the rural South, but before tenant farming, lynching, slavery, and the trauma of the middle passage, there was Africa.[35]

Romantic invocations of African soil and ancestors could certainly be heard from Chicago representatives of the Universal Negro Improvement Association (UNIA), which was led by the Jamaican black nationalist Marcus Garvey. Instead of trying to distance African Americans from the taint of "savage" Africa, Garvey and thousands of his Chicago followers (many of whom were recent arrivals from the South) celebrated a noble African past and imagined themselves members of a scattered black nation. Working out of Harlem, Garvey and the UNIA started new subsidiary organizations (such as the Black Cross Nurses, the Black Cross Flying Corps, and the Order of the Nile) and opened a series of small businesses: grocery stores, a steam laundry, a restaurant, and a newspaper called *Negro World*. He also started his own steamship company, Black Star Lines, which would not only strengthen the community economically but enable the black diaspora to return back to its original homeland, "mother Africa." All blacks would then be united as one pan-African nation, united under the famous 1920 tricolor UNIA flag, with stripes of red (symbolic of African blood that must be shed for liberation), black (representing black people), and green (symbolic of the "luxuriant vegetation of our motherland").[36]

Most Jazz Age blacks considered themselves not African but African American. Their future was in the United States. But just because they rejected Garvey's black nationalist message does not mean that they endorsed Douglass's message of uplift and his efforts to distance African Americans from "savage" Africa. As historian Clare Corbould shows, during the 1920s, large numbers of moderate African Americans began discovering their African roots. When whites portrayed Africa as an unexplored jungle of vast rivers, exotic animals, tropical plants, and savage backward people, black Americans did not respond by emphasizing progress, but rather by publically taking pride in their heritage, reminding whites of the glory of ancient Egypt, Ethiopia, and Timbuktu and embracing Africa as a cure for the ills of urban modernity. Africa, Corbould persuasively argues, "was no longer simply a place in the past, from which black Americans had come and developed. Africa was now something living and breathing within black identity and at the fore of a newly expanded and dynamic public life."[37]

In the arts, nostalgia for Africa is most often associated with the Harlem Renaissance and writer Alain Locke's call to turn to Africa and to cultivate "the ancestral arts." Although it is true that the Chicago art and literary scene during the 1920s did not have the ferment found in New York, it would be a serious mistake to think that while "New Negro" artists in Harlem turned to Africa, their counterparts in Chicago continued to emulate European models. Printmaker, educator, and founder of the Chicago Art League William McKnight Farrow taught an entire generation of black artists to turn to their own past for inspiration. He spread his message in lectures at the Wabash YMCA, but also at the Art Institute, where he was an instructor. He also organized the 1927 Art Institute "Negro in Art Week" exhibit, which featured a lecture by Locke and exhibits of Congolese sculptures alongside contemporary work from black Chicagoans. Writers also looked backward. Poet Fenton Johnson, for instance, not only wrote about great African American and Haitian leaders, but also the monuments of ancient Egypt, the fragrant groves of Libya, and the bamboo huts and date fields of Ethiopia. "No longer do the kings on couch of leopard skins await thy hour," Fenton wrote in his 1915 poem "Ethiopia." "The Gods are dead, our ancient glory dust, our altars broken, and our people gone."[38]

Historians also played a major role in reappraising the African past. Faced with a historical profession that ignored or profoundly distorted black history, Carter Woodson, the son of slaves who went on to get a Ph.D. in history from Harvard University, set about to correct the record. Working out of the basement of the Wabash YMCA with a group of like-minded colleagues, he started the Association for the Study of Negro Life and History and began publishing the *Journal of Negro History*. Later in 1926, he organized the first Negro History Week. In his work, Carter not only taught African American history to an entire generation, but he also brought his readers back to Africa, which he portrayed not as the benighted black continent, but rather the cradle of civilization.[39]

New appreciation for Africa could also be seen in black consumer culture. As historian Davarian Baldwin shows, images of Africa (in particular Egyptian queens) figured prominently in the beauty products sold by and for black women. African Americans also sometimes appropriated and reworked stereotypical portrayals of Africa they found in mass culture. The novelist Richard Wright captured just such a creative rereading in his famous realist novel, *Native Son* (1940). In the opening chapter, the protagonist, Bigger Thomas, gets some relief from the urban environment (from which he is profoundly alienated) by going to a movie theater and seeing *Trader Horn*, which in real life was the first nondocumentary film shot in Africa. Although the picture, which was released by Metro-Goldwyn-Mayer in 1931, contained all sorts of crude stereotypical portrayals of African people, Bigger sees something different in the film. He takes in "the roll of the tom-toms and the screams of black men and women dancing free and wild," but he sees "men and women who were adjusted to their soil and at home in their world, secure from fear and hysteria."[40]

Arguably the single-most-effective engine for generating race pride, popularizing black history, and invoking a noble African past was the *Chicago Defender*. Editor Robert Abbott disseminated his paper throughout the nation, including in the South, and the paper played a critical role in fueling the Great Black Migration to Chicago. Abbott disliked Garvey and his Back-to-Africa ideas and even played a role in the black nationalist's arrest, but Abbott's disapproval of Garvey and his movement does not imply that the newspaper editor was uninterested in Africa. His newspaper not only chronicled contemporary injustice throughout the United States but also introduced readers to black history (republishing chapters from Woodson's books) and published news from Africa, including archaeological finds, such as the extraordinary 1922 discovery of the tomb of King Tutankhamen (who was described in at least one article as "Negro"). And mechanically reproduced on the masthead of every single paper was Abbott's proud Egyptian sphinx.[41]

Like Europeans and Mexicans in Chicago, African Americans used rural and wild landscapes as well as urban green spaces to invoke a common ancestral past and to imagine community. Outside the city, affluent black nature tourists transformed Idlewild, the Black Eden, into a landscape

FIGURE 4.5 "Egyptian Pageant," in Ernest T. Attwell, "Recreation for Colored America," *The American City Magazine* 35 (August 1926): 162.

for the remembrance of the Negro past and the imagination of the race. While white Jazz Age tourists discovered their own North American frontier origins in wilderness parks such as Yellowstone, Starved Rock, the Indiana Dunes, and the Cook County Forest Preserves, affluent blacks, stung by racism and exclusion, gathered together in the wilderness of Michigan and imagined themselves as a people with a collective past that extended back to African soil. At the Black Eden, African American nature tourists boated, camped, hiked, and listened to some of the best jazz bands of the era, but they also attended Chautauqua-style lectures on black music, black poetry, and "The Unpublished History of the Negro versus the Published," as well as talks that stirred listeners into "greater race activity." For Du Bois, the Black Eden was a stunning natural landscape where "the sons and great-grandchildren of Ethiopia," the people within the veil, left their dress coats, servants, and formal attitudes back in the city and converged as one people, forging a "center of Negro art, conference and recreation."[42]

Back in the city, less privileged African Americans made public parks a site to remember the race's past. On Bronzeville playgrounds, African American park directors and staff conducted recreational programs similar to those in white parks, but instead of celebrating European folk culture or holding pageants celebrating America's frontier history, staff staged Egyptian pageants, with black children playing the role of pharaoh and his retainers (see Fig. 4.5).[43]

The imagination of the race can be seen even more clearly in the massive 1934 outdoor pageant, *O, Sing a New Song*, which was held in Grant Park. On the grass in the middle of Soldier's Field, a recently created open-air coliseum, a cast of 5,000 singers, actors, and dancers, including twenty-one Zulus specifically invited from South Africa, traced the history of the black race, from the African wilderness to the industrial Jazz Age city. The cast was far larger than that in earlier productions of W. E. B. Du Bois's pageant *The Star of Ethiopia*, which means that *O, Sing a New Song* was the largest black theatrical performance up to that point.[44]

Like the earlier pageant, *O, Sing a New Song* did not portray Africa as benighted or Africans as savage subhumans. Rather the pageant romanticized Africa as the original homeland of black people. The pageant begins in a peaceful African village. As dawn breaks, the villagers (played by the Zulus) slowly awake and sing an "Ode to the Sun" to the accompaniment of tribal drummers. Later in the day, the men successfully kill a lion that had threatened the village, women and children perform a fire dance, and singers greet the thunder of an approaching storm. The villagers are in thrall to the natural world, which reciprocates the Africans with abundance.

Suddenly, the peace of the African village is broken with the arrival of Portuguese slavers, who fire on the village and capture the Africans and their king. The Europeans transport the Africans to the rural South. They are now slaves on a cotton plantation where they pick their crop and sing spirituals such as "Go Down Moses" and Civil War ballads such as "John Brown's Body."

The arrival of President Lincoln ends the long suffering of the slaves. As Lincoln reads the Emancipation Proclamation and frees the people, sweeping floodlights fill the field with light and the newly released slaves sing "Rise! Shine! Give God the Glory." The last act brings the story of the race up to the Jazz Age. Booker T. Washington makes an appearance, as does the tap dance virtuoso Bill "Bojangles" Robinson. The act ends with jazz music, African American doughboys fighting in World War I, and a "mechanical ballet" representing modern industrial life.[45]

African Americans also used the green shady lawns of Washington Park to remember the black past, in particular during the annual Bud Billiken Picnic. The origin of Bud Billiken Day (which remains even today one of the most significant events in black America) dates to the 1920s, when Robert Abbott, the editor of the *Defender*, began publication of a children's section, which he named after a Billiken, a childlike figurine popular in the early twentieth century. With the children's pages, Abbott hoped to instill racial pride in younger readers, and the first Billiken Parade and Picnic in 1929 was a direct extension of this effort. To many young Chicagoans, the parade and picnic quickly became "African American New Year, Decoration Day, Fourth of July, and Mardi Gras rolled into one." At the 1933 parade, tens of thousands of spectators watched floats built by local businesses, hundreds of marching, flag-carrying Boy Scouts, Campfire Girls, and Girl Scouts, Knights of Pythias, Ancient United Knights and Daughters of Africa, soldiers of the all-black Eighth Regiment, and local luminaries, including Abbott in his Rolls Royce.[46]

After the parade, black Chicago left the city streets behind and regrouped on Bronzeville's vast front lawn for what was billed as the biggest picnic in Chicago. Once in the park, participants spread blankets on the grass and opened baskets of food, ate free ice cream, played baseball and other games organized by local playground supervisors, listened to four different jazz bands, and socialized under the shade trees. Black Chicago also welcomed a visiting Yoruba prince and his "witch doctor," both participants at the "Darkest Africa" concession at the 1933 World's Fair. Whereas white visitors to the World's Fair saw the Nigerians as savage racial others, black Chicagoans welcomed the pair to their park "with the dignity befitting a royal family." The *Defender* pronounced it "a great day for children and a great day for the race."[47]

The historians Peter M. Rutkoff and William B. Scott argue that the Bud Billiken Parade and Picnic reflects the continuation of West African traditions in industrial Chicago. They write, "The invitation to African dignitaries, the explicit recognition of Yoruba culture in the *Defender*, the parade's splendid uniforms, its Kongo-inspired high-stepping and dashing drum majors, its smartly attired officials, braided dignitaries in open cars, and the spirit of the West African dance of its majorettes sashaying side to side as they marched down South Parkway to the rhythmic encouragement of thousands of onlookers, all attested to West African cultural influences." While Rutkoff and Scott are right that the parade reflected African cultural continuities, their analysis misses a larger point: that the parade and picnic in Olmsted's Washington Park represented a crucial moment when a heterogeneous population of African Americans did the cultural work of imaging themselves as a people with common roots. Chicago's black community understood that these roots grew through the soil of the rural South, but their roots did not begin in this fraught landscape. Rather they extended from Chicago back to Africa. The park, which the poet Frank Marshall Davis described in 1937 as a verdant island that held "Chicago's Congo to its soothing breast," was yet another black Eden, a place where residents of the Black Metropolis could come together, remember that past, and envision themselves as a proud community in the present.[48]

When African Americans gathered in Idlewild and Madden, Grant, and Washington Parks and imagined "the race" during the Jazz Age, they engaged in cultural work not at all dissimilar to that of Irish, Germans, Poles, Italians, and Mexicans, all of whom used Chicago green spaces to imagine ethnicity. To imagine community in the present, European immigrant and African American leaders publically remembered a shared past, which they rooted in the soil of an original homeland.

Yet there were important differences, especially at the level of motivation. European migrants, especially those from eastern and southern Europe, certainly faced racism, but their efforts to preserve language, culture, religion, and national identity were largely born of fear. Their concern was that they and especially their children might loose connections  to homelands, Americanize, "pass" into the larger culture, and loose their identity. In sharp contrast, African Americans had tried to pass, but met increasing resistance and even violence. The forging of a distinct and positive black racial identity was fueled, then, not by threatened deracination, but by mounting antiblack racism and increasing awareness that their children could not assimilate into the American dominant culture on any terms.[49]

Although the race riot and continuing racism fueled race pride and defensive calls for black economic self-sufficiency, the Great Depression demonstrated clearly and painfully that the Black Metropolis was hardly independent of Chicago or larger economic forces. When the depression began in 1929, black financial institutions, such as the Binga Bank, collapsed leaving many penniless. At the same time, black workers, who often were the last hired and the first fired, began to lose their jobs in alarming numbers. By 1932, over 40 percent of African American workers were unemployed.[50]

The Great Depression ultimately prompted tens of thousands of African Americans to think about class in new ways and to reassess longstanding aversion to "white" unions in the stockyards and in other industries. Evidence of changing views could be seen in Washington Park. On the rolling landscape of the English park, the author Richard Wright joined growing interracial crowds gathered to listen to communist speakers. The radicals blasted racism, but they also challenged black separatism, urging workers to instead unite across lines of nationality, ethnicity, and race and  to come together in solidarity as an industrial working class. As we will see in chapter 5, 1930s radicals were hardly the first Chicagoans who viewed green space as an important site to make a working class.[51]

## CHAPTER FIVE

# The Nature of May Day
## Green Space and Working-Class Chicago

> Boom . . . boom . . . boom . . . We turned you into steel and iron.
> Be ye permeated with our sombre music, make your muscles
> into springs, and each movement of yours to fall in with the din.
> Keep turning and twisting together with the wheels, adapt your
> hand to our levers, become one of our component parts . . .
> boom . . . boom . . . boom. . . .
> And the machines further say, You must become unfeeling,
> unthinking. You must forget everything which is alien to us
> machines. Never mind that in your soul is an unsubdued cry
> about an intense desire to live, to take in the glitter of the day
> and the glory of the fields; never mind that your heart is aching
> with the gloom of years spent aimlessly, aching with the impulse
> for freedom and with the despair over a wasted youth—pluck all
> this from your breasts and turn into machines. That our clang
> and scream may become your favorite music; a substitute for the
> song of the bird and the murmur of the stream; that our
> vibrating steel lustre may substitute the sun for you. Boom . . .
> boom . . . boom. . . .
>
> —OTORMSKY, "Machines and Men," *Molodaya Rus*,
>     December 31, 1915

On Saturday May 1, 1886, nearly one hundred thousand Chicago workers went on strike. They came from a variety of national backgrounds, industries, and skill levels, and their strike was so effective it paralyzed the rapidly industrializing city. As one reporter noted, "no smoke curled up from the tall chimneys of the factories and mills, and things had assumed a Sabbath-like appearance." While soldiers, Pinkerton private police, and deputized citizens stationed on rooftops trained their Winchester rifles on the streets below and hundreds of National Guardsmen mustered in nearby armories, eighty thousand working-class people paraded through Chicago and attended numerous open-air meetings. They were members of traditional trade unions, socialists, Knights of Labor, anarchists, and unaffiliated Chicagoans, but they shared one thing in common: they all wanted a long, increasingly mechanized workday limited strictly to eight hours. In their own words, they wanted "eight hours for work, eight hours for rest, eight hours for what we will."[1]

As labor historians Philip Foner and David Roediger convincingly argue, during the late nineteenth and early twentieth centuries, the promise of reduced work hours (the eight-hour day and later the full weekend and the paid vacation) galvanized labor. As the factory floor became increasingly rationalized and work lost much of its former meaning, workers not only demanded a reprieve from long hours of toil in industrial environments, but also more time for leisure activities. They wanted time to see friends and family, pursue education, attend religious services, participate in ethnic social life, and enjoy a new world of urban amusements. But many workers in the struggle for shorter hours also had another objective, one largely missed in studies of working-class leisure: they wanted time to escape the "artificial" industrial city and enjoy the outdoors. In the verses of Otormsky, the unknown Chicago proletarian poet of our epigraph, the environment of the factory reduces the worker to a machine. Muscles become springs, hands an extension of levers. The glint of steel replaces the sun and the sounds of machines stand in for the songs of birds and the murmur of streams. But despite this, the soul cries to live, "to take in the glitter of the day and the glory of the fields."[2]

In this chapter, I argue not only that some workers fought for more leisure time so that they could escape the "artificial" city and enjoy nature but also that workers sometimes used rural and wild landscapes as well as urban green spaces to forge community and to make a working class. In previous chapters, we have seen how immigrants (Germans, Poles, Mexicans, and others), their American-born children, and African Americans used their natural places as sites to imagine community. Heterogeneous groups of workers did the exact same thing, but instead of gathering and remembering a common history rooted in a preindustrial homeland, laborers typically used green space to look forward and to imagine a reformed and sometimes utopian future. In other words, there is a little-explored "green" dimension to Chicago's vaunted labor movement.

## Alienation and the Eight-Hour Day

Labor activism in Gilded Age Chicago makes much more sense if we understand its context: the dramatic transformation of industrial capitalism in the years after the Civil War. As historian William Cronon shows, Chicago grew dramatically after the war because industrialists effectively exploited natural resources from the city's vast and ecologically diverse hinterland. Like the tentacles of an octopus, railroad lines extended out from Chicago and onto the tall-grass prairies of the Midwest; the white pine forests of northern Minnesota, Wisconsin, and Michigan; and the short-grass prairies of the Great Plains. From those distinct ecosystems, Chicago merchants and industrialists imported grain, timber, and animals. In grain elevators, lumberyards, and meatpacking houses, nature was differentiated, standardized, and ultimately affixed with a price. Grain became "#2 Spring" and dozens of other grades; white pine trees were cut, recut, and then cut again; pigs and cattle became not only packaged meat, but brushes, lard, and glue.[3]

According to Cronon, one important side effect of this conversion of nature into commodities was that urban consumers often forgot that their bread, their lumber, or their steak had originally come from a physical, animate, rural world outside the city. A steer, transformed into dressed beef, "vanished from human memory as one of nature's creatures. Its ties to the earth receded, and in forgetting the animal's life one also forgot the grasses and the prairie skies and the departed bison herds of a landscape that seemed more and more remote in space and time."[4]

But as Cronon himself would undoubtedly agree, consumers often overlooked something else: the considerable human labor required to transform wheat into bread, trees into two-by-fours, and pigs into sausage. When they cut into their steak, the American eater not only forgot the short-grass prairie, but also the immigrant packinghouse workers who labored long hours at little pay transforming living animals into standardized products. If anything, Americans then (like today) seemed far more concerned about their food's environmental context than about their dinner's connection to a dehumanizing labor process. After writing *The Jungle*, socialist Upton Sinclair was taken aback that readers of his muckraking novel came away more concerned about the "unnatural" origins of their meat than about the horrendous working conditions under which their meat was butchered. As he famously noted, "I aimed at the public's heart and by accident hit its stomach."[5]

After the Civil War, industrialists transformed the factory floor. They subdivided tasks, undercut relatively independent craftsmen, relied increasingly on unskilled labor, and brought in new labor-saving machinery. The city's business leaders not only put a price tag on the natural world, they often came to see their workers not as distinct human beings, but as interchangeable commodities that could be purchased in Chicago's labor marketplace and put to work on the factory floor. In the absence of a regulatory state, companies often demanded long, unsustainable hours of daily work, taxing workers with the same sort of reckless shortsightedness with which they culled trees in northern Wisconsin. By the time of the 1886 May Day protest, most factory workers toiled sixty hours a week, with only Sunday, the Christian Sabbath, to recuperate.[6]

Skilled and unskilled workers responded to these changes by forming unions, voting for candidates who appeared to represent their interests, making demands on employers, and sometimes striking and shutting down their places of employment. They also began the process of consciously making themselves into a working class. But in Chicago, there were many obstacles to class formation. Although workers often shared a similar experience of alienation and exploitation on the factory floor, they were frequently divided by nationality, ethnicity, language, workplace skill, sex, race, religion, and place of employment. They were also frequently at odds over politics. Traditional craft or trade unions, the Knights of Labor, socialists, and anarchists offered sometimes-conflicting remedies for the problem of an exploitative and dehumanizing labor system.[7]

Traditional craft or trade unions emerged after the outbreak of the Civil War. The war led to a labor shortage and inflation, but wages remained stagnant and hours extraordinarily long. In response, carpenters, typographers, bakers, iron molders, and other skilled workers organized unions based on their trade and demanded an eight-hour day. Worker agitation resulted in the passage of a state eight-hour law, but it was unenforced by the state; so in an effort to make the law binding, unions planned a one-week general strike to begin May 1, 1867. In what would serve as a dress rehearsal for the massive May 1, 1886, strike with which we began this chapter, ten thousand laborers joined a 7.5-mile procession and marched through the Loop and to the Lake Front. On the shores of Lake Michigan, they listened to German and English speakers talk about the "divine law" of eight hours for work, eight hours for sleep, and eight hours for recreation, and about the importance of healthy recreation given the increasing mechanization of work.[8]

Trade unionists lost their strike in 1867, but the skilled workers in the Federation of Organized Trades and Unions (the forerunner of the American Federation of Labor, or AFL) regrouped and in 1884 called for the massive May 1, 1886, strike. Although socialists, the Knights of Labor, and anarchists enjoined the strike and gave it new and radical meanings, the skilled workers in the craft unions maintained their more modest goals. They did not see the May Day strike in 1886 as the opening shot of a revolution or a dramatic reformulation of American capitalism. Rather, they merely hoped to reform an unjust system and increase the relative freedom of skilled workers by creating more leisure.[9]

Unlike the English speakers who dominated the trade union movement, German-speaking socialists offered a more radical solution. The socialist movement grew dramatically during the economic depression of 1873. While the trade unions retrenched, the socialists organized unskilled workers, supported informal communal strikes, and led the hungry, homeless, and unemployed on dramatic marches to City Hall to demand jobs and relief. Socialists, unlike trade union leaders, also took on a visible leadership role during the Railroad Strike of 1877, a bloody nationwide upheaval during which large numbers of unskilled workers rose up against their employers. Following the strike, Chicago socialists, like their brethren in Germany, not only continued to organize city workers; they also entered the political arena and put forward candidates who called for the nationalization of key industries, such as the railroads. In a series of elections during the late 1870s, socialist candidates did surprisingly well, and five were elected aldermen.[10]

Even farther to the left were the anarchists, who, unlike the socialists, sought not only to end industrial capitalism, but to destroy the state itself. During the 1877 Railroad Strike, Chicago police, instructed to protect private property, killed thirty workers, wounded two hundred, and violated the civil liberties of thousands more. This exercise of raw state power seemingly at the behest of the city's business class radicalized some socialists. In addition, incidents of voter fraud meant to keep socialist candidates from taking office led many to conclude that peaceful electoral change was futile. Having lost faith in the state, radicals formed labor militias (such as the Lehr- und Wehr-Verein [or Education and Defense Association], the Jägerverein [or Hunters Association], the Irish Labor Guards, and the Bohemian Sharpshooters) and began to prepare for an inevitable class war. The anarchists, as the radicals called themselves, looked forward to a postrevolutionary world where small economic collectives with access to cutting-edge nineteenth-century technology would spring up in the void left by the collapse of organized religion, capitalism, and the state.[11]

Between the moderate trade unions and the radical socialists and anarchists stood the Knights of Labor, which emerged in the 1870s, but exploded in popularity during the early 1880s. Unlike the trade unions, the Knights sought to organize all producers, regardless of skill, nationality, gender, and race (although they drew the line at Chinese participation). Under the motto "an injury to one is the concern of all," the Knights worked to create one big union, nationalize key industries such as the railroads, establish an income tax, provide equal pay to female workers, and end child labor. The future they envisioned was a "cooperative commonwealth" in which wage labor would disappear and workers would own the factories, mines, and shops where they worked. Although the head of the Knights, Grand Master Workman Terence Powderly, rejected the tool of the strike, his Chicago members, composed disproportionately of unskilled Irish workers on the South Side, took matters into their own hands and became enthusiastic supporters of the upcoming May 1, 1886, strike for the eight-hour day.[12]

During the warm summer months, trade unionists, socialists, anarchists, and the Knights used picnics to solidify their base and to attract new workers. Regardless of political orientation, the destination was almost always Ogden's Grove, a commercial park opened by German entrepreneur Peter Rinderer in 1865 on the Near North Side (just to the west of the intersection of Clybourn Avenue, Sheffield Avenue, and Willow Street). One police-affiliated writer of the period described the park as the "picnicking ground for labor societies, and particular for socialists, communists, and anarchists."[13]

A trip to Ogden's Grove always started with a parade through Chicago streets. Consider September 7, 1885, Chicago's first Labor Day. Under beautiful skies, around 10,000 workers from the city's trade unions and Knights of Labor set out from just west of the downtown Loop. Viewers of the parade witnessed the nattily dressed stonecutters, who escorted wagons, which carried the masons hard at work chiseling marble. They also saw the cutters' large stone tablets, inscribed with pro-labor messages such as "Capital Springs from Labor," "Don't Use Prison Made Goods," "Our Cure is the Ballot," and "Eight Hours for Work, Eight Hours for Rest, Eight Hours for Recreation." One cart carried a rich wine-drinking capitalist and a sign that said "Works Two Hours." Next to him was a miserable overworked worker with a tablet that read "Works Fourteen Hours." Viewers also saw the horseshoers. Wearing black leather hats and aprons, the men transported a miniforge and made shoes and shod horses along the parade route. On their wagon, the typographers ran off copies of the *Labor Holiday*, which they distributed to the crowd. The broom makers marched with new brooms, and the cigar makers crafted cigars of extraordinary size. The curriers and tanners, all in red shirts, demonstrated the process by which animal skin was made into leather. After finishing the final step, the tanners passed the leather backwards to the wagons of the shoemakers where the material was crafted into finished shoes. The shoemakers also transported a pair of enormous five-foot tall leather boots.[14]

The parades of social revolutionaries, in contrast, were far more confrontational. Socialists and anarchists carried signs and banners emblazoned with slogans such as "Workers of the World Unite," "Down with Capitalism, Long Live Communism," "Our Civilization—the Bullet and the Policeman's Club," "Today's Greatest Crime is Poverty," and "Land Belongs to Society." The parades also featured floats that called for worker unity and women's suffrage while lampooning capitalists, politicians, judges, and the church. Armed members of the city's various labor militias also sometimes marched in these parades. Instead of identifying principally as German, Bohemian, Irish, Swedish, or American, anarchists in particular portrayed themselves as members of an international working class inclusive not just of skilled male workers, but women, racial and ethnic minorities, the unskilled, and the unemployed. They marched not with an American flag or the flag of any nation but rather with red and black flags (symbolic of the blood of workers, on the one hand, and the negation of all national flags, on the other).[15]

Despite differences in tone, workers ended their parades at the gates of Ogden's Grove. After paying a small entrance fee, they left the city and found themselves in a beautiful wooded park along the banks of the slow-moving Chicago River. Workers (sometimes twenty thousand at a time) and their families sat at tables under the trees or reclined on blankets spread over the grass and ate picnic lunches (see Fig. 5.1). They socialized, listened to bands, danced, played sports, and, once night came, watched fireworks. They also purchased and drank beer, something forbidden in the city's much more restrictive public parks. No mere public space, Ogden's Grove was seen by workers as a natural place where they could temporarily escape the urban industrial environment and enjoy cool breezes, living oaks, and sunlight. As one German worker put it, Ogden's Grove was a place where one forgot the city and came into a world of "sunshine, woodland green and woodland shade."[16]

A PICNIC OF THE "REDS" AT SHEFFIELD.

1. Experimenting with Dynamite.   2. Getting Inspiration.   3. Engel on the Stump.   4. "Hoch die Anarchie!"
5. Mrs. Parsons addressing the Crowd.   6. Children peddling Most's Literature.   7. A Family Feast.

FIGURE 5.1 "A Picnic of the 'Reds.'" An anarchist picnic (featuring a speech by the African American labor agitator Lucy Parsons, drunken men and women, and experiments with dynamite) in Ogden's Grove, as seen through the eyes of Chicago Police Captain Michael J. Schaack. Reprinted from Michael J. Schaack, *Anarchy and Anarchists: A History of the Red Terror and the Social Revolution in America and Europe. Communism, Socialism, and Nihilism in Doctrine and in Deed. The Chicago Haymarket Conspiracy, and the Detection and Trial of the Conspirators* (Chicago: F. J. Schulte, 1889), 453.

## May Day and Labor Day

In previous chapters, we have seen how immigrant and African American leaders used urban green spaces and rural and wild landscapes to imagine ethnicity and "the race." They did this by collectively remembering a common history rooted in the soil of a preindustrial homeland. But working-class leaders in Chicago obviously could not unite industrial workers as a class by evoking a common origin. Their constituency was simply too nationally, ethnically, linguistically, and racially diverse for a joint exercise in nostalgia. The only thing that many of them shared was the common experience of exploitation on the factory floor. So when labor leaders invited workers out of the city and to green spaces, they did not look backward into the misty past, but forward into a bright future. In other words, they did not use green spaces to evoke an ancient touchstone, but rather to point towards a distant lodestar.

This orientation toward the future does not imply that workers never looked back. Trade unionists marked traditional holidays such as Independence Day, which they invested with their own meaning, principally by linking their cause to the fate of a free republic. Meanwhile, German socialists and anarchists drew on symbols from the French Revolution and remembered the Paris Commune established by workers in 1871. Sometimes workers nostalgically yearned for an earlier rural world where workers owned their own labor and lived in harmonious relationship with nature. Consider the example of the German anarchist Michael Schwab, who, in his death-row autobiography, reminisced nostalgically about his Bavarian homeland. Sitting in a miserable Chicago jail cell, he remembered the Franconia Hills covered in grape vines, the Main River and silver brooks, the grain fields and the vegetable gardens, and the "dark green forests of pure oak and beech" that villagers held in common. And he bitterly lamented that the sons and daughters of farmers had to leave the countryside and travel to cities to sell their labor. In the city, instead of "the splashing and roaring of the creeks and cataracts," and "the whispering of the air in the dark-green forests," the worker now only hears the task bell and the clattering of "noisy busy machines." While the migrant looses his health, strength, and independence, his offspring, "growing up in unhealthy surroundings, are a different race—the race of exploited, wretched wage slavers."[17]

Although Schwab and other Chicago workers certainly drew on the past, it was the future about which they were most passionate. In Ogden's Grove

under the shade trees, speakers reminded workers of present-day grievances, but told them that if they organized, they could change the present
order. Trade unionists spoke of a reformed society, a future world in
which workers would have eight hours for work, eight hours for rest, and
eight hours to do "what we will." Socialists urged workers to vote, drive
vampirelike capitalists and their agents from power, and "establish a
government of workingmen." Meanwhile, anarchist speakers talked about
the inevitability of a revolution that would destroy the state and bring
forth an entirely new world where workers would be truly free. As anarchist Samuel Fielding explained, workers would no longer have to wait
for picnics because they would have one everyday. "See to it," he told the
crowd in Ogden's Grove, "that no person shall own a private piece of
property unless each man shall have a clear title-deed to the whole
world."[18]

Despite profound differences, almost all workers in Chicago joined the
1886 struggle for an eight-hour day. Even anarchists, who initially dismissed
the movement as a palliative, eagerly joined when they saw the extraordinary enthusiasm with which common laborers greeted the movement
and the fear with which employers reacted to the prospect of shorter hours.
One reason why the eight-hour movement galvanized so many was that
it simultaneously looked like an important steppingstone to long-term
change. Socialists believed the movement would lead to socialism. The
Knights viewed it as a step toward a cooperative commonwealth. Anarchists saw May 1, 1886, as the beginnings of a violent revolution that would
bring about a stateless workers' paradise. Meanwhile, skilled, predominantly
English-speaking trade unionists believed the strike was a path to a labor
marketplace where workers would have more control in their negotiations
with employers. At the same time, the 1886 strike offered a very immedi-
ate and extremely practical short-term goal that everyone could appreciate:
more time "for what we will."[19]

What did rank-and-file workers in the eight-hour movement want to
do with their increased leisure time? Employers suggested that laborers
would use their newfound leisure to wallow in dissipation. Labor leaders
countered that long hours drove workers to drink and that with more time
for themselves, workers would have an opportunity to improve themselves
through education. Workers themselves did not explicitly answer the question of what they would do with increased leisure. They almost certainly
wanted more time for family and friends. Some probably wanted to

participate in national organizations, such as the German Turners and the Clan na Gael. Others most likely sought more time for religious observance. Still others surely wanted to enjoy the city's commercialized amusements: saloons, ethnic theater, spectator sports, and musical performances. But as the extraordinary popularity of city and commercial parks on holidays and Sundays suggests, large numbers also undoubtedly looked forward to more opportunities to leave polluted neighborhoods and enjoy sunshine, fresh air, trees, grass, and open sky.[20]

One revealing window on the importance that workers gave to having more leisure time for nature is the "Eight-Hour Song," the official anthem of the eight-hour movement. On May 1, 1886, thousands of striking workers sang it as they marched through downtown:

> We mean to make things over, we are tired of toil for naught,
> With but bare enough to live upon, and never an hour for thought;
> We want to feel the sunshine, and we want to smell the flowers,
> We are sure that God has will'd it, and we mean to have eight hours.
> We're summoning our forces from the shipyard, shop and mill,
> Eight hours for work, eight hours for rest, eight hours for what
>     we will!
> Eight hours for work, eight hours for rest, eight hours for what
>     we will!

The "Eight-Hour Song," in its entirety, described nineteenth-century industrial capitalism as a profoundly unnatural, life-destroying, and unholy force that reduced humans to physically broken slaves who envied "the beasts that graze the hillside . . . and the birds that wander free." The song also threatened that if labor was ignored, the movement could potentially take on the form of "the torrent" or "the wild tornado." Most important for the purposes of this book, the song pointed clearly to one important promise of an eight-hour day: a chance to escape unending hours of work in sunless factories, mills, and mines, get outdoors, and "smell the flowers" and "feel the sunshine."[21]

The always-uneasy alliance over the eight-hour day between radicals and more moderate groups (such as the Trades and Labor Assembly and the Knights of Labor) disintegrated only a few days after the May Day general strike in 1886. To protest police violence, the anarchists planned a meeting on the night of May 4 at Haymarket Square. The gathering was peaceful, so much so that Mayor Carter Harrison Sr., who had come to monitor the situation, declared the protest tame, instructed the police not to interfere, and left early. But following the last speech, police moved aggressively to disperse the crowd. At that moment, someone threw a pipe bomb, which exploded among the police, killing one. The confused policemen then responded with their service revolvers, hitting both workers and their own fellow officers. In the end, the evening's violence took the lives of twelve (eight police officers and four protesters) and wounded dozens more.[22]

The Haymarket bombing sparked the nation's first red scare. Chicago police arrested hundreds of people without cause, beat suspects, engaged in warrantless searches of homes and offices, opened mail, and shut newspapers. At the same time, the city banned the red flag, parades, and open-air meetings in parks and along the Lake Michigan shore that the anarchists (as well as more moderate trade unionists) had used to unite and mobilize their movement. Despite failing to find the actual bomber or any direct evidence, the state, in what is now seen as a great miscarriage of justice, sentenced seven anarchists (including Michael Schwab) to die by hanging.[23]

Despite the trial and continued police oppression, radicals during the 1890s and the first decades of the twentieth century continued to celebrate May Day in Chicago parks. Under usually sunny skies, amidst newly budding trees, socialists and anarchists left the city and returned back to nature. They picnicked, sang, danced, and enjoyed the reawakening of nature after a long Chicago winter. At these May Day gatherings, radicals certainly looked backward. Socialist William Kruse explained that the roots of the labor holiday go back to ancient Rome and sacrifices to Mai, Mother Earth, and Flora, goddess of flowers. But he noted that the day was universal, for it was born of pagan nature worship, "the very basis of all religions." The radicals also remembered the world's first May Day and the martyrdom of the Haymarket anarchists. But more important, May Day was a chance to collectively anticipate the end of the current economic regime and the birth of a utopian world. As the radical Walter Lenfersiek noted, "men meet today on May Day to celebrate the future time when we shall truly live. . . . Aye, it is something more than merely a celebration of what MAY come, it MUST and WILL come. For man will not forever suffer in hunger and cold in a world of plenty."[24]

While radicals made May Day their own and fought for a future world in which workers would no longer be alienated from their own bodies, from each other, and even from nature, the more conservative trade unions regrouped and continued the fight for the eight-hour day. Keenly aware that the entire labor movement had been tarred as dangerous and un-American, Samuel Gompers (now head of the American Federation of Labor) and other trade union leaders did everything possible to make the eight-hour movement seem American, moderate, and unthreatening. Ultimately, this objective meant abandoning May Day altogether. As radicals, both in Europe and the United States, appropriated the first of May and transformed it into an international day of labor protest, Gompers and Chicago trade unions ignored May Day in favor of Labor Day, which a reluctant President Grover Cleveland made a national holiday after federal troops broke the Pullman Strike of 1894.[25]

On Labor Day, trade unionists marched through the streets of Chicago. There were no red or black flags or revolutionary banners. Instead of singing the "Marseillaise," Labor Day bands played "The Star Spangled Banner" and "Hail Columbia" while workers marched behind American flags. After the parade, trade unionists resorted to spacious Sharpshooters Park along the Chicago River or some other commercial grove for a giant labor picnic. Labor leaders viewed the long parade as an opportunity to show labor's power to the world. At the same time, they saw the afternoon park picnic as an opportunity for workers to relax in a cool sylvan environment and bridge the ethnic and craft divisions that frequently bedeviled the movement. Like the radicals in their parks, Labor Day speakers pointed to the future. But the trade unionists did not invoke a utopian world free of capitalism and alienation. Rather, labor leaders promised a reformed future: a more humane and sustainable labor marketplace where workers would get greater relief from seemingly endless hours of industrial labor and more time for recreation.[26]

## Working-Class Wilderness

In the early twentieth century, employers played an increasing role in introducing workers to recreational landscapes outside the city. One of the first industrialists to see the value of getting workers into contact with nature was George Pullman, a maker of luxury railcars. In 1880, Pullman erected a model workers' village next to his new plant, which he built on Chicago's still-rural southern edge, where he hoped country air would invigorate his workers. In his model town, Pullman not only tried to isolate workers from drinking, gambling, and other "inappropriate" leisure-time activities, he also built them park spaces, including: Arcade Park (a formal plaza with parterres and a bandstand framed by trees); Lake Vista (an artificial lake, surrounded by trees, shrubs, and grass, fed by wastewater that had been used to cool a Corliss engine); the Playground (ten acres of flat turf intended for outdoor games); and Athletic Island (an artificial island in Lake Calumet for boating, skating, and races). Pullman also annually took his employees out of the city on a one-day minivacation to Cedar Lake, Indiana.[27]

Although twentieth-century industrialists did not replicate Pullman's authoritarian model (the 1894 Pullman Strike showed Chicago employers just how badly such overreaching paternalism could backfire), many did continue Pullman's practice of sponsoring outdoor recreation and employee vacations in Chicago's recreational hinterland. During the Progressive Era and 1920s, employers saw company outings not only as a strategy to build "team" loyalty but also as a tool to improve worker efficiency. Industrialists saw the relentless hours of work enforced by their Gilded Age predecessors as unsustainable. Echoing a finding made by John Muir in his time-motion studies back in the 1870s, they discovered that a shorter workday coupled with healthy active leisure (rather than passive "wreckreation") actually lead to greater long-term productivity. Not unlike their colleagues who extracted natural resources, the managers of "human resources" came to see the logic of conservation.[28]

Companies believed that company picnics and outings would increase corporate loyalty and make industrial workers more efficient, but this did not matter to workers, who eagerly accepted a free or subsidized pleasure trip out of the city. Revealing evidence of worker co-optation of company excursions is the 1915 Western Electric picnic, the best-documented and most ill-fated corporate outing in American history. Each year since 1911, the company had brought thousands of employees out of the city for an annual one-day vacation in Michigan City, Indiana, a beachside community just northeast of the Indiana Dunes. The outing was advertised as a chance to swim, canoe, play sports, fish, dance, listen to music, and bask "in the sunshine . . . close to mother earth." In 1915, more than 2,500 eager employees piled on the SS *Eastland*, which was moored on the Chicago River between Clark and LaSalle Streets. The top-heavy ship began to list and then suddenly capsized into the polluted river, killing 845 people, the majority of whom were female workers of Czech, Bohemian, and Hungarian descent. It was a disaster on the scale of the 1912 *Titanic* sinking, but the *Eastland* catastrophe is far less known, no doubt partly because the victims were industrial workers rather than well-heeled travelers.[29]

Not all had wanted to go to the Michigan shore. After the disaster, some complained that overzealous Western Electric foremen had compelled their underlings to purchase tickets at seventy-five cents each. But most workers appear to have eagerly anticipated the subsidized trip across Lake Michigan. Many bought tickets not only for themselves, but also for family and friends who did not work at the plant. On the morning of the disaster, the streets of the West Side were filled with "laughing parties of men and women, everybody with picnic lunch in hand," and many showed up early to get on the *Eastland*, which was the first of several steamers leaving for Michigan City that morning. Photos from previous outings show happy women and men enjoying picnics under the trees, playing outdoor games, relaxing on the beach, and swimming in the refreshing waters of Lake Michigan. In other words, the Western Electric trips and others like them were not joyless exercises in corporate compliance. Workers eagerly anticipated these outings and creatively transformed company picnics into personal holidays.[30]

Partially in response to the growing popularity of corporate outings during the Progressive Era and Jazz Age, unions and other labor organizations began sponsoring their own excursions out of the city. They also lobbied for the creation of more public wilderness parks where workers might enjoy nature without corporate oversight. Initially, organized labor had opposed the creation of the Cook County Forest Preserves, the arc of wilderness parks on Chicago's urban fringe. Unionists lobbied against the preserves not because they believed that green space was unimportant, but rather because they worried that a belt of outlying wilderness parks would deplete resources needed for the creation of additional parks in dense working-class neighborhoods. As the Building Trades Council put it in 1905, "The great need of Chicago is for small parks in the congested districts, where the children of the poor can come for air and recreation."[31]

But with the election of John Fitzpatrick as president of the CFL in 1906, things began to change. Fitzpatrick, a staunch Irish nationalist and principled defender of workers' rights, blasted nativism, opposed U.S. involvement in World War I, and worked closely with known radicals, such as the communist labor organizer William Z. Foster. Even more, drawing on the legacy of the Knights of Labor and anticipating the strategy of the Congress of Industrial Organizations (CIO), Fitzpatrick worked to erode the independence of craft-based unions and to federate and unify all workers, including the unskilled and growing ranks of African American and women workers. In the process, he pushed the CFL far to the left of its parent organization, the American Federation of Labor.[32]

Environmental historians have never placed John Fitzpatrick in the pantheon of famous early twentieth-century environmentalists. Most in my field have never heard of the labor leader, which is unfortunate because in the early twentieth century, Fitzpatrick was one of the most influential advocates of what is known today as environmental justice. Environmental historians point to Chicago settlement workers Jane Addams and Mary McDowell as founding figures of urban environmental justice, but what is often forgotten is that while Addams and McDowell lived in environmentally blighted slums, they were middle-class, Protestant, Anglo American outsiders. In contrast, Fitzpatrick was a working-class, immigrant, and Catholic advocate for environmental and social change. Partially because of his class position and his experience actually working in the packinghouses, Fitzpatrick took a more radical political position than did the settlement house workers.[33]

When Fitzpatrick announced his candidacy for mayor of Chicago in 1918, he endorsed the platform of the Labor Party (later the Farmer-Labor Party). He called for an eight-hour day and a forty-four-hour week at a living wage; equal rights for men and women; government health and life insurance plans; nationalization of transportation, communication, grain elevators, and utilities; government appropriation of large inheritances; labor representation throughout the government; international disarmament and an end to imperialism; and the "nationalization and development of basic natural resources." Locally, candidate Fitzpatrick promised that he would not only reform labor markets but also address urban environmental problems, such as poor garbage service and excessive air pollution. He also told voters that as mayor he would push not only for more urban parks, but also for the preservation of more wilderness preserves on the urban fringe.[34]

Fitzpatrick supported not only the expansion of the Cook Country Forest Preserves, but also the transformation of the Indiana Dunes into a national park. Testifying at a 1918 National Park Service hearing, a CFL representative explained that the 300,000 members of the federation do not get any vacation, "but they intend to have vacations in the future, and they want a place where they can spend them." As such, the "remarkable botanical exhibit known as the sand-dune country" ought to become a "national park and playground of the people." Presciently anticipating even more leisure (including paid vacations) and the growing popularity of wilderness recreation among workers, the CFL joined the growing national park movement and became a working-class advocate for wilderness.[35]

At the same time, the CFL challenged company outings, such as the annual Western Electric trips to Michigan, by developing its own outdoor recreation programs. The female leadership of the Women's Trade Union League (WTUL) pioneered such efforts. In the early 1920s, the WTUL built a summer camp for its members (with labor and supplies provided by the bricklayers' and painters' union) on the edge of the Palatine Forest Preserve. The camp offered horseback riding, tennis, golf, archery, and hiking. The purpose of the recreation facility was not to make union members more efficient laborers on the factory floor, but merely to unite them in a pleasurable natural setting and improve their health. As Agnes Nestor, a glove maker who helped lead the union throughout the early decades of the twentieth century, noted, at the forest preserve camp, "the factory girls could come for fresh air and relaxation, great medicine for worn-down nervous energy."[36]

During the twenties, the CFL disseminated information on vegetable and flower gardening (through its radio station WCFL and its newspaper *Federation News*), sponsored a Young People's Labor Club (which went on hikes), and purchased land for "Camp Valmar," a lakeside resort in rural Camp Lake, Wisconsin (about sixty miles outside the Loop, just across the state line) (see Fig. 5.2). Here industrial workers could escape increasingly mechanized jobs in the city and enjoy camping, swimming, boating, riding, skiing, baseball, fishing, and duck hunting. According to the CFL, the camp served as a "melting pot," a beautiful natural place where "differences will be forgotten and solidarity will be brought about."[37]

While industrial workers affiliated with the CFL vacationed in Camp Valmar or traveled to the forest preserves or the dunes, radicals not only continued to celebrate May Day in urban green spaces, but traveled from the city to their own camps. The Young Peoples Socialist League (YIPSEL) organized hikes in rural Chicago, but also opened 11-acre Camp Yipsel on Fox Lake, just north of the city. At Camp Yipsel, youth not only slept in tents, hiked, and played baseball but also participated in outdoor labor pageants where, for instance, they might sentence capitalism to die, burn an effigy of the insidious economic system at the stake, and then perform a war dance around the remaining ashes. *The Young Socialists' Maga-*

# VALMAR
## FEDERATION CLUB
### FOR MEMBERS OF ORGANIZED LABOR

Showers
Lockers
Sun Rooms
Rest Rooms
Parlors
For
Men
and
Women

Large
Assembly
Room

Screened
Porches

Refresh-
ments

## THE VALMAR FEDERATION CLUB
### For Every Member of the Family
CHICAGO OFFICE: 30 N. DEARBORN ST.    PHONE STATE 8806

FIGURE 5.2 Valmar Resort. From pamphlet advertising summer homes for members of organized labor at Camp Lake, Wisc., for the Valmar Federation Club, ICHi—68717. Courtesy of the Chicago History Museum.

zine noted that the camp, which was a model for the nation, was "the biggest vehicle for better comradeship that we ever hit on."[38]

Meanwhile, Communist Pioneers went to camp at Lake Paddock in Kenosha, Wisconsin. A journalist for the *Milwaukee Journal* noted that the red flag flew over the camp and that the young communists slept in an oak grove in tents, each of which was named after a communist hero. Everyone ate in Lenin Hall. During the day, campers sang "The Internationale" and took lessons on the history of class struggle, although labor history and talk of revolution was leavened with swimming, sports, and hikes. The reporter noted that all nationalities were represented, and that six African Americans would join the next group of campers.[39]

We might think that labor leaders such as Fitzpatrick or socialist and communist activists pushed outdoor recreation on their members.

Evidence suggests, though, that workers themselves eagerly sought opportunities to leave the city and go back to nature. The marking of Labor Day is a revealing window. As we have seen, labor leaders had long seen the annual Labor Day parade and picnic as an important opportunity to show labor's power to the rest of the city and to bridge divisions within the movement. In the late nineteenth century, these events attracted thousands of participants. But starting in the early twentieth century, the rank and file began to opt out. Attendance was so low that the Chicago Federation of Labor (CFL) permanently cancelled the annual parade in 1910. The CFL also temporarily suspended the Labor Day picnic during the 1920s.[40]

Low participation does not mean that Chicago workers had little interest in unionization or that they preferred to spend Labor Day indoors at home or at places of commercialized urban amusement. As CFL leadership made clear, what killed the parade and the picnic was not so much competition from urban amusements, but the lure of leaving the city and going even farther afield into the rural and wild landscapes surrounding Chicago. Like their privileged Anglo American counterparts, large numbers of workers saw the new holiday as a last chance to leave the city and enjoy a short vacation before the summer ended and the cold weather began. As transportation out of the city became cheaper and some workers even got access to automobiles, a parade through hot city streets followed by a labor picnic in an urban park simply could not compete with escaping the urban environment entirely and venturing into the great outdoors.[41]

When the CFL worked to preserve wilderness parks, sponsored excursions out of the city, and built working-class resorts such as Camp Valmar, they did not force outdoor recreation on a reluctant audience. Rather, they responded to member demand. And when the CFL did not listen to their members, the rank and file revolted. Asked to spend their holiday in the hot city (albeit in an urban park), increasing numbers of workers voted with their feet and opted to enjoy nature on their own terms.

## The CIO: Unity in the Outdoors

The Chicago Federation of Labor's greatest success came in organizing the meatpacking industry during World War I. Because of the European conflict, orders to Chicago packinghouses increased at precisely the moment that the availability of cheap labor (in the form of European immigrants) dried up. Workers took advantage of this situation to ask for an increase in wages, equal pay for women, and more time for leisure. After the owners of the packinghouses rebuffed the union, the CFL asked the federal government to arbitrate the dispute. Concerned that a strike would interfere with wartime production, President Woodrow Wilson appointed Judge Samuel Alschuler to mediate.[42]

After listening to workers testify about working conditions in the packinghouses (including one woman who complained not only of low wages but that after six years in Chicago she had never had enough leisure time to see a movie or visit a park or Lake Michigan), Alschuler awarded the CFL a stunning victory. The government would now ensure that workers would have a wage increase, extra pay for overtime, paid lunches, equal pay for men and women doing the same labor, a forty-eight hour week, an eight-hour day, and seven paid holidays. On Easter Sunday 1918, a large jubilant crowd of industrial workers (including Poles, Mexicans, Armenians, Lithuanians, African Americans, Greeks, and Turks of both sexes) gathered in Davis Square Park, a neighborhood athletic park built in the heart of the Back of the Yards, the polluted working-class neighborhood that adjoined the city's stockyards and meatpacking houses. President Fitzpatrick addressed the workers and looked to the future: "It's a new day, and out in God's sunshine you men and you women, black and white, have not only an eight-hour day, but you are on an equality." To further celebrate the ruling, workers renamed nearby park benches "eight-hour benches." Here they could sit in the sunshine with their children and enjoy their newly won leisure.[43]

The workers' victory, though, would prove short-lived. Despite the harmonious gathering in Davis Square Park and Fitzpatrick's talk of joint purpose, Chicago workers were still too divided along lines of skill, ethnicity, language, and race (seen most palpably during the 1919 race riot discussed in the last chapter) to form a united front. Other forces also conspired against the union. In 1921, the federal government stopped mediating labor disputes, and the vacuum enabled Chicago employers to reassert themselves. The packers and other employers fired labor organizers, exploited racial and national divisions, employed spies and private security details, engaged in red-baiting, and aggressively used the courts to undermine union initiatives. At the same time, employers tried to neutralize the labor movement with the "velvet glove" of welfare capitalism: pensions, health-care programs, company unions, profit sharing, corporate outings, and paid vacations. As a result, the Chicago labor movement remained largely chastened and subdued throughout the 1920s.[44]

With the onset of the Great Depression in late 1929, organized labor once again began to aggressively challenge employers. Managers scaled back production, laid off workers, and discontinued many popular capitalist welfare programs, including vacations and excursions. At the same time, following the election of Franklin Roosevelt in 1932, the government intervened in labor markets, defended workers' right to organize, and, to some degree, neutralized corporate repression. Onto the scene also entered the Congress of Industrial Organizations, a new national labor organization intent on unionizing industrial workers regardless of race, nationality, sex, or skill level.[45]

In her pathbreaking social history *Making a New Deal*, Lizabeth Cohen argues that the reason why the CIO succeeded while earlier efforts to unionize the meatpacking and steel industries had failed was that by the 1930s, workers were more unified as a class. More of them were born in the working-class neighborhoods of Chicago—not in Ireland, Poland, Italy, or Russia. A much larger percentage of working-class Chicagoans now spoke fluent English. During the boom years of the 1920s, many had experienced welfare capitalism, and with the onset of the Great Depression, industrial workers shared a common experience of profound insecurity: layoffs, the disappearance of employee benefits, and the collapse of the safety net formerly provided by ethnic mutual aid societies and churches. Lastly and perhaps ironically, mass culture united the rank and file. Far from homogenizing American workers into one undifferentiated mass market, consumer culture (radio programs, movies, professional sports, and the common experience of shopping in national chain stores) actually served as a *lingua franca,* allowing Chicago workers to unify as a distinct class.[46]

When CIO organizers, many of whom were communists, tried to build bridges across lines of ethnicity, race, and neighborhood, they built on this foundation of common experience. They stressed commonality at work, but even more importantly, they fostered what Cohen calls a "culture of unity" during leisure. Well aware of the importance of Jazz Age amusements in connecting working-class people from various backgrounds, the CIO made extensive use of radio, labor newspapers (which carried stories about sports heroes and movie stars), and saloons, which sometimes became impromptu union halls.[47]

But while CIO organizers cultivated a "culture of unity" through the use of radio, small newspapers, and saloons, they also pursued their objectives by organizing outings for industrial workers and their children. As we have seen, the Knights of Labor, trade unions, socialists, anarchists, and communists in Chicago had long used green spaces (such as Ogden's Grove, Sharpshooters Park, Camp Valmar, and Camp Yipsel, among others) to unite workers. During the 1930s, the CIO elaborated on these earlier practices. Organizing committees of packinghouse, steel, or farm equipment workers regularly arranged picnics at places such as Berutes Grove (now the Spears Woods Forest Preserve, located along the Chicago Sanitary Ship Canal), Frank's Grove (at what is now Merrionette Park), Wicker Memorial Park (in Hammond, Indiana), and the Eggers Woods Forest Preserve (just north of Hegewisch, near the Indiana border). CIO committees advertised multiracial and multiethnic picnics, which sometimes attracted as many as 60,000 people, as an opportunity to "bring the wife and kids and all the friends out . . . for some fresh air [and] some sunshine." Typically buses would take unionists out of working-class neighborhoods, such as Back of the Yards, and to outlying groves and forest preserves. There, participants would not only listen to speeches from organizers in multiple languages, but also enjoy enormous quantities of barbeque and ice cream, softball games and races, jazz from the Charley Straight Orchestra, labor skits, a demonstration of Mexican folk dancing, and "beer—good and plenty of it."[48]

The vast majority of these labor picnics are difficult to reconstruct because of lack of sources. But because it ended in one of the most notorious incidents of labor violence in American history, one CIO outing is remembered vividly by many unionized Chicagoans even today. In 1937, the CIO's Steel Worker's Organizing Committee (SWOC) signed a contract with U.S. Steel (the nation's largest steel maker) ensuring an eight-hour day, $5-per-day salary, time and a half for overtime, and, notably, vacations with pay. Following this considerable achievement, SWOC turned to smaller steel manufacturers, including Republic Steel, a union-busting company with a plant on Chicago's Far South Side. After SWOC struck, Republic not only got an injunction banning picketing, but also stationed Chicago police officers (whom they fed, housed, and armed) within the plant.[49]

In anticipation of a strike, SWOC threw a Memorial Day picnic on a large vacant lot or "prairie" across from the plant. Between 1,500 and 2,500 steelworkers, family members, and friends came out to show their support and enjoy a late May afternoon outdoors. One participant, Mollie West of Typographical Union Local 16, recalled: "We came out there. It was a gorgeous day, absolutely a beautiful day. People came out there, like a picnic! We were going to support the Steel Workers and we were going to enjoy a picnic day with our families. And it looked like God shone on that

FIGURE 5.3 Police clubbing workers who had gathered for a picnic on the "prairie" next to the Republic Steel mill. The Memorial Day Massacre, May 30, 1937. Courtesy of the Associated Press.

idea." After SWOC organizers gave speeches, someone in the ethnically and racially mixed crowd suggested an impromptu picket of the Republic plant. Those gathered, eager for change, approved the motion. Then the crowd, in a holiday mood and singing, began across the field, which was littered with detritus dumped by the mill. In response, three hundred Chicago police officers emerged from the plant and formed a perimeter. When the workers and their families got close to the line, the police opened fire (shooting some workers in the back) and then attacked marchers with nightsticks (see Fig. 5.3). By the end of what would later be called the "Memorial Day Massacre," police had wounded one hundred and killed ten.[50]

CIO organizers not only sponsored picnics, such as those in the forest preserves and on the prairie adjacent to Republic Steel, they also worked hard especially to give union children a summertime opportunity to escape polluted working-class neighborhoods and enjoy wilderness camping experiences. Women in the SWOC, for instance, not only brought working-class youth to picket lines, but also organized beach excursions, hikes, and camping trips to the forest preserves and other wild locations outside the city. CIO committees frequently advertised picnics in parks and forest preserves as fund-raising initiatives to send working-class children from heavily industrialized urban neighborhoods "out to the country" for camp.[51]

Meanwhile, some CIO adults went to labor summer schools. John Lewis, head of the CIO, was an enthusiastic supporter of these CIO outings, and he looked forward to the day when "all great unions of the CIO will start a program of camps to enable the workers to enjoy a vacation and to discuss questions of unionism." CIO unions sponsored labor vacations in the Pisgah National Forest in North Carolina and at Camp SWOC in the Mount Davis Recreational Camp, a Civilian Conservation Corps camp in the mountains of southern Pennsylvania. According to SWOC news, "classes were held outdoors, under a natural canopy formed by huge trees," and afternoons were "given over to swimming, baseball, tennis, or hikes through the mountains." Some Chicago industrial workers also travelled to Madison's Lake Mendota. In the morning, electrical workers took classes on economics, political action, and labor history (from none other than Philip Foner, the dean of American labor history) in outdoor classrooms, under shade trees, alongside the banks of the lake. Workers then devoted the remainder of the day to loafing, card playing, canoeing, fishing, and sunbathing. As *Chicago UE News* reported, "Rich coats of tan bloomed quickly, and warm friendships developed."[52]

Some might argue that labor leaders such as John Lewis imposed excursions to rural and wild landscapes on ambivalent industrial workers, who were principally interested in urban amusements. The evidence, though, suggests that like the welfare capitalism outings of the 1920s, CIO trips "back to nature" satisfied preexisting demand (see Fig. 5.4). As we saw in chapter 3, working-class ethnic youth during the teens and 1920s not only gravitated to movie theaters, dance halls, sports venues, pool parlors, and "black and tan" resorts, they also made extensive use of public parks, Lake Michigan beaches, commercial groves, and the wilderness forest preserves. By the Great Depression, these teenagers had grown up and become employed and unemployed industrial workers. They still enjoyed commercialized amusements, which, as Cohen so brilliantly shows, they put to their own uses. But during their leisure, workers also appropriated the landscapes of Chicago's recreational hinterland.

The Chicago Area Project (CAP) provides a revealing window on "bottom-up" demand for opportunities to know nature through leisure. In the early 1930s, sociologist Clifford Shaw and other sociologists at the

FIGURE 5.4 A CIO-SWOC Vacation Plan means fewer hours at the steel mill and more leisure time to get outdoors and fish. "What A Difference A Union Makes!" Reprinted from *Steel Labor* (April 28, 1939). Courtesy of the United Steelworkers (USW).

University of Chicago created CAP to help combat juvenile delinquency in poor and "socially disorganized" neighborhoods. Instead of the settlement house model (in which middle-class Anglo American outsiders, such as Jane Addams, moved into poor communities and established programs for inhabitants), Shaw and his colleagues opted instead to empower indigenous community leaders and give them the tools to create their own programs for at-risk youth.[53]

During the 1930s, Shaw tried this pioneering effort at community organizing in two ethnic working-class neighborhoods with high rates of juvenile delinquency: the Italian community near Hull House on the near West Side (the so-called Bloody 20th Ward) and the Polish Russell Square community located in the shadow of the mammoth U.S. Steel Corporation South Works on the far South Side (often referred to as "the Bush"). In both cases, Shaw and his colleagues worked closely with community leaders (in particular, local priests at Our Lady of Pompeii and St. Michael the Archangel Catholic Churches), hired "indigenous workers," and set in motion the development of autonomous self-directed neighborhood councils. In both cases, the CAP primed the pump, but local working-class community members who composed the councils established their own agendas and almost immediately pushed the program in new and unexpected directions.[54]

Creating opportunities to escape the city and return to nature was high on the agenda. The local members of the Russell Square Community Council and the Near West Side Community Council developed Boy Scout troops led by indigenous scoutmasters, arranged for outings, transformed abandoned lots into playgrounds, beautified neighborhoods by planting vegetation, and pushed the city to improve local public parks. But for local people the crowning achievement of their respective councils was the development of youth camps on the outskirts of Chicago. Both councils located sites where community members and their children could escape the city and come into contact with nature. Shaw disapproved of the camp idea, but members of both councils rejected his advice and moved ahead on their own. Local people found sites, raised money from within the community, built facilities, and established their own camping programs using community members as staff. As Anthony Sorrentino, a key participant in the drive for the Italian camp, put it, "It is OUR camp, crude and rustic as it is. . . . It is a place which our people own, and where they can send their children and go themselves, free from the feeling that they are being given charity or called 'underprivilged.' "[55]

FIGURE 5.5 Group of volunteers from the steel mills area ("the Bush") building a mess hall at Camp Lange, the camp of the Russell Square Community Council, ICHi-68716. Courtesy of the Chicago History Museum.

Local housewives, laborers, bricklayers, machinists, metal workers, and butchers spent spare weekends at the Polish Camp Lange (twenty-six acres of rolling, wooded land on a bluff overlooking Lake Walton, near Michigan City, Indiana) and the Italian Camp Pompeii (forty-four acres of forest interspersed with open fields adjacent to forest preserves south of the city). They cleared underbrush, laid out large vegetable gardens, planted fruit trees, dug wells, and built structures, benches, and tables. At Camp Lange (named after the priest at St. Michaels), steelworkers welded bunks together out of angle iron they brought from the South Side (see Fig. 5.5). At Camp Pompeii (named after Our Lady of Pompeii Church), women made mattresses of straw tick, men built structures from recycled wood they scavenged back in the city, and craftsmen laid cement and mosaic to create a religious grotto for a statue of the Madonna. Children hiked, camped, played sports, made crafts, grew their own food, and learned about the "mysteries of nature." At Camp Pompeii children got a reprieve from "their sun-baked, treeless streets." At Camp Lange, "the streets, its corners, its litter-strewn alleys, the booming noise of the toiling mills, the blasting echo of slag dynamite and ever present pall of smoke from the open hearth and blast furnace are forgotten," and the neighborhood children find themselves in "the eternal green of nature."[56]

In addition to these two neighborhood councils, Shaw planted seeds in 1938 for an additional project in Back of the Yards, the polluted working-class neighborhood adjacent to the stockyards. But unlike the Russell Square and the Near West Side Community Councils, the Back of the Yards Neighborhood Council (BYNC) would not represent an ethnically homogenous working-class constituency. Rather, the BYNC would have to work across national, ethnic, and racial divisions that fractured the neighborhood. Another important difference was that the CAP representative in Back of the Yards was Saul Alinsky, a radical Jewish Russian American sociologist who would go on to coin and popularize the term "community organizer" and write two significant books on pushing social change, *Reveille for Radicals* (1946) and *Rules for Radicals* (1971). In a sharp break from his mentor Shaw, Alinsky came to blame many of the community's social problems, including juvenile delinquency, not on "social disorganization," but on economic injustice.[57]

Alinsky realized that the one place that could bring such a deeply fractured community together was Davis Square Park, a five-acre neighborhood park and one of the very few green spaces in Back of the Yards. He quickly forged an alliance with the park director (Joseph Meegan, an Irish American who had grown up in a nearby working-class neighborhood), and the two, working together, made this park into a commons or green where representatives of local organizations (everything from conservative Catholic priests, immigrant nationalists, gang leaders, and communist organizers working with the CIO) could come together and discuss common issues. Community members did not have a common origin, but they did share very real grievances in the present and a sense that together they could create a better future. Revealingly, the BYNC chose as its motto: "We the people will work out our own destiny."[58]

As in the Bush and the Bloody 20th Ward, local people created the agenda and pushed the council in new directions. From this island of green situated in the midst of an extraordinarily harsh industrial environment, the BYNC addressed local juvenile delinquency problems, organized a job bank, lobbied for more National Youth Administration and Civilian Conservation Corp jobs, tracked down negligent landlords, established a health and dental clinic, published their own community newspaper, and started a credit union. At the same time, the BYNC attempted to ameliorate the urban environment by distributing trash cans free of charge, improving the Back of the Yards sewage system, rerouting garbage trucks, and investigating environmental nuisances. It also established outdoor recreation programs (including Boy Scout and Girl Scout troops) and created more urban green spaces in the bleak industrial neighborhood. They planted trees, bushes, and grass on bare earth and converted two vacant lots into parks with ball fields, grass, trees, flowers, and benches.[59]

Like the community members of the Russell Square Community Council and the Near West Side Community Council, members of the BYNC made it a top priority to acquire a campground where local residents could escape the industrial city and retreat back to nature. Ultimately, though, the BYNC was unable to acquire the equivalent of a Camp Pompeii or Camp Lange, so it opted instead to turn to the CIO, which helped subsidize summer vacations for children. With CIO funding, the BYNC could send its kids out of the polluted Yards and to Camp Pottawatomie, a National Park Service camp on Indiana's Tippecanoe River. Next to one of the few remaining groves of old growth white pine in the greater Chicago region, the children of packinghouse workers—Polish, Lithuanian, Mexican, and African American—spent two weeks camping together, undoubtedly enjoying contact with the wilderness along the Tippecanoe, but also learning that despite their differences, they could come together as a working-class community and work out their own destiny.[60]

From the Gilded Age to World War II, workers in Chicago struggled for more leisure: an eight-hour day, weekends, and paid vacations. They wanted this leisure for a variety of reasons, including the enjoyment of urban amusements. But many, as we have seen, also wanted time to escape increasingly mechanized work and dense urban neighborhoods and get outside. In the words of the "Eight-Hour Song," workers wanted more leisure to "smell the flowers" and "feel the sunshine." During the Gilded Age and Progressive Era, they typically enjoyed cool breezes, sunshine, shade trees, grass, and moving water in urban parks, but especially as their hours of leisure grew and transportation became more accessible, they left the city entirely for forest preserves, the Indiana Dunes, and wilderness camps.

During their limited leisure, Chicago workers not only appropriated American mass culture, they also imbued the rural and wild landscapes and urban green spaces of "nature's nation" with new meanings. In forgotten places such as Ogden's Grove, Sharpshooters Park, Camp Valmar,

Camp Yipsel, and Camp Pottawatomie, rank-and-file Chicagoans picnicked, drank beer, played sports, listened to music, fished, hunted, and camped. But they also used these places to imagine community and make themselves into a working class. They did not create unity in the present by evoking common origins in the soil of the United States, Ireland, Germany, Greece, Mexico, Africa, or any other homeland. Rather, diverse workers in Chicago green spaces made themselves into a class by recalling common grievances and imagining a better future. For some, it was a socialist government that would nationalize industries. For others, it was a "cooperative commonwealth" in which producers owned the means of production. For still others, it was violent revolution followed by a worker's paradise in which every day would be May Day. But for most, it was simply the promise of a reformed world in which there would be more time "to do what we will."

# Conclusion

## *What We Can Learn from Chicago's Cultures of Nature*

> We the people will work out our own destiny.
> —Motto of Back of the Yards Neighborhood Council, 1939

The social history of nature in industrial Chicago offers several lessons. First, I hope my scholarship speaks to sociobiologists. As we have seen, nature was an object of desire for not just affluent Anglo Americans, but immigrants, minorities, and working-class people. Some might conclude that this amounts to further confirmation of the so-called biophilia hypothesis, the idea that yearning for nature is a hardwired product of human evolution. But just because desire for nature can cut across nation, ethnicity, race, sex, and class in interesting and surprising ways does not mean that biology was the fundamental driver in Chicago. Not everyone in Chicago was in love with nature, but more to the point, history offers us a far more compelling explanation for subaltern nature romanticism than does genetics. As I hope I have made clear, my subjects' desire for contact with nature was not innate but rather a reaction to unique historical circumstances: sudden immersion in a harsh, fast-paced, seemingly artificial urban environment, subjugation to new "unnatural" industrial work regimes, feelings of dislocation and homesickness born of migration, and exposure to transnational variants of romantic nationalism.[1]

Second, I hope *Urban Green* informs the work of social historians of leisure. As we have seen, immigrants, minorities, and working-class people did not see public parks as mere public or recreational spaces, as extensions of the city rather than its antipode. On the contrary, during their scarce leisure, large numbers of Chicagoans actually sought to escape the industrial city. They did this most often by venturing into urban parks, but when they had the means, they left the physical confines of the city and eagerly visited the Cook County Forest Preserves, the Indiana Dunes, and the lakes, prairies, and forests of Wisconsin and Michigan. They also vacationed at Turner Camp, Camp Sokol, Camp Chi, Idlewild, and the Chicago Federation of Labor's Valmar Resort. In addition, they sent their children to wilderness camps located throughout Chicago's far-reaching recreational hinterland. We should be wary then of characterizing fights over urban parks as battles between nature-loving Anglo Americans (such as Frederick Law Olmsted) and sports- or amusement-loving workers and immigrants. If instead we follow the marginalized out of the city and back to nature (even if that nature was an urban park), we will get a richer sense of the ways marginalized people reacted to industrial urban environments. At the same time, we will open a revealing window on the cultural construction of immigrant, minority, and working-class identities.

Third, I hope *Urban Green* contributes to the field of environmental history. As we have seen, marginalized Chicagoans knew nature not only through work but also through leisure. This conclusion alone should be of interest to scholars in the field. But environmental history's central charge is exploring the dance between humans and the environment over time. Scholars in the field study how humans acted on the land and how nonhuman actors (infectious diseases, soil, insects, animals, climate, etc.) shaped human history. So although environmental historians are interested in the ways people think about nature, they take even more notice when ideas result in significant ecological change.

Like privileged Anglo Americans, marginalized Chicagoans drew an ecologically problematic line between the "artificial" city and nature and sought to cross it during their leisure. That said, it is important to note exactly where my subjects drew the line. Wealthy nature tourists could visit the rural landscapes and classical and Gothic ruins of Europe, travel to pastoral New England, escape to the wilderness of Wisconsin or Michigan, or take the train to a distant national park such as Yellowstone. They often drew the line far from where they actually lived and worked. In contrast, my subjects often did not have the time or money to travel great distances. Sometimes they took streetcars, railcars, and produce trucks to the forest preserves or the Indiana Dunes or working-class and ethnic resorts. Most Chicagoans, though, retreated to green spaces within the physical confines of the city. Because they had no other choice, they came to appreciate the nature they found close to home, even if home was one of the most polluted industrial neighborhoods on the planet. Like our urban ranger Leonard Dubkin, they came to see that "whether one goes to nature for truth, or for beauty, for knowledge, or relaxation, these things can be found in a yard in the city as well as in a tropical jungle."[2]

Long before mainstream environmentalists abandoned their focus on wilderness and began to see urban density as an important answer for twenty-first century environmental challenges, my subjects sought out, appropriated, and defended urban places they saw as green. It is true that when they went through park gates, they hoped to escape the city and travel. But it is also the case that many of the places they loved (public parks, urban forests, the north branch of the Chicago River, vacant lots, and the wild-urban interface that is the Lake Michigan shore) provided herculean ecosystem services for the city of Chicago. Their landscapes of leisure often absorbed and filtered polluted storm-water runoff; cleansed the air of particulates; provided habitat for plant and animal communities, including pollinating insects and birds; diminished urban heat island effects; metabolized mountains of organic waste; sequestered carbon; and not least, provided food for hungry city residents. Unintentionally, my subjects became important early champions of Chicago's overtaxed green infrastructure.[3]

Fourth, I think *Urban Green* can inform American studies investigations into landscape. Classic works such as *Virgin Land, The Machine in the Garden*, and *Wilderness and the American Mind*, among others, suggested that representations of nature are the key to unlocking a singular American culture, character, civilization, or "mind." According to Perry Miller, nature was "*the* American theme" and "the obsessive American drama." For historian Roderick Nash, "wilderness was the basic ingredient of American culture."[4]

As historian and American studies scholar Patricia Limerick noted in 2000, the problem with these traditional accounts is that they "concentrated wholeheartedly on the thinking of English-speaking, westward-moving, literate, record-keeping middle and upper-class, pre-twentieth century, white men. Offered as studies of American attitudes toward landscape, these standard works were in fact investigations into the mind of a minority." Limerick argued that such parochialism was now untenable and that we need a more multicultural approach.[5]

I hope that my book partially answers Limerick's call for studies of the American landscape that address diversity. I want readers of my book to clearly see that the United States was home not to a culture of nature but rather *cultures* of nature. That said, simply making room for American cultures of nature is not enough. One of the most striking things one sees in Chicago is the degree to which marginalized people yearned for landscapes outside the physical boundaries of the United States: the dark forests, silver brooks, and hills of Franconia; the dunes of Lithuania's Baltic Coast; the bird-filled forests of Michoacán. In Chicago parks, my subjects remembered the landscapes of Greek villages, regions of Norway, nations, such as Poland, Ireland, and Mexico, and even entire continents, such as Africa.

In using landscape to imagine themselves as German, Irish, Polish, or Mexican, my subjects confirmed something many historians of nationalism have known for a long time: we might think of nations as growing organically out of the soil of a given homeland, but in reality nations are fragile, modern institutions. As such, nationalists must continually do the cultural work of convincing a far-flung group of strangers that they are a community. Nationalists do this ideological work in part by pointing to a national origin in the soil and then narrating a history of the homeland. For this reason, nations are such prolific producers of historical and landscape effects. Chicagoans showed not only that the United States was home to multiple cultures of nature, but also that outside the U.S. there were in fact many nature's nations, and in each, nature became an obsessive drama. In other words, the United States was simply not that unique or exceptional.[6]

But my subjects went even farther. When immigrants used Chicago city parks to remember distant homelands, they crossed national borders and implicitly made "American" parks into transnational spaces. The anarchists who gathered in Ogden's Grove were even more explicit. Not only did they view themselves as members of an international proletariat, they explicitly branded the idea of the nation as a fiction or opiate invented by the powerful to forestall revolution. On May Day, they represented this position by flying the black flag, symbolizing the negation of all national flags. Chicago immigrants, black nationalists, and anarchists showed that America was no island isolated from the rest of the world. In so doing they pose a significant challenge to those American studies scholars and U.S. historians who continue to view "America" as a coherent, self-contained, and unproblematic unit of study.[7]

Fifth, I think evidence from Chicago sheds light on white middle-class nature nostalgia during the 1950s and 1960s. As is well established, following World War II, large numbers of European Americans left cities and relocated to new bucolic suburbs on the urban fringe. One of the most famous was the Chicago suburb of Park Forest, which served as the central case study for William Whyte's sociological classic, *The Organization Man* (1956). The developers of Park Forest sold the new community as a place where families could live in a parklike environment with big yards and easy access to the adjoining forest preserve wilderness but within easy commuting distance of the Loop. As the developer Philip Klutznick put it in 1946, a resident of Park Forest could labor in the "fuming and belching furnaces" of Chicago while living in the "tree-studded, cleansed environment of the smokeless town. . . . close to the earth." Thousands of Anglo and European Americans answered the call.[8]

Postwar middle-class suburbanites not only enjoyed the outdoors in their own backyards, they also perused Sierra Club coffee table books filled with photographs of the nation's wilderness wonders, and they watched nature documentaries and television shows, such as Disney's *True-Life Adventure* and Marlin Perkin's *Zoo Parade* (broadcast originally from Chicago's Lincoln Park Zoo) and later *Mutual of Omaha's Wild Kingdom*. The suburbs also served as a base for further forays into the great outdoors. During the summer, midcentury middle-class suburbanites and their children piled into station wagons and traveled to national parks in such numbers that some critics began complaining that "the masses" were "loving the wilderness to death." Lastly, significant numbers of middle-class suburban whites and their children joined nature organizations, defended wilderness areas, and fueled the emergent environmental movement of the 1960s.[9]

The first historians and American studies scholars to explore postwar suburbanization and nature tourism viewed both as distinctively American phenomena that trickled down from "the classes to the masses." When newly middle-class white Americans left the industrial urban environment for parklike suburbs, they simply emulated affluent Anglo Americans who had moved to the first suburbs following the Civil War. When the new suburbanites watched nature shows, car camped in the wilderness, or joined environmental groups such as the National Wildlife Federation or the Sierra Club, they simply followed in the footsteps of Victorian nature tourists and ultimately pioneering romantics, such as Henry David Thoreau.[10]

Evidence from Chicago supports recent research suggesting that there were important "bottom-up" components to this midcentury culture of nature. There is no doubt that when newly middle-class, ethnically diverse whites moved to Park Forest or visited a national park, they drew on Anglo American precedent. Roots of 1950s and 1960s nature nostalgia undoubtedly go back to Walden Pond. But we also must consider that these roots also extended back to the Irish, Jewish, Polish, and Italian slums of industrial Chicago. The new suburbanites may have channeled Thoreau, but they also learned to appreciate nature from their working-class parents and grandparents who responded to seemingly unnatural urban conditions by making Sunday forays into urban parks.[11]

Chicago's history also demonstrates that the notorious whiteness of mid-century suburbs and wilderness parks was hardly inevitable. The 1950s exodus out of the city and back to nature amounted to "white flight." But things could have gone differently. As we have seen, Chicagoans had long used rural and wild landscapes and urban green space as a commons or a green, as a place where participants built bridges (sometimes based on "creative misunderstanding") across lines not only of class, religion, nationality, and neighborhood, but also of race. Think of July 4th, 1892, in Lincoln Park, the site of a massive outdoor gathering inclusive of immigrants from almost every European nation, but also of African Americans, Chinese, Persians, and Arabs. Or think of Camp Pottawatomie and the children of Mexican, Polish, Lithuanian, and African American meatpackers who camped in the wilderness along the Tippecanoe River. When postwar Chicagoans decamped for the "tree-studded, cleansed environment of the smokeless town. . . . close to earth," they (along with already established Anglo Americans) could have used the new peri-urban environment to imagine different and far more racially inclusive forms of community. Chicagoans had used landscape to imagine such communities in the past, and they could have done it again in 1950s suburbs such as Park Forest. But instead of finding inspiration in the CIO example of unity in nature, the new suburbanites drew on a very different model: the ethnically mixed but racially white 1920s social athletic club defending its local neighborhood park, its "turf," against outsiders.[12]

I hope *Urban Green* prompts readers to think differently about Chicago's past. But I also hope that that my social history of nature illuminates the present. Today, a majority of the earth's population lives in cities, and each week, another million more people make the move from country to city. According to United Nations' projections, the planet will be 70 percent urban by 2050. Like migrants to Chicago one hundred years ago, today's urban migrants are pushed out of rural areas by war, persecution, ecological degradation, natural disasters, and especially the growth of large-scale, technologically intensive, market-oriented agriculture. And like Chicagoans such as those in Back of the Yards, today's migrants face stark inequalities and extraordinary environmental challenges, more so in fact because of the beginnings of global climate change.[13]

If industrial Chicago is a distorted mirror of the present, which I think in many ways it is, we can learn a great deal from the historical experience of marginalized Chicagoans. Especially worth remembering today is the example of the Back of the Yards Neighborhood Council, which operated out of arguably the most polluted neighborhood in industrial America. In the face of a community deeply divided along lines of nation, ethnicity, religion, generation, and race, Saul Alinsky, Joseph Meegan, and female communist organizers appropriated Davis Square Park, which they transformed into a commons or green where neighbors could cross the lines that divided them and organize themselves into a working-class urban community. In this island of green, community members did not look backward to some imaginary origin in the mist-shrouded past, but forward toward a brighter future. In the park community members learned that "we the people will work out our own destiny."

Davis Square Park became an important launching pad in the CIO struggle to organize Polish, Lithuanian, Irish, Mexican, and African American male and female workers and to challenge the industrialists who ran the meatpacking industry. At the same time, from the park, the community fought for jobs, better housing, and improved policing. But they also fought for a cleaner urban environment. In what we might see as an early and class-based environmental justice fight, members of the BYNC demanded better sewage and trash infrastructure, investigated environmental nuisances, raised money to send their children to a CIO wilderness camp on the Tippecanoe River, and worked to green "the Jungle" by planting trees and grass, constructing community gardens, and transforming vacant lots into new parks.

At the dawn of the twenty-first century, we find ourselves in an increasingly urban world with extraordinary social inequalities and mounting environmental challenges. In fighting simultaneously for social justice and a greener city, the Back of the Yards Neighborhood Council gives us a model of activism well worth emulating.

# Notes

## Abbreviations

| | |
|---|---|
| ASP | Anthony Sorrentino Papers, Chicago Historical Society, Chicago, Ill. |
| CAPP | Chicago Area Project Papers, Chicago Historical Society, Chicago, Ill. |
| *CD-L* | *Chicago Defender (Local Edition)* |
| *CD-N* | *Chicago Defender (National Edition)* |
| CFLPS | Chicago Foreign Language Press Survey, Special Collections Research Center, Joseph Regenstein Library, University of Chicago, Chicago, Ill. |
| CHS | Chicago Historical Society, Chicago, Ill. |
| *CT* | *Chicago Tribune* |
| EBP | Ernest W. Burgess Papers, Special Collections Research Center, Joseph Regenstein Library, University of Chicago, Chicago, Ill. |
| FITZ | John Fitzpatrick Papers, Chicago Historical Society, Chicago, Ill. |
| FLOP | Papers of Frederick Law Olmsted, Manuscripts Division, Rare Books and Special Collections Reading Room, Library of Congress, Washington, D.C. |
| IAC | Italian American Collection, Daley Library Special Collections, University of Illinois at Chicago, Chicago, Ill. |
| IWPN | Illinois Writer's Project: The Negro in Illinois, Vivian Harsh Collection, Carter G. Woodson Regional Library, Chicago, Ill. |
| NAACPR | Records of the National Association for the Advancement of Colored People, Rare Books and Special Collections Reading Room, Library of Congress, Washington, D.C. |
| NHRC-B | Neighborhood History Research Collections, Back of the Yards, The Special Collections and Preservation Division, Harold Washington Library, Chicago, Ill. |
| NHRC-C | Neighborhood History Research Collections, City Wide Community Collections, The Special Collections and Preservation Division, Harold Washington Library, Chicago, Ill. |
| NHRC-R | Neighborhood History Research Collections, Ravenswood–Lake View Community Collection, Special Collections, Sultzer Library, Chicago, Ill. |
| NNWSCCP | Near North West Side Community Council Papers, Daley Library Special Collections University of Illinois at Chicago, Chicago, Ill. |

OHACP     Oral History Archives of Chicago Polonia, Chicago Historical Society, Chicago, Ill.

RRP     Robert Redfield Papers, Special Collections Research Center, Joseph Regenstein Library, University of Chicago, Chicago, Ill.

SBP     Stephen S. Bubacz Papers, Daley Library Special Collections, University of Illinois at Chicago Special Collections, Chicago, Ill.

## Introduction

1. On the Indiana Dunes, see Engel, *Sacred Sands*.

2. Mather, "Report on the Proposed Sand Dunes National Park Indiana."

3. Ibid., 58, 57.

4. Cronon, *Nature's Metropolis*, 380–81.

5. Nash, *Wilderness and the American Mind*. Smith, *Virgin Land*; Miller, *Errand into the Wilderness*; Huth, *Nature and the American*; and Marx, *The Machine in the Garden*.

6. On dispossession, see, e.g., Ramachandra, "Radical American Environmentalism and Wilderness Preservation"; Cronon, "The Trouble with Wilderness"; Warren, *The Hunter's Game*; Spence, *Dispossessing the Wilderness*; Johnson, "Conservation, Subsistence, and Class at the Birth of Superior National Forest"; Jacoby, *Crimes Against Nature*; Klingle, *Emerald City*, 44–85; Chiang, *Shaping the Shoreline*. On identity, see, e.g., Haraway, *Primate Visions*, 26–58; Cronon, "The Trouble with Wilderness"; Davis, *Spectacular Nature*; Price, *Flight Maps*, 167–206; Mitman, *Reel Nature*; Shaffer, *See America First*. On environmental problems, see, e.g., Cronon, "The Trouble with Wilderness"; White, "Are You an Environmentalist or Do You Work for a Living?"; Price, *Flight Maps*, 167–206.

7. See, e.g., Gottlieb, *Forcing the Spring*, 83–120; Hurley, *Environmental Inequalities*; Hurley, "Fiasco at Wagner Electric"; Hurley, "Busby's Stink Boat"; Hurley, "Floods, Rats, and Toxic Waste"; Davis, *Ecology of Fear*, 93–148; Stroud, "Troubled Waters in Ecotopia"; Greenberg, "Reconstructing Race and Protest"; Pellow, *Garbage Wars*; Gandy, *Concrete and Clay*, 153–228; Washington, *Packing Them In*; Colten, *An Unnatural Metropolis*; Platt, *Shock Cities*, 299–498; Davis, *Planet of Slums*, 121–50; Klingle, *Emerald City*; Chiang, *Shaping the Shoreline*; Mitman, *Breathing Space*, 130–66.

8. Lévi-Strauss, *Totemism*, 89. For work on leisure in nature from "the bottom up" and the use of landscape to forge subaltern identities, see, e.g., Limerick, "Disorientation and Reorientation"; Pulido, *Environmentalism and Economic Justice*; Fisher, "African Americans, Outdoor Recreation, and the 1919 Chicago Race Riot"; Lipin, *Workers and the Wild*; Smith, *African American Environmental Thought*; Sze, *Noxious New York*; Montrie, *Making a Living*, 13–34, 91–112; Chiang, "Imprisoned Nature"; Fisher, "Nature in the City"; Young, "'A Contradiction in Democratic Government'"; Kahrl, *The Land Was Ours*; McCammack, "Recovering Green in Bronzeville." Women are another marginalized group whose outdoor recreational practices need much more exploration by scholars. On middle-class and affluent women, gender, and leisure in nature, see Schrepfer, *Nature's Altars*.

9. For early, seminal works that explored the popular culture of the marginalized, see, e.g., Thompson, *The Making of the English Working Class*; Gutman, "Work, Culture and Society in Industrializing America"; Rawick, *From Sundown to Sunup*. On commercialized amusements, see in particular Peiss, *Cheap Amusements*; Cohen, *Making a New Deal*; Lipsitz, *Time Passages*. Also see Baldwin, *Chicago's New Negroes*; Rabinovitz, *For the Love of Pleasure*. For a good overview of this historiography, see Enstad, "Popular Culture."

10. Rosenzweig, *Eight Hours for What We Will*, 127–52; Rosenzweig and Blackmar, *The Park and the People*. Also see Hardy, *How Boston Played*; Riess, *City Games*; Gems, *The Windy City Wars*; Bachin, *Building the South Side*.

11. Rosenzweig and Blackmar, *The Park and the People*. For quote, see Blackmar and Rosenzweig, "The Park and the People," 129.

12. On the distinction of knowing nature through leisure versus knowing nature through work, see White, "Are You an Environmentalist or Do You Work for a Living?"; White, *The Organic Machine*.

## Chapter 1

1. On the concept of recreational hinterland, see Cronon, *Nature's Metropolis*, 380–83.

2. Ibid.

3. On the concept of the urban ranger, see "Los Angeles Urban Rangers," http://www.laurbanrangers.org (accessed January 3, 2014). The LA Urban Rangers is an organization, led in part by historian Jennifer Price, which deconstructs the line between nature and culture in Los Angeles. On Dubkin, see Yearwood, "Family Memoir," 4–5; Greenberg, "Leonard Dubkin," 287–88. Dubkin's six books were *Wolf Point, The White Lady, The Natural History of a Yard, The Murmur of Wings, My Secret Places,* and *Enchanted Streets.*

4. On the ideology behind nineteenth-century park building in Chicago, see Bluestone, *Constructing Chicago*, 7–35; Bachin, *Building the South Side*, 127–38. Also see Rosenzweig and Blackmar, *The Park and the People*, 15–37; Young, *Building San Francisco's Parks*, 1–30; Bender, *Toward an Urban Vision*, 159–88; Schuyler, *The New Urban Landscape*, 59–76.

5. Rauch, *Public Parks*; for quotes, see 32, 80, 19.

6. For quote on awful cliffs, see Frederick Law Olmsted, *Yosemite and the Mariposa Grove, 1865* in Dilsaver, *America's National Park System: The Critical Documents,* 16. On Olmsted's focus on the Yosemite Valley, see Olwig, "Reinventing Common Nature," 394; also see Beveridge, "The California Origins of Olmsted's Landscape Design Principles," 451, 464–69. On Niagara, see Irwin, *The New Niagara*, 84–89. For quote on rugged ground, see Olmsted, *Public Parks and the Enlargement of Towns*, 23.

7. For Olmsted quote, see Frederick Law Olmsted, "Preliminary Report on the Proposed Suburban Village at Riverside, near Chicago," in Schuyler and Censer, *The Years of Olmsted, Vaux & Company*, 276. For Cleveland quote, see Cleveland, *The Public Grounds of Chicago*, 13. On nineteenth-century landscape architects' view

of native landscapes in Chicago, see Bluestone, *Constructing Chicago*, 37–52; Grese, *Jens Jensen*, 29–33.

8. On English park history, see Lasdun, *The English Park.*

9. See Williams, *The Country and the City*, 22, 96–107, 120–26, 141. On enclosure and emparkment, also see Franklin, *The Liberty of the Park*, 145–47; Barrell, *The Dark Side of the Landscape,* 3–4.

10. On the spread of the English park abroad, see Hunt, *The Picturesque Garden in Europe*. For quote, see Frederick Law Olmsted, "Public Parks," in *The American Cyclopaedia: A Popular Dictionary of General Knowledge*, ed. George Ripley and Charles A. Dana, vol. 12 (1876), reprinted in Beveridge and Hoffman, *Writings on Public Parks, Parkways, and Park Systems*, 309.

11. On Lincoln Park, see Bluestone, *Constructing Chicago*, 44, 46; Grese, *Jens Jensen*, 32–33; Bachrach, *The City in a Garden*, 105–11; Pullen, "Parks and Parkways of Chicago," 416, 423; Simon, *Chicago, the Garden City*, 15–39; I. J. Bryan, ed., "Report of the Commissioners and a History of Lincoln Park" (Chicago, 1899), box 23/13, NHRC-R. For quote on windswept sand hills, see *Report of Lincoln Park Commissioners*, n.d., quoted in *Picturesque Chicago*, 146. For quote on lake, see Pullen, "Parks and Parkways," 416. For quote on great beauty, see "Souvenir of Lincoln Park: An Illustrated and Descriptive Guide" (Chicago: Illinois Engraving, 1896), 7, box 23/12, NHRC-R.

12. On Jenney and the West Parks, see Rainey, "William Le Baron Jenney and Chicago's West Parks," 57–79; Turak, *William Le Baron Jenney*, 75–95; Bluestone, *Constructing Chicago*, 46–52; Grese, *Jens Jensen*, 33–35; Simon, *Chicago, the Garden City*, 60–89; Bachrach, *The City in a Garden*, 55–59, 63–67, 81–87, 153–55; Pullen, "The Parks and Parkways of Chicago," 416. On Parisian park building under Napoleon III, see Chadwick, *The Park and the Town*, 152–62. For quote on velvety lawn, see Pullen, "The Parks and Parkways of Chicago," 416. For quote on the man of business, see *Second Annual Report of the West Chicago Park Commission* (Chicago 1871), 62, quoted in Rainey, "William Le Baron Jenney," 66.

13. On the South Parks, see Bluestone, *Constructing Chicago*, 39–44; Grese, *Jens Jensen*, 30–32; Ranney, *Olmsted in Chicago*, 15–35; Bachrach, *The City in a Garden*, 93–101, 157–61; Pullen, "Parks and Parkways of Chicago," 412, 416; Holt, "Private Plans for Public Spaces," 181–82; Simon, *Chicago, the Garden City*, 40–59. For quote on flat and treeless prairie, see Frederick Law Olmsted, Calvert Vaux, and Company, *Report Accompanying Plan for Laying Out the South Park* (Chicago: Chicago South Park Commission, 1871) in Sutton, *Civilizing American Cities*, 165. For quote on pleasing slopes, see "Report of the South Park Commissioners to the Board of County Commissioners of Cook County, for Nine Months, from March 1st to December 1st, 1872" (Chicago: Jameson and Morse, 1873), 8–9, file 1, box 34, NHRC-C.

14. On Jackson Park, see Grese, *Jens Jensen*, 38; Ranney, *Olmsted in Chicago*, 31–39; Olmsted and Vaux, *Report Accompanying Plan for Laying Out the South Park*; Holt, "Private Plans for Public Spaces," 181. For quote on the Thames, see Frederick Law Olmsted to partners, July 17, 1892, General Correspondence, 1892–1994 (microfilm), FLOP. See also Frederick Law Olmsted to Henry Codman, May 25, 1892, General Correspondence, 1892–1994 (microfilm), FLOP. For Olmsted's plans for Chicago,

see Olmsted, "Memorandum as to What Is to Be Aimed at in the Planting of the Lagoon District," 602–4; also see Frederick Law Olmsted, "A Report upon the Landscape Architecture of the Columbian Exposition to the American Institute of Architects," *American Architect and Building News* 41 (September 1893), reprinted in Sutton, *Civilizing American Cities*, 180–96.

15. Dubkin, *My Secret Places*, 1–14; Dubkin, *The Murmur of Wings*, 9–13; Dubkin, *Enchanted Streets*, 64–68.

16. On the Municipal Science Club and the Special Parks Commission, see Doty, "Ecology, Community, and the Prairie Spirit," 9, 12; McCarthy, "Politics and the Parks," 160–63; McArthur, "The Chicago Playground Movement," 377–82; McArthur, "Parks, Playgrounds, and Progressivism," 10–11. Tippens and Sniderman, "The Planning and Design of Chicago's Neighborhood Parks," 21–22. On the growing vogue for wilderness recreation, see, e.g., Nash, *Wilderness and the American Mind*, 141–60; Cronon, "The Trouble with Wilderness; or, Getting Back to the Wrong Nature," 69–90.

17. See Perkins, *Report of the Special Park Commission*. On the history of the forest preserves, see Hayes, "Development of Forest Preserve District," 22–24, 29, 69, 211, 216, 233; Christy, "Wide-Awake Dreaming"; Perkins, *Perkins of Chicago*, 104–20; Retzlaff, "The Illinois Forest Preserve District Act," 433–55.

18. Mather, "Report on the Proposed Sand Dunes National Park, Indiana," 36–39; quotes on 36, 38.

19. On the preserves, see Forest Preserve District of Cook County, *The Forest Preserves of Cook County*; Sauers, "A People's Paradise of Fifty-One Square Miles of Woodland," 288. On the dunes, see Engel, *Sacred Sands*; Cockrell, *A Signature of Time and Eternity*; Cohen and McShone, eds., *Moonlight in Duneland*.

20. For quote on Indian paradise, see Forest Preserve District of Cook County, *The Forest Preserves of Cook County*, 27. On Indian ruins in the preserves, see Forest Preserve Commissioners, *Forest Preserve Accompaniment* (Chicago: Forest Preserve Commissioners, 1925), Cook County, Illinois Board of Forest Preserve Committee— Miscellaneous Pamphlets, CHS; Forest Preserve District of Cook County in the State of Illinois, *The Forest Preserves of Cook County*, 14–24, 27, 49, 52, 70, 80–81.

21. On sewage, see Todd, Byron, and Vierow, *Private Recreation*, 23–24, 34, 164. On the introduction of native species, see Forest Preserve District of Cook County, *The Forest Preserves of Cook County*, 57–61. On the extermination of top predators in the national parks, see Sellars, *Preserving Nature in the National Parks*, 71–75.

22. On early Native Americans see Lace, "Native Americans in the Chicago Area," 23–27.

23. Ransom Kennicott, unpublished paper, November 26, 1920, Unpublished Papers from the Booster Club, CHS, 4 for quotes, 3–4 for description of "Indian Day."

24. On Anglo Americans' view that U.S. Indians were a "vanishing race," see Dippie, *The Vanishing American*. On the Prairie Club and playing Indian, see Monroe, "Festivals—Masques—Pageants," 109; and Anderson, "Canoeing," 194–96; Doeserich, "Dunes Camp," 90; Wassekigig (Thomas W. Allinson), "The Tribe of Ha Ha No Mak," 197; Engel, *Sacred Sands*, 14–26, 68–69. On the national phenomenon of playing Indian, see Deloria, *Playing Indian*.

25. On the relationship between Anglo-American nostalgia and actual American Indian lives, see, e.g., Deloria, *Indians in Unexpected Places*. On legal action against the city, see "Indians' Suit for Strip on Lake Front Rejected," *CT*, March 19, 1914; "Two Indians, 223 Years Old, Claim Land in Chicago," *CT*, October 30, 1923.

26. On the Chicago playground movement, see Draper, "The Art and Science of Park Planning in the United States"; Tippens and Sniderman, "The Planning and Design of Chicago's Neighborhood Parks," 21–28; Pacyga, "Parks for the People," 15–19; McArthur, "Parks, Playgrounds, and Progressivism," 9–14; McArthur, "The Chicago Playground Movement," 376–95; McCarthy, "Politics and the Parks," 158–72; Bachin, *Building the South Side*, 138–59; Pacyga, *Chicago: A Biography*, 167–70; Cranz, *The Politics of Park Design*, 61–99; Cranz, "Models for Park Usage."

27. For accounts of playgrounds that stress social control, order, and/or rationalization, see Finfer, "Leisure as Social Work in the Urban Community," Boyer, *Urban Masses and Moral Order in America*, 241–51; Goodman, *Choosing Sides*; Cavallo, *Muscles and Morals*; Cranz, *The Politics of Park Design*, 98–99; Bachin, *Building the South Side*, 138–59; Young, *Building San Francisco's Parks*, 4–6, 8–9, 10–12, 137–69; Gems, *The Windy City Wars*, 104. For a critique of such accounts, see Mrozek, "The Natural Limits of Unstructured Play, 1880–1914."

28. On field house architecture, see Tippens and Sniderman, "The Planning and Design of Chicago's Neighborhood Parks," 21–27; Draper, "The Art and Science of Park Planning," 100–119.

29. For an example of activities, see, e.g., De Groot, "Suggestions to Instructors in Municipal Playgrounds and Gymnasiums," 98–105; quote on 101.

30. On Kent, see *Hull House Bulletin* 6 (Midwinter 1904–1905): 19; Nash, "John Muir, William Kent, and the Conservative Schism." On Olmsted, see Tippens and Sniderman, "The Planning and Design of Chicago's Neighborhood Parks," 22–23. For Roosevelt's statement, see Taylor, "Recreation Developments in Chicago Parks," 88. On Roosevelt and wilderness, see Nash, *Wilderness and the American Mind*, 150–51.

31. Hall, *Adolescence*, xiii. On Hall's philosophy of play, see Hall, *Adolescence*, 202–36; also see Hall, "Recreation and Reversion." On Hall, also see Ross, *G. Stanley Hall*. See also Higham, "The Reorientation of American Culture in the 1890s"; Lears, *No Place of Grace*, 147–49. For quote, see Addams, *Twenty Years at Hull-House*, 16–18. On Addams's nostalgia for the countryside of her youth, see Spears, *Chicago Dreaming*, 149–73.

32. On the mental, physical, and moral issues attendant commercialized recreation, see, e.g., Addams, *The Spirit of Youth and the City Streets*.

33. "Chicago Playgrounds and Park Centers," 6.

34. Theodore Roosevelt, untitled address, in Playground Association of America, *Playground* (September 1908): 4. On playgrounds and efficiency, see also Richards, "Chicago's Recreation Problem as Related to a City-Wide Organization," 468–85.

35. For Olmsted quote on labor, see Frederick Law Olmsted, "Preliminary Report in Regard to a Plan of Public Pleasure Grounds for the City of San Francisco," March 11, 1866, in Ranney, *The California Frontier*, 522. Also see Frederick Law

Olmsted and Calvert Vaux, "Preliminary Report to the Commissioners for Laying Out a Park in Brooklyn, New York: Being a Consideration of Circumstances of Site and Other Conditions Affecting the Design of Public Pleasure Grounds," in Fein, *Landscape into Cityscape*, 100. On Muir's time-motion study, see Wolfe, *Son of the Wilderness*, 101–2; Turner, *John Muir*, 123–25. For quote on work, see John Muir, "Summering in the Sierra," *Daily Evening Bulletin*, July 20, 1876. On the utilitarian argument for national parks, see Runte, *National Parks*, 82–89. For Muir quote on pendulum, see "Chart of One Day's Labor," John Muir Collection, Wisconsin Historical Society Archives Collection, Madison Wisconsin.

36. On Chicago playground landscapes, see Tippens and Sniderman, "The Planning and Design of Chicago's Neighborhood Parks." On nature study, scouting, and playground trips to the "wilderness," see, e.g., Seman, "Chicago's Program for Meeting Its Recreational Needs," 505; Osborn, "The Development of Recreation in the South Park System of Chicago," 75; Chicago Park District, *Annual Report 5* (1939), 44, 46, 62; Allen, "Saturday Afternoon Walks," 99–103; Holman, "What We Did on a Summer Playground in Chicago"; Sheridan, "Hiking in Chicago"; Richards, "Public Recreation," 102.

37. For an account of Jensen's rejection of European landscaping and the creation of the American Garden in Union Park, see Jensen, "Natural Parks and Gardens," 18–19, 169–70. See also Grese, *Jens Jensen*, 1–9, 62–94; Eaton, *Landscape Artist in America*, 1–18, 29–45; Doty, "Ecology, Community, and the Prairie Spirit," 8–17; Sniderman, "Bringing the Prairie Vision into Focus," 19–31; de Wit and Tippens, "Prairie School in the Parks," 33–41.

38. On Columbus Park, see Collier, "Jens Jensen and Columbus Park"; Grese, *Jens Jensen*, 80–86; Eaton, *Landscape Artist in America*, 38–41; Sniderman, "Bringing the Prairie Vision into Focus," 28. For quote, see Dean, "A 'Swimming Hole' in Chicago," 138.

39. For quotes, see "A German Sunday," *CT*, June 29, 1874. On beer gardens, see Duis, *The Saloon*, 154–55; Duis, *Challenging Chicago*, 210–18; Melendy, "The Saloon in Chicago," 303–5; Sawislak, *Smoldering City*, 220–21; Ensslen, "German-American Working-Class Saloons," 174–76.

40. On Sharpshooters Park, see Duis, *Challenging Chicago*, 212–13; "Grounds of the Chicago Sharpshooters Association," n.d., box 24/4, NHRC-R; Haugh, *Riverview Amusement Park*, 9–18; "Opening of the North Chicago Schuetzenverein's Park," *Illinois Staats-Zeitung*, September 22, 1879, file: German, CFLPS; "Wilhelm Schmidt," *Abendpost*, December 12, 1924, file: German, CFLPS. For quote on delightful grove, see "Opening of the North Chicago Schuetzenpark" *Illinois Staats-Zeitung*, August 22, 1879, file: German, CFLPS. On memories of landscape, see "John Drury's North Side Notebook," *Lincoln-Belmont Booster*, n.d., box 24/4, NHRC-R.

41. On reformers concern with amusement parks, see Kassen, *Amusing the Million*, 98–105; Nasaw, *Going Out*, 93; Duis, *Challenging Chicago*, 217. On Riverview, see Haugh, *Riverview Amusement Park*; Griffin, "The Ups and Downs of Riverview Park," 14–22; Barker, "Paradises Lost," 26–49; Rabinovitz, *For the Love of Pleasure*, 137–67. On Tivoli Gardens, see Benson, *Tivoli Gardens*.

42. For quote on sunshine, see "The Desplaines Hall Workers Club Picnics in Ogden's Grove," *Der Westen*, July 22, 1869, quoted in Keil and Jentz, *German Workers in Chicago*, 207. For quote on woodland garden, see "Wright's Grove," n.d., box 22/10, NHRC-R. For quote on foaming stein, see "Harms' park to Bow to March of Time," n.d., box 23/11, NHRC-R. On the shooters park in Palos Park, see Keating, *Chicagoland*, 121; "Picnic at Palos Park Held by the Grand Lodge of C.S.P.S.," *Denní Hlasatel*, August 4, 1908, file: Bohemian, CFLPS.

43. On the park at Thirty-seventh and Indiana, see Darby, "Emigrants at Play," 54–57. For quote on the home of Irish sports, see "Gaelic Park Opens Sunday Next May 19," *Chicago Citizen*, May 17, 1918, reprinted in Flanagan, "The History of the Development and Promotion of Irish Dancing," 202; "A Study of Gaelic Park," file 7, box 129, EBP; Bachin, *Building the South Side*, 163; Fanning, Skerret, and Corrigan, *Nineteenth Century Chicago Irish*, 34. On the Feis, see Hellsmuth, "Feis." On the Chicago Hebrew Institute (later the Jewish People's Institute), see Cutler, *The Jews of Chicago*, 88; Pacyga and Skerrett, *Chicago*, 212; Gerald Gems, "Sport and the Forging of a Jewish-American Culture." On the grounds of the Chicago Hebrew Institute, see *Chicago Hebrew Institute Observer*, "Grounds," November 1912, file: Jewish, CFLPS. For quote, see "The Institute Buildings and Grounds," *Chicago Hebrew Institute Messenger*, November 1, 1909, file: Jewish, CFLPS. On Pilsen Park, see Pacyga, "Chicago's Pilsen Park"; Nemecek, "The Pilsen Brewery and Pilsen Park in Chicago History," 1, 12; Horak, "Assimilation of Czechs in Chicago,"19; "Pilsen Park in the Making," *Denní Hlasatel*, December 8, 1907, file: Bohemian, CFLPS.

44. On ethnic cemeteries, see Sclair, "Ethnic Cemeteries: Underground Rites"; Hucke and Bielski, *Graveyards of Chicago*; Simon, *Chicago, the Garden City*, 111–86. Also see "The Call of the Hungarian Cemetery Association," *Magyar Tribune*, file: Hungarian, CFLPS; "Sunday Causerie," *Denní Hlasatel*, September 16, 1915, file: Bohemian, CFLPS; "Polish Youngsters Marching Out to the Cemetery on Memorial Day," *Dziennik Chicagoski*, May 23, 1905, file: Polish, CFLPS; "At the Swedish Cemetery," *Svenska Nyheter*, file: Swedish, CFLPS. For a description of the Chinese shrine, see *Chicago Tribune*, "Dedicate A Shrine," August 29, 1892. On Chinese burial practices in Chicago, see Moy, "The Chinese in Chicago," 381–82; Ho and Chinese-American Museum of Chicago, *Chinese in Chicago*, 28; Fan, "Chinese Residents in Chicago," 50–51. On picnic parties, see Vojan, *The Semi-Centennial Jubilee of the Bohemian National Cemetery Association*, 41–42, 66. Keating, *Chicagoland*, 123–25; Duis, *Challenging Chicago*, 210; Melendy, "The Saloon in Chicago," 305–6. On Anglo American use of cemeteries for recreation, see Bender, "The 'Rural' Cemetery Movement"; Sachs, *Arcadian America*, 19–61.

45. On vacant lots, see Dubkin, *My Secret Places*, xvi, 53–54; Dubkin, *Enchanted Streets*, 51, 59, 103–4, 136–37.

46. On the river, see Dubkin, *My Secret Places*, 15–27. For quote on the strangeness of time, see Dubkin, *My Secret Places*, 23. On the bat grotto, see Dubkin, *My Secret Places*, 27–40; Dubkin, *The White Lady*.

47. On the history of Northerly Island, see Wille, *Forever Open, Clear, and Free*, 99–102. On Northerly Island, Dubkin, *My Secret Places*, 41–59; Dubkin, *Enchanted Streets*, 80–89. For quotes, see Dubkin, *My Secret Places*, 56, 57.

48. Dubkin, *My Secret Places*, 60–76; Dubkin, *Wolf Point*. For quote, see Dubkin, *My Secret Places*, 72–73.

49. On Mrs. Grossetti, see Dubkin, *Enchanted Streets*, 138. On birds in the city, see Dubkin, *The Murmur of Wings*. On insects, see Dubkin, *Enchanted Streets*, 23. On backyard animals, see Dubkin, *Enchanted Streets*, 126; Dubkin, *The Murmur of Wings*, 112. On sumac and other foliage in the city, see Dubkin, *Enchanted Streets*, 139–40. On rats, see Dubkin, *Enchanted Streets*, 43–48.

50. Dubkin, *Enchanted Streets*, 138.

51. Dubkin, *A Natural History of a Yard*, 6.

52. Dubkin, *My Secret Places*, 72–73.

## Chapter 2

1. On immigrants and environmental history, see Warren, *The Hunter's Game*, 21–47; Washington, *Packing Them In*, 75–99; Chiang, *Shaping the Shoreline*; Rome, "Nature Wars, Culture Wars"; Chiang, "Imprisoned Nature"; Rawson, *Eden on the Charles*, 157–59. Handlin, *The Uprooted*; quotes on 110, 104, 8.

2. See Bodnar, *The Transplanted*. See also Vecoli, "Contadini in Chicago."

3. On the invention of ethnicity, see Sollors, "Introduction: The Invention of Ethnicity"; Conzen, "Ethnicity as Festive Culture"; Conzen, Gerber, Morawska, Pozzetta, and Vecoli, "The Invention of Ethnicity"; Schultz, *Ethnicity on Parade*. For quote, see Conzen, "The Invention of Ethnicity," 4–5. Also see Anderson, *Imagined Communities*.

4. On transnationalism, see, e.g., Gabaccia, "Liberty, Coercion, and the Making of Immigration Historians"; Tyrell, "American Exceptionalism in an Age of International History"; Wyman, *Round-Trip to America*; Jacobson, *Special Sorrows*; Hsu, *Dreaming of Gold, Dreaming of Home*; Gerber, "Forming a Transnational Narrative." Although many immigrants were in fact emigrants, I will use the more traditional term *immigrants*.

5. For quote, see McNeill, "Observations on the Nature and Culture of Environmental History," 17–18. On efforts to internationalize American history, see Bender, *Rethinking American History in a Global Age,* as well as "The Nation and Beyond: Transnational Perspectives on American History," special issue, *Journal of American History* 86 (December 1999): 1015–307.

6. See Bodnar, *The Transplanted,* 1–56. On the economic effects of cheap American grain on Europe, see O'Rourke, "The European Grain Invasion." On Chicago farm machinery and the global marketplace, see Heikkonen, *Reaping the Bounty*.

7. For quotes, see Wells, *The Future in America*, 59, 60.

8. Sinclair, *The Jungle*. On Back of the Yards, see Slayton, *Back of the Yards*; Jablonsky, *Pride in the Jungle*; Barrett, *Work and Community in the Jungle*.

9. For quote on odor, see Sinclair, *The Jungle*, 32. On environmental hazards, see Phillips, "Mary McDowell as We Knew Her in the Yards," 120; McDowell, "City Waste"; Slayton, *Back of the Yards*, 15, 26–28; Jablonsky, *Pride in the Jungle*, 1–24; Washington, *Packing Them In*, 81–85.

10. For quote on bubbles, see Sinclair, *The Jungle*, 112.

11. On the changing nature of factory labor in Chicago, see Schneirov, *Labor and Urban Politics*, 17–24, 32–33. On the changing nature of work in meatpacking, see Barrett, *Work and Community in the Jungle*, 13–31.

12. On indoor immigrant leisure in Chicago, see Cohen, *Making a New Deal*, 99–158; Duis, *Challenging Chicago*, 204–10, 218–37; Vaillant, *Sounds of Reform*, 190–233; Rabinovitz, *For the Love of Pleasure*, 68–136; Duis, *The Saloon*; Skilnik, *The History of Beer and Brewing in Chicago*, 67–76, 88–89; Addams, *The Spirit of Youth and the City Streets*; Heiss, "Popular and Working-Class German Theatre in Chicago," 181–202.

13. "Out in the Sunshine," *CT*, July 4, 1892.

14. On the Continental Sunday, see McCrossen, *Holy Day, Holiday*, 41–46.

15. On changing Anglo American ideas about leisure, see Rogers, *The Work Ethic in Industrial America*, 94–124. On changing views of Sunday, see McCrossen, *Holy Day, Holiday*. On the situation in Chicago, see Bohlmann, "Sunday Closings." On Sundays and parks, see Hardy, *How Boston Played*, 59–60, 93–94, 106; Rosenzweig and Blackmar, *The Park and the People*, 238–59. On Anglo American private gardens and promenading in Lake Front Park, see Bluestone, *Constructing Chicago*, 8–20.

16. Renner, "In a Perfect Ferment"; Pierce, *From Town to City*, 437–39; Flinn and Wilkie, *History of the Chicago Police*, 70–79; Seeger, *Chicago: The Wonder City*, 108–15. On park rules, see Gems, "Sports and Culture Formation in Chicago," 112; Bachin, *Building the South Side*, 136. For quote on cricket, see Gary, *Law and Ordinances Governing the City of Chicago*, 298. On updated rules, see Mann, *Municipal Code of the South Park Commissioners*, 32–41.

17. Renner, "In a Perfect Ferment,"161–70; Pierce, *A History of Chicago*, 437–39; Flinn and Wilkie, *History of the Chicago Police*, 70–79; Seeger, *Chicago: The Wonder City*, 108–15.

18. On the fire and the Sunday law during the 1870s, see Sawislak, *Smoldering City*, 217–59; Schneirov, *Labor and Urban Politics*, 51–52; Smith, *Urban Disorder and the Shape of Belief*, 103–4. For quote from Hesing, see Ahern, *The Great Revolution*, 99.

19. "Humboldt Park: The Formal Opening," *CT*, July 15, 1877; "Humboldt Park: The Informal Dedication by the Citizens Themselves: An Immense Crowd," *CT*, July 16, 1877; Simon, *Chicago, the Garden City*, 77. On outrage, see "Sabbath Desecration," *CT*, July 16, 1877. Also see Bluestone, *Constructing Chicago*, 32.

20. "The Origin of Picnics," *Chicagoer Arbeiter-Zeitung*, June 27, 1883, quoted in Keil and Jentz, *German Workers in Chicago*, 205, 206.

21. On music, see "Sunday-Concerts," *CT*, September 1, 1872; Vaillant, *Sounds of Reform*, 67–73. On liberalization of rules and creation of space for sports in parks, see Halsey, *The Development of Public Recreation in Metropolitan Chicago*, 20–21; Gems, *The Windy City Wars*, 80; Riess, "Introduction: The History of Sports in Chicago," 9. On the liberalization of park rules on Sundays, see "Sunday Games in Parks," *CT*, July 15, 1905. For quote, see Farwell, "Chicago's Candidacy for the 1892 World's Fair," 54. Also see, "Keep off the Grass"; Simon, *Chicago, The Garden City*, 52.

22. *Illinois Staats-Zeitung*, September 22, 1879, file: German, CFLPS. On the importance of the spatial context of sports, see Bale, *Sports Geography*, esp. 142–75.

23. For preserve stats, see Todd, Byron, and Vierow, *Private Recreation*, 1:166. For national park stats, see Steiner, "Recreation and Leisure Time Activities," 920. On ethnic politicians, see, e.g., "Professor Szymczak Is Pleased with New Appointment," *Dziennik Zjednoczenia*, June 3, 1927, file: Polish, CFLPS; "Rocco De Stefano," *Chicago Evening Post*, November 16, 1929; Lewis and Smith, *Chicago*, 427–28.

24. On hunting and fishing clubs, see, e.g., "Club Activities," *Abendpost*, August 25, 1924, file: German, CFLPS; "German Clubs and Societies of Chicago," *Abendpost*, July 6, 1935; J. R. Christianson, "Danes"; "Polish Activity in Chicago," *Dzienniki Chicagoski*, December 22, 1890, file: Polish, CFLPS; "Polish Societies in America: Polish Hunters' Club of Chicago, Illinois, *Dziennik Chicagoski*, August 5, 1892, file: Polish, CFLPS; Anna Masley, "Study of Ukrainians, A Nationality Group of Chicago and Vicinity," box 157, file 6, EBP; "Shooting Competition Results," *Denní Hlasatel*, June 6, 1911, file: Bohemian, CFLPS. For quote on woods, see Czeslawa Kowalewski, box 4, OHACP.

25. For quote, see "In the Foreground," *Svenska Tribunen-Nyheter*, August 2, 1922, file: Swedish, CFLPS. For more on Swedish painters, see "Among Swedish Artists in Chicago," *Svenska Tribunen-Nyheter*, December 28, 1921, file: Swedish, CFLPS; "The Swedish Art Show," *Svenska Tribunen-Nyheter*, February 7, 1923, file: Swedish, CFLPS. On Tunis Ponsen, see Gerdts, *The Lost Paintings of Tunis Ponsen*. On Armin, see Engel, *Sacred Sands*, 106–7; Jacobson, *Thirty-five Saints and Emil Armin*. On the Umlecky Klub, see "Art Club Sponsors Lectures," *Denní Hlasatel*, April 1, 1917, file: Bohemian, CFLPS.

26. On Helmuth, see "An Inestimable, Scientific Work of a Chicagoan," *Illinois Staats-Zeitung*, April 22, 1892, file: German, CFLPS. On Sala, see "A Czech's Gift to the Field Museum," *Denní Hlasatel*, November 25, 1917, file: Bohemian, CFLPS.

27. On Chicago Hebrew Institute/Jewish People's Institute, see "Open Natural History Museum at J.P.I.," *Chicago Jewish Chronicle*, November 3, 1933, file: Jewish, CFLPS. For quote on sunken gardens, see Seman, *Jewish Community Life*, 89. For quote on academy, see "Resurrection Sisters' Academy," *Narod Polski*, August 15, 1917, file: Polish, CFLPS.

28. On Jensen, see Grese, *Jens Jensen*.

29. For quote from Sauer, see "Expect 500,000 to Visit Forest Preserve Today," *CT*, June 16,1935. For picnics, also see "400,000 to Picnic in Forests Today," *CT*, July 14, 1935; "42,600 to Attend Picnics Today," *CT*, July 23, 1939; "200,000 to Picnic in Woods Today," *CT*, July 21, 1940. See also Cutler, *The Jews of Chicago*, 227–28; "Activities of the Mexican Methodist Church," *El Nacional*, August 6, 1932, file: Spanish, CFLPS; "About 10,000 Attend Croatian Day Held at East Side Forest Preserve," *Daily Calumet*, August 27, 1934, file: Croat, CFLPS; "The Messinians," *Saloniki-Greek Press*, July 31, 1929, file: Greek, CFLPS; "Splendid Picnic of the Vereinigte Maennerchoere,"*Abendpost*, September 10, 1934, file: German, CFLPS; "Cerny Club of Town of Lake to Hold Picnic," *Osadne Hlasy*, July 24, 1931, file: Slovak, CFLPS; "Italian Picnic in the Forest Preserve, c. 1920s," file 60.16.1, box 56, IAC; "Josef Sowa," box 9, OHACP. Sandburg, "Happiness."

30. On the concept of the recreational hinterland, see Cronon, *Nature's Metropolis*, 380–82. On ethnic resorts in Michigan, see Thomopoulos, *Resorts of Berrien*

*County, Michigan,* 8, 17, 22–27, 34, 40, 42; Thomopoulos, *St. Joseph and Benton Harbor,* 112. On South Haven, see Kraus, *A Time To Remember*; Cutler, "The Jews of Chicago," 158–59. On Norwegians, see "Scandia Beach, June 11, 1927, file: Norwegian, CFLPS; "Ski Club Celebrates," Scandia, November 19, 1912, file: Norwegian, CFLPS. On Skansen, see "From 'Skansen'," *Svenska Tribunen-Nyheter,* July 24, 1929, file: Swedish, CFLPS; "Skansen Colony Retains Spirit of Native Sweden," *Milwaukee Journal,* October 7, 1934. On Bosnians, see Puskar, *Bosnian Americans of Chicagoland,* 33; quote on 32.

31. Thomopoulos, "Summer Memories." Also see "At the Summer Resorts," July 27, 1932, file: Greek, CFLPS.

32. "The Hypocrite's Holiday," *Svenska Nyheter,* August 30, 1904, file: Swedish, CFLPS.

33. On Anglo American tourism in England, see Lockwood, *Passionate Pilgrims*; Strout, *The American Image of the Old World,* 86–156. Also see Lears, *No Place of Grace,* 141–81. On New England, see for instance, Brown, *Inventing New England.* On national park landscapes and nationalism, see, e.g., Belasco, *Americans on the Road,* 71–104; Hyde, *An American Vision*; Sears, *Sacred Places,* 122–81; Shaffer, *See America First.* For quote, see Yard, *Our Federal Lands,* 231.

34. "The Desplaines Hall Workers Club Picnics in Ogden's Grove," *Der Westen,* July 22, 1869, in Keil and Jentz, *German Workers in Chicago,* 206–10.

35. See Vecoli, "Prelates and Peasants"; Orsi, *The Madonna of 115th Street*; Conzen, "The Invention of Ethnicity," 22–23, 26–27; Hsu, *Dreaming of Gold*; Sanchez, *Becoming Mexican American,* 17–37.

36. For *landsmanshaften* organizations, see Cutler, *The Jews of Chicago,* 226, 236. For Polish village associations, see Josef Sowa, box 9, OHACP. For Greek village and regional picnics, see, e.g., "Third Annual Picnic of the Cretans Society," *Saloniki,* September 1, 1928, CFLPS; "The Klepaitons' Picnic," June 19, 1929, CFLPS; "The Baltetsian Picnic," *Greek Press,* July 10, 1929, CFLPS; "The Riziotian Agkyra Picnic," *Greek Press,* July 17, 1929; "The Messians," *Greek Press,* July 31, 1929. On the persistence of regional/village identity in Chicago, see Yeracaris, "A Study of the Voluntary Associations of the Greek Immigrants of Chicago."

37. On Italian *festas,* see Orsi, *The Madonna of 115th Street.* On Chicago, see Vecoli, "Chicago's Italians Prior to World War I," 211–16; Vecoli, "Cult and Occult in Italian American Culture," 31–32; Cohen, *Making a New Deal,* 88–94. See also Zaloha, "A Study of Persistence of Italian Customs among 143 Families of Italian Descent," 99–101; *Golden Jubilee of the Feast of Our Lady of Mt. Carmel*; "Pin Money on a Statue," *CT,* July 29, 1901; "Great Parade in Suburb," *CT,* July 25, 1904; "Parade by Court Order," *Chicago Chronicle,* July 24, 1905; "Italians Have Feast Today," *CT,* July 28, 1901. For quote on Italian families, see Vecoli, "Chicago's Italians Prior to World War I," 211; Nelli, "The Role of the 'Colonial' Press in the Italian-American Community of Chicago," 83–86. For quote from participant, see *L'Italia,* July 28–29, 1894, quoted in Vecoli, *Chicago's Italians Prior to World War I,* 211–12.

38. On *bygdelag,* see Lovoll, *The Promise of America,* 184; Lovoll, *A Century of Urban Life,* 253, 255. For *Heimat* associations in Chicago, see Lekan, "German Landscape";

quote on 149. On *Heimat* associations in Germany, see Rollins, *A Greener Vision of Home*; Lekan, *Imagining the Nation in Nature*, 3, 6–8, 11, 13–17, 20–21, 24, 34, 40, 56–57, 74–75, 80–87, 122, 131, 142–46, 150–51, 254.

39. See "Schwaben-Verein Organized in 1878," box 17/14, NHRC-R; Hofmeister, *The Germans of Chicago*, 117–18; Keil and Jentz, "Picnics"; "The Cannstatter Volksfest," *Chicagoer Arbeiter-Zeitung*, August 21, 1879, in Keil and Jentz, *German Workers in Chicago*, 210; "Caanstatter Volksfest: A Move to Brand's Park.—Lively Debate between Representatives of the Older and Younger Generations in the Schwaben-Verein, *Chicagoer Arbeiter-Zeitung*, January 19, 1905, in Keil and Jentz, *German Workers in Chicago*, 211–12; "'S Schwabenlaendle," *CT*, August 20, 1883; "German Rejoicings," *CT*, August 18, 1884; "A Suabian Holiday," *CT*, August 16, 1886; "Drank the Royal Wine, *CT*, August 10, 1891; "Schwabens Have Fun," *CT*, August 20, 1894; "Quaff King's Own Wine," *CT*, August 24, 1896; "Suabians Keep Their Ancient Harvest Festival," *CT*, August 22, 1898; "Gala Day for Swabians," *CT*, August 21, 1899; "Celebrating Schwaben Festival at Sharpshooters' Park," *CT*, August 17, 1903; "People's Festival," *Chicago Arbeiter Zeitung*, August 30, 1880, file: German, CFLPS; "The Caanstatters National Festival," *Abendpost*, August 21, 1911, file: German, CFLPS; "The Cannstatt Festival," September 1, 1879, file: German, CFLPS. For quote on great fest, see "Cannstatter National Festival," *Abendpost*, August 22, 1910, file: German, CFLPS.

40. On the forces shaping the invention of nationalism, see Conzen et al., "The Invention of Ethnicity"; Schultz, *Ethnicity on Parade*.

41. On Our Lady Day in Harvest in Chicago, see Funchion, "Irish Chicago," 67; Jerome, "The Significance of Recent National Festivals in Chicago," 83. On the day, also see "They Honor Dr. Cronin," *CT*, August 16, 1891; "Fun and Patriotism," *CT*, August 14, 1892; "United Irish Societies' Picnic," *CT*, August 16, 1896; "United Irish to Celebrate," *CT*, August 15, 1898; "Unite to Seek Erin's Freedom," *CT*, August 16, 1901; "Irish at Rival Picnics," *CT*, August 16, 1904; "'Fish' Chief of Picnic," *CT*, August 13, 1906; "Observe Old Irish Holiday," *CT*, August 16, 1908. On nationalistic speeches at Our Lady in Harvest, see, e.g., "United Irish Societies' Picnic," *CT*, August 16, 1896; "Make Britain a Target," *CT*, August 19, 1898. On Lughnasa, see MacNeill and Irish Folklore Commission, *The Festival of Lughnasa*; MacCulloch, *The Religion of the Ancient Celts*, 272–74.

42. See "The German Peace Celebration," *CT*, May 7, 1871; "Yesterday's German Procession," *CT*, May 30, 1871; "Peace," *CT*, May 30, 1871. For quote, see "The Festival," *CT*, May 30, 1871.

43. On the origins of *midsommar*, see Scott, *Sweden: The Nation's History*, 350–51. On the festival in Chicago, see "Swedish Midsummerfeast," *Svenska Tribunen*, June 28, 1899, file: Swedish, CFLPS; "Swedish National Association's Midsummer Festival," *Svenska Nyheter*, June 23, 1903, file: Swedish, CFLPS; "Around the Mayple," *Svenska Nyheter*, June 27, 1905, file: Swedish, CFLPS; "The Swedish Midsummer Festival," *Svenska Tribunen*, June 26, 1906, file: Swedish, CFLPS; "Swedish National Midsummer Festival," June 25, 1907, file: Swedish, CFLPS; "Festival of the Swedish National League," *Svenska Tribunen-Nyheter*, June 28, 1910, file: Swedish, CFLPS; "The Midsummer Festivals," *Svenska Tribunen-Nyheter*, June 22, 1915, file: Swedish, CFLPS.

For quote on Midsummer sun, see "Swedish Midsummerfeast," *Svenska Tribunen*, June 28, 1899, file: Swedish, CFLPS.

44. For quotes on fondness of nature and festivals, see Horak, "Assimilation of Czechs in Chicago," 30–31, 48. On Posvícení and other country fairs at Pilsen Park, see "An Old Fashioned Czech Feast—A Plain People's Festival," *Denní-Hlasatel*, September 4, 1917, file: Bohemian, CFLPS; "Posvícení," *Denní-Hlasatel*, September 9, 1918, file: Bohemian, CFLPS; "What Is Posvícení?," *Denní-Hlasatel*, September 14, 1920, file: Bohemian, CFLPS; "Extensive Preparations for the National Pilgrimage," *Denní-Hlasatel*, August 16, 1922, file: Bohemian, CFLPS; "The Most Significant Event of the Season," *Denní-Hlasatel*, September 14, 1922, file: Bohemian, CFLPS; "Old Country Czech Festival a Success," *Denní-Hlasatel*, September 20, 1922, file: Bohemian, CFLPS. For quote, see "Tomorrow Is the National Pilgrimage in Pilsen Park," *Denní-Hlasatel*, August 19, 1922, file: Bohemian, CFLPS. For quote on incorporating everything colorful, see V. Hnatek, "Posvícení," *Denní-Hlasatel*, September 9, 1918, file: Bohemian, CFLPS. For quote on reliving, see "Tomorrow is the National Pilgrimage in Pilsen Park," *Denní-Hlasatel*, August 19,1922, file: Bohemian, CFLPS.

45. Pacyga, "Chicago's Pilsen Park and the Struggle for Czechoslovak Independence during World War One"; Pacyga, *Chicago*, 189–90, 193. On the use of Pilsen Park in the independence struggle, also see Nemecek, "The Pilsen Brewery and Pilsen Park in Chicago History," 1, 12; Jahelka, "The Role of Chicago Czechs in the Struggle for Czechoslovak Independence," 385. For the sacred urn, see "Festival to Commemorate the Bringing of Soil of Czechoslovakia to Chicago," *Denní Hlasatel*, November 16, 1922, file: Bohemian, CFLPS.

46. On the celebration of Mexican Independence in Chicago, see Jones, *"Conditions Surrounding Mexicans in Chicago,"* 51; Arredondo, *Mexican Chicago*, 161; "The Festival of September 15th," *El Nacional*, August 22, 1931; "Mexico's Independence Feasts in Chicago," *El Nacional*, September 24, 1932; "Festival for Today," September 16, 1932, CFLPS. On Mexican nationalism in Chicago, see Arredondo, *Mexican Chicago*, 153–65. For quotes on the duties of the citizen, see "The Mexican Fraternal Society of Chicago," *El Heraldo de las Américas*, November 1, 1924, folder 2, box 1, RRP. On the land of the Aztecs, see *México*, September 16, 1926, quoted in Arredondo, *Mexican Chicago*, 161.

47. On American ethnic identities and homemaking, see Øverland, *Immigrant Minds, American Identities*. On immigrant nationalism, see Jacobson, *Special Sorrows*.

48. On binationalism of late nineteenth and early twentieth century Chicago immigrants, see Litwicki, " 'Our Hearts Burn with Ardent Love for Two Countries.' " For mother/wife analogy, see "Germans Cry 'Hoch,' " *CT*, June 16, 1893.

49. On parks named after ethnic/national heroes, see "Humboldt Park," *Illinois Staats-Zeitung*, July 16, 1877, file: German, CFLPS; Simon, *Chicago the Garden City*, 77; Bachrach, *The City in a Garden*, 81, 133; Vaillant, *Sounds of Reform*, 155–56; "50 Norwegian Groups Name Roald Amundsen Park Today," *CT*, October 29, 1933; "Appeal to Our Countrymen," *Dziennik Zwiazkowy*, December 4, 1914, file: Polish, CFLPS; and "Chopin Park Opening Celebration Held Yesterday," *Dziennik Zjednoczenia*, October 4, 1926; Bachin, *Building the South Side*, 163. For quote on themes, see Taft, "The Monuments

of Chicago," 124–25. On sculptures in Chicago parks, see Moses and Kirkland, *The History of Chicago, Illinois*, 509–12; Johannesson, "The Flower King in the American Republic," 267–69; Lovoll, *A Century of Urban Life*, 240–41; Bachin, *Building the South Side*, 163–64; Graf and Skarpad, *Chicago's Monuments, Markers, and Memorials*.

50. Kammen, *The Mystic Chords of Memory*, 481–514.

## Chapter 3

1. Farrell, *Studs Lonigan*. Although Farrell's fiction is inspired by real people, locations, and events, it is driven by a sociological impulse to capture the texture of everyday Irish American life in the South Side.

2. Ibid.; quote on 113.

3. Ibid.; quote on 847.

4. Ibid.; quote on 466.

5. On using Farrell's fiction as a primary source, see Fanning and Skerrett, "James T. Farrell and Washington Park."

6. Addams, *The Spirit of Youth and the City Streets*; quotes on 69, 68.

7. Park, "The City: Suggestions for the Investigation of Human Behavior in the Urban Environment," 40.

8. On the play movement and the preservation of Anglo American games, see Glassberg, "Restoring a 'Forgotten Childhood.'" For quote on old games, see Brown and Boyd, *Old English and American Games for School and Playground*, 4. On old Anglo American games, see Taylor, "How They Played at Chicago," 5. On flag in the playground, see, e.g, "Dedication Day in Davis Park," *CT*, May 14, 1905. On dances and husking bee, see for instance "Trip Old Time Steps at Harvest Festival," *CT*, November 30, 1914. On playing Indian, see "Mimic Indians at the Third Annual Children's Play Festival at Garfield Park," *CT*, October 10, 1909. On holidays, see Rainwater, *The Play Movement in the United States*, 209; "Patriotism in the Parks," *CT*, February 13, 1909. On the pageant, see Rainwater, *The Play Movement in the United States*, 267. On historical pageantry at this time, see Glassberg, *American Historical Pageantry*. On playgrounds, democracy, and good citizenship, see Gulick, "Play and Democracy"; Lee, "Play as a School of the Citizen"; South Park Commissioners, *Annual Report*, 72. For quote on the flag, see "Children Rule for a Day," *CT*, June 11, 1905.

9. On the play festivals, see Taylor, "Recreation Developments in Chicago Parks"; Taylor, "How They Played at Chicago"; Tarbell, "An Old World Fete in Industrial America," 546–48; Taylor, "The Chicago Play Festival"; Millet, "A Meeting and Mingling of Peoples"; "Chicago's Third Play Festival." For quote on bright-colored garments, see Addams, *The Spirit of Youth and the City Streets*, 102. For quote on hallowed by tradition, see Tarbell, "An Old World Fete in Industrial America," 548.

10. On Puritanism and Elizabethan play, see Glassberg, "Restoring a 'Forgotten Childhood.'"

11. On prohibition on foreign languages, see "What I Have Noticed," *Lietuva*, April 10, 1908, file: Lithuanian, CFLPS. For quote, see Hofer, "The Significance of Recent National Festivals in Chicago," 85. For a somewhat problematic analysis of Chicago Progressives and pluralism, see Shpak-Lissak, *Pluralism and Progressives*.

12. On the push for consent during the war years, see Kennedy, *Over Here*, 45–92. On the See American First movement, see Shaffer, *See America First*, 45–92.

13. On Independence Day Americanization events, see for instance "City Observes Fourth, Sane but Patriotic," *CT*, July 5, 1917; "Melting Pot Fourth to Boil with Loyalty: Over Million Here to Join in Fetes of Americanism," *CT*, July 3, 1918; and "City's Hordes of All Bloods Exalt Liberty: Melting Post Helps Consecrate Day of Freedom," *CT*, July 5, 1918. For quote on crucible, see "City's Hordes," *CT*, July 5, 1918. On Americanization in the small parks, see Becker, "Teaching Good Citizenship in Chicago's Parks and Playgrounds"; Pacyga, "Parks for the People," 15–19; Halsey, *The Development of Public Recreation in Metropolitan Chicago*, 168; Loomis, *Americanization in Chicago*; Glassberg, "Restoring a 'Forgotten Childhood.'"

14. On Columbus Park, see Collier, "Jens Jensen and Columbus Park," 233–34; Grese, *Jens Jensen*, 80–86; Eaton, *Landscape Artist in America*, 38–41; Sniderman, "Bringing the Prairie Vision into Focus," 28. On trips out of the parks, see, e.g., Seman, "Chicago's Program for Meeting Its Recreational Needs," 505; Osborn, "The Development of Recreation in the South Park System of Chicago," 75; Chicago Park District, *Annual Report*, 44, 46, 62; Allen, "Saturday Afternoon Walks"; Holman, "What We Did on a Summer Playground in Chicago"; Sheridan, "Hiking in Chicago"; Richards, "Public Recreation," 102.

15. On the body, see, e.g., "The Turner Movement," *Skandinaven*, July 29, 1900, file: Norwegian, CFLPS. "The Power of Athletics," *Star*, March 10, 1905, file: Greek, CFLPS; "Do Jews Value Physical Culture," *Daily Jewish Courier*, April 23, 1923, file: Jewish, CFLPS; "The Saloons, Sports, and the Pleasures of Our Youth," *Narod Polski*, March 28, 1900, file: Polish, CFLPS. On fears of American leisure, see Cohen, *Making a New Deal*, 54–55, 96.

16. For quotes, see Miller, "Nature and the National Ego," 205, 204. On the concept of "nature's nation," see Miller, *Nature's Nation*. Also see Smith, *Virgin Land*; Huth, *Nature and the American*; Marx, *The Machine in the Garden*; Nash, *Wilderness and the American Mind*; Runte, *National Parks*; Schmitt, *Back to Nature*.

17. On Jahn and the Turners, see Mosse, *The Nationalization of the Masses*, 128, 129; Denker, "Popular Gymnastics and the Military Spirit in Germany, 1848–1871"; Goltermann, "Exercise and Perfection"; Lempa, *Beyond the Gymnasium*; Ueberhorst, *Friedrich Ludwig Jahn and His Time*; McMillan, "Germany Incarnate."

18. On the place of nature in the Turner movement, see Eichberg, "The Enclosure of the Body"; and Eichberg and Idraetshojskøle, "Race-Track and Labyrinth," 249–52. For quote on open fields, see Friedrich Ludwig Jahn and Ernst Eiselen, *Die deutsche Turnkunst* (1816; Fellbach, 1967), 169, quoted in Eichberg and Idraetshojskøle, "Race-Track and Labyrinth," 250. On the *Tie*, see Mosse, *The Nationalization of the Masses*, 128–29. On *Turnfahrt*, see Phillips, "Friends of Nature," 56; McMillan, "Germany Incarnate," 62–63, 427, 443; Hagen, *Preservation, Tourism and Nationalism*, 78. On walking, see Lempa, *Beyond the Gymnasium*, 163–93.

19. On this transformation, see Eichberg, "The Enclosure of the Body," 54–57; and Eichberg and Idraetshojskøle, "Race-Track and Labyrinth," 252–57. On the fin-de-siècle vogue for nature, see Rollins, *A Greener Vision of Home*, 73. On gymnastics, English sport, and the development of handball, see Van Bottenburg,

*Global Games,* 72–75. On the *Wandervogel* movement, see Laqueur, *Young Germany*; Heineman, "Gender Identity in the Wandervogel Movement"; Williams, *Turning to Nature in Germany,* 107–216. For quote on *Wandervogel,* see Mosse, *The Nationalization of the Masses,* 133.

20. On the Sokol movement in Slavic nations, see Nolte, *The Sokol in Czech Lands*; Nolte, "All for One! One for All!"; Jones, "Forerunners of the Komsomol," 64–65; Matusik, "Der polnische 'Sokół'"; Liponski, "Still an Unknown European Tradition," 11–16; Dabrowski, *Commemorations and the Shaping of Modern Poland,* 166, 179–81, 198, 204–6; Mathur, "Women and Physical Culture in Modern Poland," 24–25, 29, 34–35, 71–72, 139, 148–50. On gymnastics in the Scandinavian nations, see Eichberg, "Body Culture and Democratic Nationalism"; Goksøyr, "Phases and Functions of Nationalism," 131–32. On Italy, see Gori, *Italian Fascism and the Female Body,* 34–35; Teja and Impiglia, "Italy"; Van Dalen and Bennett, *A World History of Physical Education,* 342. On Greece, see Koulouri, "Athleticism and Antiquity," 142–49; Kaimakamis, Duka, Kaimakamis, Anastasiou, "The Birth of the German Gymnastics System and Its Introduction in the Modern-Greek State"; Van Dalen and Bennett, *A World History of Physical Education,* 338. On France, see Weber, "Gymnastics and Sports in Fin-de-Siècle France." On Jewish gymnastics, see Presner, *Muscular Judaism,* 106–54; Berkowitz, *Zionist Culture and West European Jewry,* 107–9.

21. On early Czech Sokol outings, see Nolte, *The Sokol in the Czech Lands,* 40–42, 51–52, 58, 61, 63, 103. On the importance of Říp Mountain, see Sayer, *The Coasts of Bohemia,* 142. On the Sokol and the outdoor life movement, see Nolte, *The Sokol in the Czech Lands,* 126; Jandásek, "The Sokol Movement in Czechoslovakia," 68; Roberts, *From Good King Wenceslas to the Good Soldier Svejk,* 157; Martin, Turčová and Neuman, "The Czech Outdoor Experience" 198–202. Also see, Helen Hrachovska, "'Sokol,' Gymnastic Organization in Czechoslovakia," box 145, EBP.

22. On Polish outings, see Zaborniak, "An Outline of Development of Tourism." On Hungarian student tourism, see Vari, "From Friends of Nature to Tourist-Soldiers," 72–81. On Slavic scouting, see Kerr, *The Story of a Million Girls,* 129–41, 252–61, 293–302, 325–28, 344–48, 354–60; Moynihan, *An Official History of Scouting,* 132, 141; Jones, "Forerunners of the Komsomol" 56–61; Zaborniak, "An Outline of Development of Tourism," 62; Nolte, *The Sokol in the Czech Lands,* 149; Roberts, *From Good King Wenceslas to the Good Soldier Svejk,* 73; Martin, "The Czech Outdoor Experience," 201–2; Scheidlinger, "A Comparative Study of the Boy Scout Movement," 744–46; Subtelny, *Ukraine: A History,* 439–40; Mathur, "Women and Physical Culture in Modern Poland," 24, 29, 34–35, 70, 148–49; Redlich, *Together and Apart in Brzezany,* 48; Liponski, "Still an Unknown European Tradition," 16; Vari, "From Friends of Nature to Tourist-Soldiers," 77–79; Meehan, "The World Brotherhood of Boys."

23. On Jewish gymnastics and Jewish outdoor life, see Presner, *Muscular Judaism*; Nur, "Hashomer Hatzair Youth Movement." For quote from Scholem, see *Die Jüdische Turnzeitung* 6 (1908): 112, quoted in Presner, *Muscular Judaism,* 135. On the *Blau Weiss,* a German Jewish version of the *Wandervogel,* see Laqueur, *A History of Zionism,* 485. On Jewish scouting, see Scheidlinger, "A Comparative Study of the Boy Scout Movement," 748–49.

24. On the Gaelic Athletic Association, see Cronin, *Sport and Nationalism in Ireland*, 70–116; Mandle, "The IRB and the Origins of the Gaelic Athletic Association"; Mandle, *The Gaelic Athletic Association and Irish Nationalist Politics*. On the connection between the GAA and the *Fianna Eireann*, see Sisson, *Pearse's Patriots*, 115–30. For quote, see "A Word about Irish Athletics," *United Ireland* (October 1884), quoted in Mandle, "The IRB and the Origins of the Gaelic Athletic Association," 418.

25. See Goksøyr, "Phases and Functions of Nationalism"; Sørlin, "Nature, Skiing and Swedish Nationalism"; Löfgren, "Know Your Country"; Löfgren, "Materializing the Nation in Sweden and America," 178–79; Nolin, "Stockholm's Urban Parks," 118–19. On Scouting in Scandinavia, see Kerr, *The Story of a Million Girls*, 72–84, 101–16, 210–13; Moynihan, *An Official History of Scouting*, 138–39.

26. On the formation of ethnic sports organizations in Chicago, see Riess, *City Games*, 93–102; Riess, "Ethnic Sports"; Gems, "Not Only a Game"; Gems, *The Windy City Wars*, 9–12, 24–28, 185–88. On Germans, see Hofmeister, *The Germans of Chicago*, 176; Jentz, "Turnvereins." On Bohemians, see Nolte, "Our Brothers across the Ocean," 17; McCarthy, "The Bohemians of Chicago," 24–25, 44, 46. On Swedes, see Beijbom, *Swedes in Chicago*, 270–71. On Poles, see Pienkos, *One Hundred Years Young*, 24–69. On the Irish, see Darby, "Emigrants at Play," 52–54. On Norwegians, see Lovoll, *A Century of Urban Life*, 133–35; Strand, *History of the Norwegians of Illinois*, 206–7. On Slovaks, see Droba, *Czech and Slovak Leaders*, 211. On Ukrainians, see Kuropas, "Ukrainian Chicago," 211–12; "Short Review of the Sitch Organization in the United States," *Sichovi Visty*, July 13, 1918, file: Ukrainian, CFLPS. On Greeks, see "Many Thrills in Store," *Greek Press*, January 29, 1931, CFLPS. On Italians, see Puzzo, "The Italians in Chicago," 66.

27. See, e.g., "The 13th District Turn Festival," *Abendpost*, January 28, 1890, file: German, CFLPS. On Lincoln and Douglas Parks, see "Chicago Turngemeinde," *Illinois Staats-Zeitung*, March 5, 1892, file: German, CFLPS; "Gymnastic Grounds in the Park," *Abendpost*, June 26, 1895, file: German, CFLPS; "Sherman Park," folder 20, box 4, MCD; "Sokol Rozvoj Inducted into the National Sokol Union," *Denní Hlasatel*, August 21, 1911, file: Bohemian, CFLPS; "Public Gymnastic Exhibition of the Chicago Sokol Union," July 3, 1922, file: Bohemian, CFLPS; "A Sokol Tournament in Douglas Park, *Denní Hlasatel*, July 11, 1922, file: Bohemian, CFLPS; Todd, Byron, and Vierow, *Public Recreation*, 166. On immigrant soccer in Chicago, see Gems, *The Windy City Wars*, 110, 129, 180–81; Logan, "The Rise of Early Chicago Soccer," 760–61. For quote on picnics, see Helen Hrachovska, "Some Experiences from American Sokol" (1931), 12, file 1, box 145, EBP. Also see "The Sokol Havlicek-Tyrs Prepares for an Excursion," *Denní Hlasatel*, August 25, 1922, file: Bohemian, CFLPS. On Jewish excursions, see Seman, *Jewish Community Life*, 71, 74, 89, 90; Cutler, *The Jews of Chicago*, 235–36. For Cwik quote, see Lillian Cwik, box 2, OHACP. For quote on appreciation of nature, see "Polish Falcons of America," *Dziennik Zjednoczenia*, March 21, 1928, file: Polish, CFLPS.

28. On Polish scouting in the United States, see Zachariasiewicz, "Organizational Structure of Polonia," 657–58; Scheidlinger, "A Comparative Study of the Boy Scout Movement," 746–48. On Polish troops in Chicago, see "Polish Scouting," *Narod Polski*, April 26, 1916, file: Polish, CFLPS; "Reporter's Notes," *Dzienni Chicgoski*, February 10, 1910, file: Polish, CFLPS; George Fields, "History of the Triangle Community Or-

ganization," file Jan-116, box 4, OHACP; Zglenicki, *Poles of Chicago*, 143; "St Michael's Boys' Club. Boy Scout Troop 750," folder 8, SBP. For quote on camping expedition, see "Polish Scouting," *Narod Polski*, April 26, 1916, file: Polish, CFLPS. On Jews, see *Sentinel*, September 8, 1911, file Jewish, CFLPS; Weinberg, "Jewish Youth in the Lawndale Community," file 3, box 140, EBP. On Bohemians, see "A Bohemian Troop of Boy Scouts," *Denní Hlasatel*, June 18, 1911, file: Bohemian, CFLPS. On Germans, see *Program and Chronological History*, 159, 161; M. H. Johnson, "Boys Clubs and the House of Happiness" (1930), file 4, box 155, EBP. On Greeks, see "Greek Boy Scouts of Chicago," *Saloniki*, September 19, 1914, file: Greek, CFLPS. On Hungarians, see "The Verhovay Fraternal Society," *Otthon*, August 23, 1935, file: Hungarian, CFLPS. On Ukrainians, see "The Ukrainian Catholic Boy and Girl Scouts of America," *Ukrainian Youth*, December 5, 1935, file: Ukrainian, CFLPS. On Italians, see "Activiites of the Garibaldi Institute," *Vita Nuova*, June 1927, file: Italian, CFLPS. On Chinese, see Todd, Byron, Vierow, *Private Recreation*, 93.

29. On Camp Sokol, "A Camp of Sokol Plzen," *Denní Hlasatel*, August 3, 1913, file: Bohemian, CFLPS; "Camp News of the Pilsen Sokol, *Denní Hlasatel*, August 2, 1922, FLPS; Shabowski, "Camp Sokol"; "Public Gymnastic Exhibition of the Pilsen Sokol," *Denní Hlasatel*, August 30, 1922, file: Bohemian, CFLPS; "Camp News of the Pilsen Sokol," *Denní Hlasatel*, August 2, 1922, file: Bohemian, CFLPS; "The Pilsen Sokol Gives Its Victorious Junior Team a Free Vacation," *Denní Hlasatel*, July 16, 1922, file: Bohemian, CFLPS; Cada, "Czechs of Chicago," 137. On the Harcerstwo Camp, see "Commemorate Pilsudski's Battle with the Reds Today," *CT*, August 4, 1935; Todd, Byron, Vierow, *Private Recreation*, 102. On the Illinois Turner Camp, see Jentz, "Turnvereins," 836; *50th Anniversary of the Socialer Turnverein*, 17, 22; "About the Illinois Turner Camp"; "Turner Society Wins the Association Prize," *Abendpost*, June 25, 1928, file: German, CFLPS; "Illinois Turnbezirk Eleventh Convention at Lincoln Turner Hall," Abendpost, April 28, 1919, file: German, CFLPS; "Turner Instructor Alfred Wild Dead after Long Illness," *Abendpost*, May 15, 1935, file: German, CFLPS. For quote on high rolling banks, see "Summer Let Down," *Lincoln Turner*, June 1931, in box 17/16, NHRC-R. On hiking, see *50th Anniversary of the Socialer Turnverein*, 15.

30. On Jewish camping, see Chubat, "On the Stage at Camp Kinderland," 6–7, 14; Magida and Magida, "Memories of Camp Interlaken"; Lebeson, "Recall to Life," 36; Seman, *Jewish Community Life*, 90–103; "On the Public Rostrum, *Daily Jewish Courier*, June 22, 1923, file: Jewish, CFLPS; "Register Your Children for the Children's Colony of the Workmen's Circle Schools," *Forward*, June 23, 1923, file: Jewish, CFLPS; "Camp Chi," *Chicago Hebrew Institute Observer*, 1928, file: Jewish, CFLPS; "Poale Zion Juniors Celebrate the Fourth at the Y.P.Z.A. Camp," *Sunday Jewish Courier*, July 10, 1927, file: Jewish, CFLPS; "My Work as a Counselor at Camp Chi," *Chicago Hebrew Institute*, 1929, file: Jewish, CFLPS. Zola, "Jewish Camping"; Sarna, "The Crucial Decade in Jewish Camping"; Isaacman, "Development of Jewish Camping." For quote, see S. Kirson Weinberg, "Jewish Youth in the Lawndale Community: A Sociological Study," file 4, box 140, EBP.

31. "Speech on Greek Schools," *Saloniki*, September 25, 1917, file: Greek, CFLPS.

32. On youth excursions by Poles, Germans, Italians, Scandinavians, French, and Czechs, see "The Polish National Alliance Youth Excursion to Poland," *Weekly Zgoda*,

February 26, 1931, file: Polish, CFLPS; "Let Us Send the Youth to Motherland," *Weekly Zgoda*, January 1, 1931, file: Polish, CFLPS. Also see "New Polish Enterprise," *Dziennik Chicagoski*, March 30, 1893, file: Polish, CFLPS; "Sokol Excursion to Homeland," *Denni Hlasatel*, September 27, 1906, file: Bohemian, CFLPS; "Those Whom the Heart Unites, the Sea Cannot Divide!," *Denni Hlasatel*, June 5, 1912, file: Bohemian, CFLPS; "Home Again," *Denni Hlasatel*, August 30, 1920, file: Bohemian, CFLPS; "Exchange of Students," *Svenska Tribunene-Nyheter*, September 11, 1929, file: Swedish, CFLPS; "To the Rhine," *Abendpost*, April 30, 1926, file: German, CFLPS; "Speech by John D. Dristas, March 25," *Saloniki-Greek Press*, March 29, 1934, file: Greek, CFLPS; Chebithes, *AHEPA and the Progress of Hellenism in America*, 129–30. For quote, see "Send Your Children to Poland for a Vacation," *Weekly Zgoda*, February 19, 1931, file: Polish, CFLPS.

33. On Anglo American views of women and sport, see Mrozek, *Sports and American Mentality*, 136–60. On immigrant women and sports, see Gems, "Sport and the Americanization of Ethnic Women in Chicago"; Harzig, "German-American Women in Chicago," 219; Harzig, "The Ethnic Female Public Sphere," 144–45. For quote on Lithuanian women, see "The Question of Women's Gymnastics Clubs," *Lietuva*, December 11, 1914, file: Lithuanian, CFLPS. For quote on tame lions, see "The Egg Will Teach the Chicken," *Dziennik Chicagoski*, February 18, 1896, file: Polish, CFLPS.

34. See Harzig, "German-American Women in Chicago," 219; Harzig, "The Ethnic Female Public Sphere," 144–45; "The Aurora Turnverein," *Der Westen: Frauen-Zeitung*, November 15 and 22, 1896, reprinted in Keil and Jentz, *German Workers in Chicago*, 163. On Sokols, see Nolte, " 'Every Czech a Sokol!,' " 265–88; also see Nolte, "Our Brothers across the Ocean," 26. On Polish women, see Maria Sielski, box 9, OHACP.

35. On the culture of the streets during the 1920s, see Cohen, *Making a New Deal*, 143–47; Diamond, *Mean Streets*, 65–118; Thrasher, *The Gang*, 394. On the development of a distinct culture among middle-class youth, see Fass, *The Damned and the Beautiful*.

36. Cohen, *Making a New Deal*; quote on 147.

37. Thrasher, *The Gang*, 3–78.

38. On mass culture, see Thrasher, *The Gang*, 98, 102–3. On green spaces, see Thrasher, *The Gang*, 116–46; for quotes, see 135, 116.

39. See Thrasher, *The Gang*, 138, 143, 164–70; for quotes see 165, 142–43. Also see, Francis Sweeney, "Remembrance of Boyhood," folder 5, box 148, EBP. For more on "jungles," see Anderson, *The Hobo*, 16–26.

40. For quotes, see Shaw, *The Jack-Roller*, 137, 121. On excursions see, "A Study of Non-Delinquents in a Delinquency Area" (1941), file 21, box 2, ASP; "Sammy La Monica," folder 5, box 136, EBP; Thrasher, *The Gang*, 168; "An Intensive Study of a Member of the Swan Street Gang," file 268 Addenda, file 1, EBP. For quote, see M. A. Rachwalski, box 8, OHACP.

41. On the importance that young people gave to urban green space, see Jablonsky, *Pride in the Jungle*, 109; Suttles, *The Social Order of the Slum*, 99–118; Gems, *The Windy City Wars*, 105–8. Thrasher, *The Gang*, 142–43.

42. On appropriation of parks, see Thrasher, *The Gang*, 142–43. On Mark White Square, see "Rowdies Reign in Park," *CT*, August 17, 1905. On North Side playground,

"Pelt Police with Tacks," *CT,* September 5, 1903. On Fulton Playground, see "Recreation in Chicago," file 12, box 200, EBP. On Raster Playground, see Recreation in Chicago," file 12, box 200, EBP. On park rules aimed at delinquents, see Osborn, "The Development of Recreation in the South Park System," 60.

43. On gangs and ethnic antagonism, see Riess, *City Games,* 145–46; Gems, *The Windy City Wars,* 106; Thrasher, *The Gang,* 195–97, 200. Also see, Howitt, *Let Them Call Me Rebel,* 6; Riess, "Ethnic Sports," 545; Riess, "Sports and the American Jew," 17–18; Asbury, "The Life, Times, and End of Dion O'Banion," 381; Cutler, "The Jews of Chicago," 157; "Gang of Polish Youths Attack Jews in Douglas Park," *Daily Jewish Courier,* June 3, 1919, file: Jewish, CFLPS; "Chicago Poles Prepared a Pogrom for Today; Police Will Not Permit It," *Sunday Jewish Courier,* June 8, 1919, file: Jewish, CFLPS; "Judge Suggests that Douglas Park Be Closed," *Daily Jewish Courier,* June 6, 1919, file: Jewish, CFLPS. For Miller quote, see "Chicago Poles Could Not Stage a Pogrom Yesterday," *Daily Jewish Courier,* June 9, 1919, file: Jewish, CFLPS. For quote on solidarity, see Thrasher, *The Gang,* 197.

44. Zorbaugh, *The Gold Coast and the Slum,* 31; "An Encounter on the North Side," *Svenska Nyheter,* July 17, 1904, file: Swedish, CFLPS. For quote on brigades, see Abbott, *The Tenements of Chicago,* 94.

45. Farrell, *Studs Lonigan;* quote on 624.

46. On the importance of neighborhood place ties to American-born ethnic youth, see Thrasher, *The Gang,* 327; Jablonsky, *Pride in the Jungle,* 109; also see Suttles, *The Social Order of the Slum,* 3–9. On interethnic gangs, see Gems, "The Neighborhood Athletic Club," 37–38; Barrett and Roediger, "The Irish and the 'Americanization' of the 'New Immigrants,'" 14; Edward Ross Scribano, "The 'Back O' the Yards' Gangs" (1931), file 1, box 162, EBP; Thrasher, *The Gang,* 327; Walter F. Mitchell, "A Sociological Study of a Gang" (1933), file 6, box 159, EBP. For quote on Americanization, see Thrasher, *The Gang,* 217. Girls and young women also sometimes formed interethnic gangs. See for instance, Shaw, *Delinquency Areas,* 149–51.

47. Shiffman, "Ethnic Competitors in Studs Lonigan," 67–79.

48. On Gaelic Park, see "Season Opens at New Gaelic Field," *CT,* May 4, 1908; "'Twas a Big Day for the Irish," *CT,* January 24, 1916; "Irish-Americans to Hold Annual Picnic Tomorrow," *CT,* August 31, 1928; Edward Ross Scribano, "The 'Back O' the Yards' Gangs" (1931), file 1, box 162, EBP; Paul G. Cressey, "A Study of Gaelic Park," file 7, box 130, EBP; "Staged Irishmen Barred at Fete," *CT,* July 29, 1912. Also see Bachin, *Building the South Side,* 163; White, *Remembering Ahanagran,* 199–204. On the Feis, see Hellsmuth, "Feis."

49. Paul G. Cressey, "A Study of Gaelic Park," file 7, box 130, EBP.

50. Ibid. Thrasher, *The Gang,* 194–95.

51. On gangs and masculinity, see Diamond, *Mean Streets,* 32–39.

52. For statistics, see "Girls Compose One-Tenth of School Gangs," *CT,* April 16, 1927. On female gangs, also see Jean C. Rosenbluth, "An Attempt to Study Child Life at the Russell Square Field House," 5–6, file 2, box 149, EBP; Thrasher, *The Gang,* 224–29; Meyerowitz, *Women Adrift,* 107–08. On female delinquency, see Odem, *Delinquent Daughters.* Paul G. Cressey, "A Study of Gaelic Park," file 7, box 130, EBP. On working-class femininity, see Peiss, *Cheap Amusements;* Meyerowitz, *Women*

*Adrift*, 92–116. For quote from Addams, see Addams, *The Spirit of Youth and the City Streets*, 8.

53. For the percentage of mixed-race gangs, see Thrasher, *The Gang*, 191. On ethnically mixed neighborhoods, see Pacyga, "Chicago's Ethnic Neighborhoods," 606. On racial segregation in housing, see Philpott, *The Slum and the Ghetto*, 111–208; Arredondo, *Mexican Chicago*, 55–58; Moy, "The Chinese in Chicago," 383, 388. On the recreation of Chinese youth, see Soong, "A Survey of the Education of Chinese Children in Chicago" (Ph.D. diss., University of Chicago, 1931), 24, 27, 71, 86, 88–89. On Mexican gangs and SACs, see Baur, "Delinquency among Mexican Boys in South Chicago"; also see Innis-Jiménez, "Organizing for Fun"; Slayton, *Back of the Yards*, 181.

54. Farrell, *Studs Lonigan*; quote on 196.

55. Roediger, *The Wages of Whiteness*; Jacobson, *Whiteness of a Different Color*; Barrett and Roediger, "The Irish and the 'Americanization' of the 'New Immigrants' "; Guglielmo, *White on Arrival*.


Chapter 4

1. A. Wilberforce Williams, "Keep Healthy," *CD-L*, August 2, 1913.

2. On nineteenth-century black life, see Spear, *Black Chicago*, 5–7; Philpott, *The Slum and the Ghetto*, 116; Tuttle, *Race Riot*, 160–61; Reed, *Black Chicago's First Century*, 241–66.

3. On use of Oswald's Grove, see, e.g., "The Colored Waiters," *CT*, August 23, 1888; "Get Your Ticket and Avoid the Rush," *Illinois Record*, August 20, 1898; "First=Annual=Picnic," *Illinois Record*, August 27, 1898. For quote on ice cream, see "Colored Pythian Knights Picnic," *CT*, September 11, 1888.

4. On the emergence of the color line, see Spear, *Black Chicago*, 11–27; Philpott, *The Slum and the Ghetto*, 113–45; Grossman, *Land of Hope*, 123–27. On housing conditions and environmental hazards, see "Filthy Chicago," *Illinois Record*, September 3, 1898; Chicago Commission on Race Relations, *The Negro in Chicago*, 152–230; Tuttle, *Race Riot*, 157–83; Philpott, *The Slum and the Ghetto*, 156–60, 180, 248–50; Grossman, *Land of Hope*, 127, 133–39, 145, 166; Washington, *Packing Them In*, 129–52. On prostitution, see Baldwin, *Chicago's New Negroes*, 26; Bachin, *Building the South Side*, 250, 254–60; Diamond, *Mean Streets*, 45–46, 50–53, 80–83; Spear, *Black Chicago*, 25; Mumford, *Interzones*, 23–35.

5. On black migration to Chicago during World War I, see Grossman, *Land of Hope*, 13–119. On population, see Philpott, *The Slum and the Ghetto*, 116, fig. 3.

6. See Grossman, *Land Of Hope*, 181–207.

7. On black pastors' rejection of leisure, see Du Bois, "The Problem of Amusement"; Wright, "Social Work and Influence of the Negro Church," 92. On concern about leisure in black Chicago, see Grossman *Land of Hope*, 130–32, 140–41; Baldwin, *Chicago's New Negroes*, 28–31, 51, 99, 102–08, 129–31; Williams, "Social Bonds in the 'Black Belt' of Chicago," 40. On the Stroll, see Grossman, *Land of Hope*, 86, 117, 131–32; Bachin, *Building the South Side*, 247–97; Baldwin, *Chicago's New Negroes*, 21–52. For quote, see Hughes, *Big Sea: An Autobiography*, 33.

8. "Spring," *CD-L*, May 16, 1914. On use of green space, see, e.g., Washington Intercollegiate Club of Chicago, *The Negro in Chicago*, 261; "Walter's A.M.E. Church," *CD-L*, July 20, 1912; "With the Picknickers," *CD-L*, July 27, 1912; "Outing for Children," *CD-L*, June 13, 1914; and "St. Luke M.E. Church," *CD-L*, August 1. 1914; "Big Revival in Chicago Baseball," *CD-L*, March 1, 1919; "Frederick Douglass Center," *CD-L*, July 6, 1912; "The Clotee Scott Settlement," *CD-L*, January 23, 1915; "YMCA News," *CD-L*, June 15, 1918; "YMCA News," *CD-L*, August 24, 1918; "YMCA News," *CD-L*, August 31, 1918; and "Leaves for Vacation Camp," *CD-L*, July 6, 1918; "Boy Scouts," *CD-L*, June 8, 1912; "Boy Scout Notes," *CD-L*, June 29, 1918.

9. See Tuttle, *Race Riot*, 156–83; Philpott, *The Slum and the Ghetto*, 162–80; Pacyga, *"Chicago's 1919 Race Riot,"* 204–5; and Spear, *Black Chicago*, 147–50.

10. On gangs, SACs, and ethnic antagonism, see Thrasher, *The Gang*, 200; Riess, *City Games*, 145–46; Gems, *The Windy City Wars*, 106.

11. On gang violence and the parks, see Chicago Commission on Race Relations, *The Negro in Chicago*, 288–95; Spear, *Black Chicago*, 206; Diamond, *Mean Streets*, 47–48; Fisher, "African Americans, Outdoor Recreation, and the 1919 Chicago Race Riot," 67–68; McCammack, "Recovering Green in Bronzeville," 105–14. For quote, see "Race Girls Brutally Assaulted by Whites in Washington Park," *CD-L*, June 8, 1918.

12. For quote on Lake Michigan waters, see Bowen, *The Colored People of Chicago*, 274. For material on projectile-throwing whites, see Chicago Commission on Race Relations, *The Negro in Chicago*, 286–88. For quote on polluting the water, see "Color Line Drawn at Bathing Beach," *CD-L*, August 28, 1915. For quote on white ruffians, see "Aldermen Have Protection Placed to Preserve Order at Beaches," *CD-L*, July 27, 1918. Also see "White Boys Start Trouble on Beach," *CD-L*, August 5, 1916; "Our Bathing Beaches," *CD-L*, September 2, 1916.

13. On the tension in parks and beaches in 1919, see Tuttle, *Race Riot*, 235–39; Diamond, *Mean Streets*, 19–20; Spear, *Black Chicago*, 206; Chicago Commission on Race Relations, *The Negro in Chicago*, 289–90. On Carter Playground, see Chicago Commission on Race Relations, *The Negro in Chicago*, 283; also see "Boys Fight on South Side," *CD-L*, June 7, 1919. For quotes, see "Ruffianism in the Parks," *CD-L*, July 12, 1919.

14. For quote on Beutner Playground, see Chicago Commission on Race Relations, *The Negro in Chicago*, 277. For quote from aldermen, see "Aldermen Have Protection Placed to Preserve Order at Beaches," *CD-L*, July 27, 1918. For statistics on attendance, see Chicago Commission on Race Relations, *The Negro in Chicago*, 275, fig. 17. For lifeguard and dunking, see "Color Line Drawn at Bathing Beach," *CD-L*, August 28, 1915. On police and parks, also see Chicago Commission on Race Relations, *The Negro in Chicago*, 277–78; Spear, *Black Chicago*, 205. For attempted rape, see "Race Girls Brutally Assaulted by Whites in Washington Park," *CD-L*, June 8, 1918. On racial exclusion in the park, see also Chicago Playgrounds and Park Centers," *City Club Bulletin* 2 (March 4, 1908): 10. On segregation and public pools, see Wiltse, *Contested Waters*, 63–65, 186–87.

15. On the plan to close Beutner and create a new park, see Special Park Commission, *Annual Report*, 6; Chicago Commission on Race Relations, *The Negro in Chicago*, 277.

16. On the emergence of segregation in the Cook County Baseball League, see Washington Intercollegiate Club of Chicago, *The Negro in Chicago*, 261; "Color Line Drawn Again," *CD-L*, June 15, 1912. On segregation in the Boy Scouts and the YMCA and YWCA, see Philpott, *The Slum and the Ghetto*, 307. On separate Mexican and Asian troops, see C. H. Humphrey, "Project Study" (1931), file 6, box 180, EBP. For Prairie Club quote, see *Social Service Directory*, 126.

17. On carrying weapons in picnic baskets during the Fourth of July, see Taylor, "Chicago in the Nation's Race Strife," 695. On the melee, see Tuttle, *Race Riot*, 5–6.

18. Tuttle, *Race Riot*, 3–5.

19. Ibid., 6–10.

20. On the ensuing events, see Chicago Commission on Race Relations, *The Negro in Chicago*, 1–52; and Tuttle, *Race Riot*, 32–66.

21. Travis, *An Autobiography of Black Chicago*, 26.

22. On clubs, see "In Days of Old," *Illinois Record*, July 2, 1898; "Notice," *Illinois Record*, October 8, 1898; Reed, *Black Chicago's First Century*, 273; "Chicago Recreation and Sports," file 3, box 40, IWPN. See also "News in Brief," *Illinois Record*, November 19, 1998; "Chicago Weekly Letters," August 10, 1998. On the West Michigan Resort and other prewar black resorts in the Midwest, see Foster, "In the Face of 'Jim Crow,'" 138–39. For quote on breathing spot, see "Vacation Time," *CD-L*, May 3, 1913. For quote on sentiment, see "Last Girl Cottager Riots in Sentiment," *CD-L*, September 14, 1912. For quote on Arcadia, see "The West Michigan Resort," *CD-L*, July 22, 1911.

23. On white trade sign, see "And This Is Civilization," *CD-L*, September 7, 1929. On resorts, see, e.g., "A. L. Jackson Wins Jim Crow Suit against Resort Owner," *CD-N*, December 31, 1932. For quote, see the Associated Negro Press, *Annual Survey, December 30, 1925*, in Claude A. Barnett Papers, Part 1: Associated Negro Press Releases, 1928–1964, Series A, Chicago Historical Society, Chicago, Ill.

24. For quote from Du Bois, see Du Bois, "Hopkinsville, Chicago, and Idlewild," 158–60. On Idlewild, see Wilson, "Idlewild," 33–37; Wilson and Walker, *Black Eden*; Foster, "In the Face of 'Jim Crow,'" 138; Fisher, "African Americans, Outdoor Recreation, and the 1919 Chicago Race Riot," 74; and McCammack, "Recovering Green in Bronzeville," 159–190. The second-most-popular vacation destination for black Chicago was Ivanhoe, in rural Wisconsin. On Ivanhoe, see Gonzales, "A Black Community in Wisconsin."

25. On black scouting, see, e.g., "Boy Scout News," *CD-N*, October 31, 1925; "Boy Scout News," *CD-N*, November 21, 1925; "Girl Scout Notes," *CD-L*, July 14, 1934; "Camping Solves Many Hot Weather Problems," *CD-L*, July 15, 1939. Also see Todd, Byron, and Vierow, *Private Recreation*, 77. For quote on hike to dunes, see "Boy Scout News," *CD-L*, November 7, 1925. On Y trips and Camp Wabash, see "Y.M.C.A. News," *CD-L*, July 10, 1920; "YWCA," *CD-L*, August 7, 1920; "YMCA," *CD-L*, May 30, 1925; "Camp Wabash News," *CD-L*, July 27, 1926. For quote on Camp Wabash, see "Defender Newsboys to Get Free Vacation Trip," *CD-L*, July 7, 1934. On efforts by black organizations to get children back to nature, see Fisher, "African Americans, Outdoor Recreation, and the 1919 Chicago Race Riot," 70–71, 74–75; and McCammack, "Recovering Green in Bronzeville," 195–222.

26. For recommendation, see Chicago Commission on Race Relations, *The Negro in Chicago*. For quote from director of Fuller Park, see Chicago Commission on Race Relations, *The Negro in Chicago*, 295. On Armour Square, see Chicago Commission on Race Relations, *The Negro in Chicago*, 294. For quote from Callahan, see Chicago Commission on Race Relations, *The Negro in Chicago*, 295. Also see Osborn, "The Development of Recreation in the South Park System," 108, 115, 117.

27. For quote on rock, see Chicago Commission on Race Relations, *The Negro in Chicago*, 286. For trouble at beaches, also see "Trouble Point at 39th Street Beach," *CD-N*, July 9, 1921; "Breeding Trouble," *CD-L*, July 18, 1925; "What the People Say," *CD-N*, August 10, 1929; "Colored Leaders Ask Equal Rights at City Beaches," *CT-L*, August 12, 1929; "Bathing at Jackson Park," *CD-N*, September 1, 1928; "No Jim Crow Beach," *CD-N*, August 8, 1931. On Spencer Castle, see "Chicago 'Lily-Whites' Open Fight on Oakwood Bathing Beach Site," *CD-L*, May 6, 1933; and "Hyde Park Astir over Race Mixing at Beach," *CD-L*, May 20, 1933. On Artman, see "On Guard White Voters," flyer, Charles E. Merriam Papers, box 103, folder 2, University of Chicago, quoted in Guglielmo, *White on Arrival*, 101. On the fence, see Drake and Clayton, *Black Metropolis*, 105. For quote on preventing race riot, see "Police Object to Mixing of Race on Beach; Arrest 18," *CD-L*, July 14, 1934. For quote on singing, see "End Battle over Jim Crow Beach Party," *CD-N*, December 22, 1934. On tension in the parks after the 1919 riot, see Fisher, "African Americans, Outdoor Recreation, and the 1919 Chicago Race Riot," 72–74; and McCammack, "Recovering Green in Bronzeville," 238–46.

28. On equal access, see "Colored Leaders Ask Equal Rights at City Beaches," *CT-L*, 12 August 1929; "Bathing at Jackson Park," *CD-N*, September 1, 1928; "No Jim Crow Beach," *CD-N*, August, 8 1931; "An Open Letter to Bathers," *CD-L*, June 10, 1933; "Young Gangster Hoodlums," *CD-N*, September 2, 1939.

29. For quote on sunshine, see "A Park for South Side," *CD-L*, February 5, 1927. For quote on moving colored life, see Bond, "The Chicago Board of Education," 211. The health survey results are reported in Charles S. Johnson, *The Negro in American Civilization*, 306. For more on the inadequacies of parks for blacks in Chicago, see "Recreation," Special Subject Files, 1912–1939, Series A, NAACPR; Frazier, *Recreation and Amusement*, 101–3; Daniel E. Day and Sherman Briscoe, "Is the South Side Doomed?," *CD-L*, July 29, 1939.

30. On 1908 request, see Special Park Commission, *Annual Report*, 6. On push for parks, see "Playground, Park Assured South Side," *CD-L*, May 23, 1925; "Slight Prospect of Playgrounds," *CD-L*, July 24, 1926. On Madden Park, see "Name Park in Honor of Late Martin B. Madden," *CD-N*, May 5, 1928; "Build Madden Park Now, Plea of Urban League," *CD-L*, December 13, 1931; "Season is Open at Madden Park," *CD-L*, May 6, 1933; "Madden Park Plans 'Open House' Week," *CD-L*, June 10, 1933; "New Park under Construction," *CD-N*, July 4, 1936. On local residents involvement in cleaning up and landscaping the park, see "New Park Leads Near South Side in Beauty Drive," *CD-L*, August 21, 1932; "200 Jobless Aid in Dressing up South Park Way," *CD-L*, October 30, 1932. On Madden Park, see Fisher, "African Americans, Outdoor Recreation, and the 1919 Chicago Race Riot," 75; and McCammack, "Recovering Green in Bronzeville," 137–40, 260–64.

31. On Farrell's work and the Irish-American exodus, see Fanning and Skerrett, "James T. Farrell and Washington Park." On Booker T. Washington Park, see Bontemps and Conroy, *They Seek a City*, 151; Frazier, *Recreation and Amusement*, 102. For quotes on Washington Park, see Drake and Clayton, *Black Metropolis*, 603, 380. On black use of Washington Park, see Fisher, "African Americans, Outdoor Recreation, and the 1919 Chicago Race Riot," 75–76; and McCammack, "Recovering Green in Bronzeville," 114–30.

32. On the race riot and whiteness, see Guglielmo, *White on Arrival*, 42–43; Diamond, *Mean Streets*, 25–26; Barrett and Roediger, "The Irish and the 'Americanization' of the 'New Immigrants,' " 7–16; Hirsch, "E Pluribus Duo?," 8–20, 35. On African Americans and the reimagination of "the race" during this period, see Baldwin, *Chicago's New Negroes*, 14–15.

33. On "Afro-Saxons," see Reed. *"All the World Is Here!,"* xiv. On racial uplift, see, Gaines, *Uplifting the Race*; Mitchell, *Righteous Propagation*. On the assimilationist position of elite black Chicagoans, see in particular Spear, *Black Chicago*, 51–89. On African Americans and the exposition, see Rudwick and Meier, "Black Man in the 'White City' "; Massa, "Black Women in the 'White City' "; Paddon and Turner, "African Americans and the World's Columbian Exposition"; Ballard, "A People without a Nation"; Rydell, "Editor's Introduction"; and Reed, *"All the World Is Here!"* For quote on progress, see Frederick Douglass, "Frederick Douglass's Speech at Colored American Day (August 25, 1893)," reprinted in Reed, *"All the World Is Here!,"* 194. In a pamphlet called *The Reason Why the Colored American Is Not in the World's Columbian Exposition,* Douglass went further, lamenting as "if to shame the Negro, the Dahomians are also here to exhibit the Negro as a repulsive savage." See Wells, Douglass, Penn, and Barnett, *The Reason Why the Colored American Is Not in the World's Columbian Exposition*, 9.

34. On this shift, see Spear, *Black Chicago*, 51–89.

35. On problems of black southern pastoralism, see e.g., Dixon, *Ride Out the Wilderness*, 2; Bennett, "Anti-Pastoralism, Frederick Douglass, and the Nature of Slavery"; Griffin, *"Who Set You Flowin'?"*; Outka, *Race and Nature*, 171–200; Smith, *African American Environmental Thought*, 149–54. On anti-environmental black thought, see Glave, *Rooted in the Earth*, 5–6. On how this history of violence and exploitation on the land might influence African American outdoor recreation, see White, "Black Women and the Wilderness." Despite recognizing the problems of black southern pastoralism, U.S. environmental historians and ecocritics have focused their attention on strained nostalgia for southern landscapes at the expense of exploring how alienation could displace nostalgia onto the Caribbean (in particular Haiti) and Africa. For three otherwise excellent works in this vein, see Outka, *Race and Nature*, 171–200; Smith, *African American Environmental Thought*, 149–54; and McCammack, "Recovering Green in Bronzeville," 21, 90, 157, 250–51. On the importance of what we might call the African (and Caribbean) pastoral to Jazz Age African Americans, see Corbould, *Becoming African Americans*; Ladino, *Reclaiming Nostalgia*, 80–81.

36. On Garvey and the UNIA, see Grant, *Negro with a Hat*. On Garvey and his followers' views of Africa, see Corbould, *Becoming African Americans*, 18–56. On Gar-

vey and Chicago, see Spear, *Black Chicago*, 193–97; Drake and Cayton, *Black Metropolis*, 752; Grossman, *Land of Hope*, 264; Baldwin, *Chicago's New Negroes*, 41. For quote on flag, see Universal Negro Improvement Association and McGuire, *Universal Black Men Catechism*, 37, as quoted in Martin, *Race First*, 45.

37. Corbould, *Becoming African Americans*; quote on 214.

38. On Harlem and the arts, an excellent starting place is Lewis, *When Harlem Was in Vogue*. On the Chicago "renaissance" in the arts, see Bone and Courage, *The Muse in Bronzeville*; Knupfer, *The Chicago Black Renaissance and Women's Activism*; Reed, *The Rise of Chicago's Black Metropolis*, 201–8; Tracy, *Writers of the Black Chicago Renaissance*. On Farrow and Locke, see Bone and Courage, *The Muse in Bronzeville*, 69–71. Johnson, "Ethiopia," 42.

39. On Woodson, see Goggin, *Carter G. Woodson*; Dagbovie, *The Early Black History Movement*. On Woodson and Africa, see Corbould, *Becoming African Americans*, 88–128. On Woodson's views of Africa, see Woodson, *The Negro in Our History*, 1–14; Woodson, *African Myths and Proverbs*; Woodson and Jones, *African Heroes and Heroines*.

40. Baldwin, *Chicago's New Negroes*, 53–90. On *Trader Horn*, see Erb, *Tracking King Kong*, 93–101. On *Native Son* and black environmental thought, see Smith, *African American Environmental Thought*, 182–84. See Wright, *Native Son*; quote on 36.

41. See "King Tut Was Married at 5; Dead at 15: Egypt's Ruler Proven to Be Mere Boy," *CD-N*, December 5, 1925; "First Photos of King Tut Arrive in United States," *CD-N*, March 6, 1926; "Tut-Ankh-Amen Known as First Real Booker T.," *CD-N*, March 10, 1923. On the *Defender*, see Ottley, *The Lonely Warrior*; Grossman, *Land of Hope*, 74–89; Stovall, "The *Chicago Defender* in the Progressive Era," 166. On the *Defender* and imagined racial community, see Baldwin, *Chicago's New Negroes*, 14.

42. On camping in national parks and nationalism, see Belasco, *Americans on the Road*, 92–103; Shaffer, *See America First*, 225–41. For quotes, see Du Bois, "Hopkinsville, Chicago, and Idlewild," 159–60.

43. On Egyptian pageants, see Attwell, "Recreation for Colored America," 162.

44. On *O, Sing a New Song*, see "Greatest Pageant in the History of the Race Was Staged Saturday," *CD-N*, September 1, 1934; "Africans to Aid Pageant," *CD-N*, August 11, 1934; "Expect 75,000 to See Negro Pageant Tonight," *CT*, August 25, 1934; "O, Sing a New Song Spectacle Greatest in History," *CD-N*, September 1, 1934; Ford, *Soldier Field*, 159–64. On the size of the cast in *The Star of Ethiopia*, see Krasner, *A Beautiful Pageant*, 81–96.

45. Unfortunately, no script survives. For the plot, see "Greatest Pageant in the History of the Race Was Staged Saturday," *CD-N*, September 1, 1934; "Expect 75,000 to See Negro Pageant Tonight," *CT*, August 25, 1934; "O, Sing a New Song Spectacle Greatest in History," *CD-N*, September 1, 1934; Ford, *Soldier Field*, 159–64.

46. On the parade and picnic, see Rutkoff and Scott, "Pinkster in Chicago"; Ottley, *The Lonely Warrior*, 351–54. On the Billiken, see Leach, *Land of Desire*, 230. For quote on holidays, see Rutkoff and Scott, "Pinkster in Chicago," 316. On the 1933 parade, see "50,000 Hail the Chicago Defender Billikens," *CD-N*, August 26, 1933.

47. On Nigerians, see "African Royalty Did Their Part for Picnic," *CD-N*, August 26, 1933. On Darkest Africa exhibit and the 1933 Chicago World's Fair, see Rydell,

*World of Fairs*, 84, 167; Ganz, *The 1933 Chicago World's Fair*, 112. For quote on great day, see "50,000 Hail the Chicago Defender Billikens," *CD-N*, August 26, 1933.

48. Rutkoff and Scott, "Pinkster in Chicago," 321. Frank Marshall Davis, "Washington Park, Chicago" (1937), in Davis, *Black Moods*, 73.

49. On this distinction in the context of consumer culture, see Cohen, *Making a New Deal*, 156. On anti-European racism, see for instance Jacobson, *Whiteness of a Different Color*, 39–90; Guglielmo, *White on Arrival*, 59–92.

50. On the effect of the Great Depression on blacks, see Cohen, *Making a New Deal*, 215, 242; Deutsch, "Great Depression."

51. On Washington Park and communists, see Drake and Clayton, *Black Metropolis*, 603; Drake, *Churches and Voluntary Associations* (Chicago: Works Progress Administration, 1940), 3; Wright, *Black Boy (American Hunger)*, 294–97.


## Chapter 5

1. See Avrich, *The Haymarket Tragedy*, 186–87; Schneirov, *Labor and Urban Politics*, 183–200; Green, *Death in the Haymarket*, 164. For quote, see Calmer, *Labor Agitator*, 79.

2. Foner and Roediger, *Our Own Time*. Otormsky, "Machines and Men," *Molodaya Rus,* December 31, 1915, file: Russian, CFLPS.

3. Cronon, *Nature's Metropolis*.

4. For quote, see Cronon, *Nature's Metropolis*, 256–57.

5. For quote, see "'The Jungle' and the Way Out."

6. On the changing nature of work in nineteenth-century Chicago, see Schneirov, *Labor and Urban Politics,* 17–24, 32–33; Jentz and Schneirov, *Chicago in the Age of Capital*, 13–51. On work hours, see Daniels, *The Work Ethic in Industrial America*, 106.

7. On class formation, see Thompson, *The Making of the English Working Class*. On class formation in Chicago specifically, see Schneirov, *Labor and Urban Politics,* 17–40. On divisions in Chicago, see Schneirov, *Labor and Urban Politics,* 25–29.

8. Schneirov, *Labor and Urban Politics,* 33–35; Montgomery, *Beyond Equality*, 306–10; Haverty-Stacke, *America's Forgotten Holiday*, 15–16; "The Eight-Hour Movement," *CT,* May 2, 1867; "On the Lake Shore," *CT*, May 2, 1867.

9. Schneirov, *Labor and Urban Politics*, 17–46; Jentz and Schneirov, *Chicago in the Age of Capital*, 53–116.

10. Schneirov, *Labor and Urban Politics*, 69–76, 81–94; Jentz and Schneirov, *Chicago in the Age of Capital*, 157–64; Nelson, *Beyond the Martyrs*, 9–76; Avrich, *The Haymarket Tragedy*, 26–52.

11. Avrich, *The Haymarket Tragedy*, 55–177; Nelson, *Beyond the Martyrs*, 9–51; Schneirov, *Labor and Urban Politics*, 173–79.

12. Schneirov, *Labor and Urban Politics*, 76–81, 99–135. On the culture of the Knights, see Weir, *Beyond Labor's Veil*.

13. On the origins of Ogden's Grove, see Duis, *The Saloon*, 154. For quote, see Flinn and Wilkie, *History of the Chicago Police*, 249.

14. "Knights of Labor: A Monster Demonstration by the Local Trade and Labor Organizations," *CT*, September 8, 1886; Messer-Kruse, *The Haymarket Conspiracy*, 152–53. On other trade union parades to Ogden's Grove, see "Very Successful," *CT*, August 22, 1881; "The Trade-Unions: Second Annual Picnic at Ogden Grove," *CT*, August 25, 1879; "Men of Muscle," *CT*, July 28, 1884; "The Trade-and-Labor Demonstration at Ogden Grove," *CT*, July 5, 1882; "Labor's Holiday: The Arrangements for Monday's Great Demonstration," *CT*, September 6, 1885.

15. See "The Red Flag," *CT*, June 23, 1879; "The Picnic," *CT*, June 16, 1878; "The Socialists," *CT*, September 8, 1879; "Anarchists in Array, *CT*, July 27, 1885; "Eight-Hour Law: The Ogden's Demonstration," *CT*, July 5, 1879; "A Picnic and Jubilee: Socialists Enjoy a Day of Recreation," *CT*, June 8, 1885; "The Last Ditch: A Dismal Failure Was the Communist Picnic Yesterday," *CT*, June 13, 1881; Nelson, *Beyond the Martyrs*, 127–52.

16. "The Red Flag," *CT*, June 23, 1879; "Very Successful," *CT*, August 22, 1881; "The Trade-Unions: Second Annual Picnic at Ogden Grove," *CT*, August 25, 1879; "The Socialists," *CT*, September 8, 1879; "The Socialists: Second Day's Picnic and Demonstration," *CT*, July 6, 1879; "The Socialists; Their Three–Days' Picnic Brought to a Close," *CT*, July 7, 1879; "Men of Muscle," *CT*, July 28, 1884; Nelson, *Beyond the Martyrs*, 127–52. For quote, see "The Desplaines Hall Workers Club Picnics in Ogden's Grove," *Der Western*, July 22, 1869, quoted in Keil and Jentz, *German Workers in Chicago*, 207, 209.

17. On labor republicanism, the Paris Commune, and the French Revolution, see Schneirov, *Labor and Urban Politics*, 3, 4, 9–10, 55, 175–76, 236–40, 298–99. On Schwab, see Michael Schwab, "Autobiography of Michael Schwab," 135–74; quote on 135; also see Avrich, *The Haymarket Tragedy*, 87–88.

18. "Knights of Labor: A Monster Demonstration by the Local Trade and Labor Organizations," *CT*, September 8, 1886; "The Red Flag," *CT*, June 23, 1879; "The Trade-Unions: Second Annual Picnic at Ogden Grove," *CT*, August 25, 1879; "The Socialists," *CT*, September 8, 1879; "The Communists," *CT*, August 20, 1877; "The Socialists; Their Three–Days' Picnic Brought to a Close," *CT*, July 7, 1879; "The Wage-Workers: Address of Ira Steward, of Boston, to the Trades-Unions of this City," *CT*, July 10, 1879; "A Picnic and Jubilee: Socialists Enjoy a Day of Recreation," *CT*, June 8, 1885; "Socialistic Array," *CT*, June 30, 1884; "The Trade-and-Labor Demonstration at Ogden Grove," *CT*, July 5, 1882; "The Last Ditch: A Dismal Failure Was the Communist Picnic Yesterday," *CT*, June 13, 1881. For quote on government of workingmen, see "The Socialists; Their Three-Days' Picnic Brought to a Close," *CT*, July 7, 1879. For quote on private property, see "A Picnic and Jubilee: Socialists Enjoy a Day of Recreation," *CT*, June 8, 1885.

19. On the popularity of the eight-hour-day movement and the response of the anarchists, see Schneirov, *Labor and Urban Politics*, 177–78, 183–200; Avrich, *The Haymarket Tragedy*, 181–96; Nelson, *Beyond the Martyrs*, 180–81.

20. On Gilded Age working-class recreation, see for instance Keil and Jentz, *German Workers in Chicago*, 151–69, 175–81, 203–20, 276–90; Barrett, *The Irish Way*, 157–94; Nelson, *Beyond the Martyrs*, 127–52; Ensslen, "German-American Working-Class

Saloons"; Heiss, "Popular and Working-Class German Theater"; Wagner, "Turner Societies and the Socialist Tradition."

21. On the full lyrics of the "Eight-Hour Song," see Foner, *American Labor Songs of the Nineteenth Century*, 581–82.

22. Avrich, *The Haymarket Tragedy*, 197–214; Green, *Death in the Haymarket*, 174–91.

23. Avrich, *The Haymarket Tragedy*, 215–93; Green, *Death in the Haymarket*, 192–230. Schwab, it should be noted, later had his sentence commuted to life in prison and thus escaped the gallows.

24. On the history of May Day, see Haverty-Stacke, *America's Forgotten Holiday*; Kruse, "The Flag of May Day"; Walter Lenfersiek, "May Day," Socialist Party (U.S.), Miscellaneous Pamphlets on May Day, CHS.

25. On the eight-hour struggle of the 1890s, see Schneirov, *Labor and Urban Politics*, 304–7. On efforts to create distance, see Gompers, *Seventy Years of Life and Labor*, 294. On the tension between May Day and Labor Day, see Kazin and Ross, "America's Labor Day," 1303–5; Haverty-Stacke, *America's Forgotten Holiday*, 44–72.

26. See also "Labor-Day Parade," *CT*, May 2, 1890; "The Eight Hour Demonstration," *CT*, May 2, 1890; "Speeches at the Lake-Front," *CT*, May 2, 1890; "Dress Parade of Labor," *CT*, September 5, 1899.

27. See Lindsey, *The Pullman Strike*, 47–48, 56; Pesavento, "Sport and Recreation in the Pullman Experiment," 38–62; Riess, *City Games*, 83–84; Gems, "Welfare Capitalism and Blue-Collar Sport," 44–45.

28. On employers' increasing cognizance of the link between outdoor recreation and productivity, see Brandes, *American Welfare Capitalism*, 76–77; Weller, "Recreation in Industries," 250–52; Aron, *Working at Play*, 202.

29. On the Eastland, see Hilton, *Eastland*. For quote on "mother earth," see "'Twas to Be a Whale of a Big Club Picnic," *CT*, July 25, 1915.

30. On aggressive foremen, see "Forced on Boat Through Fear of Jobs, Many Say," CT, July 27, 1915. For quote, see "'Twas to Be a Whale of a Big Club Picnic," *CT*, July 25, 1915. For photos from previous trips, see the images in Wachholz, *The Eastland Disaster*.

31. On CFL resistance, see Riess, *City Games*, 140; Bachin, *Building the South Side*, 166. For quote on children, see *Chicago Examiner*, November 4, 1905, quoted in Bachin, *Building the South Side*, 166.

32. See Keiser, "John Fitzpatrick"; McKillen, "Chicago Federation of Labor"; Foner, *History of the Labor Movement*, 259–63.

33. On environmental justice and settlement house workers, see Gottlieb, *Forcing the Spring*, 98–106; Pellow, *Garbage Wars*, 21–39; Washington, *Packing Them In*, 85–96.

34. On the Labor Party, see Keiser, "John Fitzpatrick"; McKillen, *Chicago Labor*, 126–192; McKillen, "Chicago Federation of Labor," 225–27; Montgomery, "The Farmer-Labor Party," 73–82; "Labor's 14 Points," *New Majority*, January 11, 1919. On Fitzpatrick's local campaign platform, see "Labor Forms a Party; Urges Many Reforms," *CT*, December 30, 1918.

35. For quotes on dunes, see Mather, "Report on the Proposed San Dunes National Park, Indiana," 89, 90.

36. On competition with employers, see "Recreational Activities of Labor Organizations," *Monthly Labor Review*. On the WTUL, see "Recreational Activities of Labor Organizations," 900; "Women's Trade Union League in Conference," *New Majority*, September 13, 1919; "Women's Trade Union League Camp Opens," *Federation News*, June 9, 1928. For quote, see Nestor, *Woman's Labor Leader*, 270.

37. On working-class gardening, see "Summer Invites You to Grow Flowers at Home," *Federation News*, May 5, 1928; "There Is Still Time to Plant Your Annuals," *Federation News*, May 19, 1928. On the Young People's Labor Club, see "Bike Hike Sunday," *New Majority*, November 8, 1919. On the Valmar club and camp, see "Labor Group to Have Club Near Antioch," *CT*, March 18, 1928; Valmar Federation Club, *Health, Wealth, and Happiness for You!*, CHS; "Organized Labor's Country Club Completes Organization," *Federation News*, May 12, 1928; Cohen, *Making a New Deal*, 210. For quote on solidarity, see "Show Interest in Valmar Club Project," *Federation News*, July 14, 1928.

38. On Camp Yipsel, see "Summer Camp for Yipsels Opened in Chicago"; "Chicago Campers in Action"; National Secretary, Young Peoples Socialist League, to Emil Wingenburg, July 14, 1917, in Victor L. Berger, *Hearings before a Special Committee of the House*, 2:222. For quote on comradeship, see "Camp Yipsel Has a Very Successful Season."

39. On the Young Pioneer camp, see "Establish Child's Soviet on Lake Near Kenosha," *Milwaukee Journal*, July 25, 1929; "Young Communists Get Training in Wisconsin Camp," *CT*, July 28, 1929. On the Young Pioneers, see Mishler, *Raising Reds*.

40. Kazin and Ross, "America's Labor Day," 1306. On the canceling of the parade in Chicago, see "'Labor Sunday' Fills Pulpits," *CT*, September 4, 1910; "Labor Day and Its Origin," September 5, 1927, box 16, FITZ.

41. "Labor Day and its Origin," September 1927, box 16, FITZ; Haverty-Stacke, *America's Forgotten Holiday*, 78. On extent of exodus out of the city, see "Thousands Flee to Country for Labor Day Rest," *CT*, September 6, 1925.

42. On the struggle in the stockyards during World War I, see Barrett, *Work and Community in the Jungle*; Cohen, *Making a New Deal*, 44–46; Halpern, *Down on the Killing Floor*, 44–72; Brody, *The Butcher Workmen*, 75–106.

43. On worker testimony about Lake, see "Life's Hardships Told by Women of Stockyards," *Philadelphia Press*, February 14, 1918, as quoted in Brody, *The Butcher Workmen*, 81. On scene in park, see Chenery, "Packington Steps Forward," 37; McDowell, "Easter Day After the Decision." "The Foreign Born," MCD, box 2, folder 12. On quote on new day, see Chenery, "Packington Steps Forward," 37. On eight-hour benches, see Montgomery, *The Fall of the House of Labor*, 384.

44. On divisions within labor, see Barrett, *Work and Community in the Jungle*, 202–31; Cohen, *Making a New Deal*, 40–52; Halpern, *Down on the Killing Floor*, 76–85. On the government pullout and the corporate response, see Barrett, *Work and Community in the Jungle*, 202–31, 240–63; Cohen, *Making a New Deal*, 44–46, 160–83; Halpern, *Down on the Killing Floor*, 65–72, 76–95. On welfare capitalism during the 1920s, see

Barrett, *Work and Community in the Jungle*, 202–31, 240–63; Cohen, *Making a New Deal*, 44–46 160–183; Halpern, *Down on the Killing Floor*, 65–72, 76–95.

45. Cohen, *Making a New Deal*, 214–49.

46. Ibid., 252–321.

47. Ibid., 323–60.

48. On picnics, see, e.g., "Yards Workers Will Attend Picnic Sunday," *Journal of the Town of Lake*, July 8, 1937; "Chicago Shifts Picnic Date to July 23," *CIO News, PWOC Edition*, June 26, 1939; "Ahoy, for S.W. Picnic," *Chicago UE News*, June 21, 1945; "60,000 Attend Celebration of Calumet District Unions," *Steel Labor*, September 29, 1939; untitled, *Women in Steel*, October 1937; "Chicago to Have Annual Picnic at Berutes Grove, June 16," *CIO News, PWOC Edition*, May 27, 1940; "Much Fun and Frolic at 'June Jamboree,'" *CIO News, PWOC Edition*, June 26, 1935; Drake and Clayton, *Black Metropolis*, 339; Cohen, *Making a New Deal*, 341; Zivich, "Fighting Union," 32–34. For quote on ribs, see "Chicago Council Holds Annual Picnic," *CIO News, PWOC Edition*, June 10, 1940. For quote on beer, see advertisement, file: "South Works Closing 1992," box: "U.S. Steel 'Making Steel Killing Men' and 'Steel Yard Blues' Steel Info," SHS.

49. On steel and unionization during the 1930s, see Cohen, *Making a New Deal*, 293–96; Newell, *Chicago and the Labor Movement*, 115–47; Clark, Gottlieb, and Kennedy, *Forging a Union of Steel*. On Republic Steel's response to SWOC, see Sofchalk, "The Memorial Day Incident," 4–10.

50. For quote from Mollie West, see "The Great Depression: Mean Things Happening." On the Memorial Day Massacre, see Bernstein, *The Turbulent Years*, 432–98; Leab, "The Memorial Day Massacre"; Sofchalk, "The Memorial Day Incident"; Newell, *Chicago and the Labor Movement*, 134–47; Quirke, "Reframing Chicago's Memorial Day Massacre." On black participation, see Drake and Clayton, *Black Metropolis*, 322–23.

51. On camp and outings for children, see "Children in Steel," *Women in Steel*, September 1937; "CIO Juniors to Camp," *CIO News, PWOC Edition*, August 14, 1939; "More than 100 Children May Go to CIO Camp," *Back of the Yards Journal*, June 13, 1940; Halpern, *Down on the Killing Floor*, 157. On picnic fundraisers for camp, see, e.g., "Chicago to Have Annual Picnic at Berutes Grove, June 16," *CIO News, PWOC Edition*, May 27, 1940; "Much Fun and Frolic at 'June Jamboree,'" *CIO News, PWOC Edition*, June 26, 1935. For quote on country, see "First Chicago Kids Off to Summer Camp," *CIO News, PWOC Edition*, July 22, 1940.

52. For quote from Lewis, see "SWOC Camp Brings Members from New York to Cincinnati Plants," *Steel News*, July 28, 1939. On outdoor labor schools, see "SWOC to Open Training 'School': Union Members Given Chance to Hear Outstanding Speakers and Enjoy Mountain Vacation," *Steel Labor*, June 17, 1938; "Two Hundred Steel Workers Attend School in Mountain," *Steel News*, August 19, 1938; "SWOC Summer Camp," *Steel News*, April 28, 1939; "SWOC Summer Camp to Open July 2," *Steel News*, June 23, 1939; Denning, *The Cultural Front*, 258–59; Altenbaugh, *Education for Struggle*. For quote on tans, see *Chicago UE News*, "'School Never Like This' Say UE Members at Resort," July 13, 1944.

53. On the philosophy behind the Chicago Area Project, see Schlossman and Sedlak, *The Chicago Area Project Revisited*, viii–x; Pacyga, "The Russell Square Community Committee," 162–65; Horwitt, *Let Them Call Me Rebel*, 48–51.

54. On the two community councils, see Schlossman and Sedlak, *The Chicago Area Project Revisited*, 3–99; Pacyga, "The Russell Square Community Committee," 159–84; Horwitt, *Let Them Call Me Rebel*, 49–53.

55. On Shaw's reservations, see Pacyga, "The Russell Square Community Committee," 174. For quote, see Anthony Sorrentino, "It's an Inside Job: The Story of the Near West Side Community Committee: An Italian American Community Action Program" (1950), box 1, ASP.

56. On Camp Lange, see Pacyga, "The Russell Square Community Committee," 173–77; Schlossman and Sedlak, *The Chicago Area Project Revisited*, 56–58; "Report of the History and Work of the Russell Square Community Council," file 10, box 95, CAPP; "Report of the RSCC Submitted to the Chicago Ass'n of Commerce (c. 1945), file 10, box 95, CAPP; John Lulinski and the Russell Square Community Committee, "A New Adventure in Community Organization," (1946), file 4, box 96, CAPP; "Russell Square Community Committee, Development of Camp Lange," file 5, box 96, CAPP; "Camp Lange Closes 1939 Season," file 11, SBP; "Camp Lange Report 1941," file 11, SBP. On Camp Pompeii, see Anthony Sorrentino, "It's an Inside Job: The Story of the Near West Side Community Committee: An Italian American Community Action Program" (1950), box 1, ASP; Anthony Sorrentino, "For a Better Community," reprint, *American Citizen* (October 1941), in file 3, box 2, ASP; "Program of the West Side Community Council," file 1, box 102, CAPP; "Statistical Report of the Program of the West Side Community Council, June 1, 1939–June 30, 1940," file 1, box 102, CAPP; "Annual Report of the West Side Community Council, 1940," file 1, box 102, CAPP; "West Side Community Committee," file 1, box 102, CAPP; "Boys Discover Work Is Fun as They Make Camp," *CT*, August 23, 1942; "Just One Hour from Chicago," box 617, NNWSCCP. For quote on mysteries on nature, see "Camp Lange Closes 1939 Season." For quote on sun-baked streets, see "West Side Community Committee." For quote on booming noise, see "Russell Square Community Committee, Development of Camp Lange," 1.

57. On Alinsky, see Horwitt, *Let Them Call Me Rebel*. On the Back of the Yards Neighborhood Council, also see Jablonsky, *Pride in the Jungle*, 134–46; Slayton, *Back of the Yards*, 189–223.

58. On the importance of Davis Park, see Horwitt, *Let Them Call Me Rebel*, 63.

59. On the use of Davis Square Park, see Jablonsky, *Pride in the Jungle*, 135, 139, 145; Horwitt, *Let Them Call Me Rebel*; Slayton, *Back of the Yards*, 63–66, 147–62. On the beautification program and the conversion of vacant lots, see "47th St. Corner to Be Made a Place of Play," *Journal Town of Lake*, December 14, 1939; "New Playground to Be Ready for Use in Spring," February 22, 1940, Joseph B. Meegan Scrapbook, microfilm reel 10, NHRC-B; "Back O' Yard Aid Gets Jobs for 2,400," November 14, 1940, Joseph B. Meegan Scrapbook, microfilm reel 10, NHRC-B; "Recreation Lot Taking Definite Form," April 25, 1940, Joseph B. Meegan Scrapbook, microfilm reel 10, NHRC-B; "Playlots to Be Done for Summer Use," May

9, 1940, Joseph B. Meegan Scrapbook, microfilm reel 10, NHRC-B; Close, "Back of the Yards: Packingtown's Latest Drama: Civic Unity," 612.

60. On camping, see "Back of the Yards Girls Turn to Scouting Work," April 7, 1941, Joseph B. Meegan Scrapbook, microfilm reel 10, NHRC-B; "BYNC Sends 90 Boys, Girls to Summer Camp," July 2, 1941 Joseph B. Meegan Scrapbook, microfilm reel 10, NHRC-B; "Send 70 Kids to Camp—CIO Picnic Goal," June 5, 1940, Joseph B. Meegan Scrapbook, microfilm reel 10, NHRC-B; "PWOC Kids to Get Two Weeks at Camp," *CIO News, PWOC Edition*, July 8, 1940; "What Is It That Youth in BY Is Going to Do to Solve Local Problems," *Journal Town of Lake*, November 9, 1939; "Industrial Areas Foundation," file 1, box 74, CAPP.

## Conclusion

1. On biophilia, see Wilson, *Biophilia*; Kellert and Wilson, *The Biophilia Hypothesis*.

2. Dubkin, *The Natural History of a Yard*, 6.

3. On green infrastructure and ecological services, see Bolund and Hunhammar, "Ecosystem Services in Urban Areas"; Wolf, "Metro Nature"; Bunster-Ossa, "The Importance of Landscaping"; Pouyat, Yesilonis, and Nowak, "Carbon Storage by Urban Soils"; Davis, *Planet of Slums*, 134; Benedict and McMahon, *Green Infrastructure*, 57–84; Beatley, *Green Urbanism*, 94–99.

4. Smith, *Virgin Land*; Marx, *The Machine in the Garden*; Nash, *Wilderness and the American Mind*. For quotes on theme and drama, see Miller, *Errand into the Wilderness*, 205, 204. For quote on wilderness, see Nash, *Wilderness and the American Mind*, xi.

5. For quote, see Limerick, "Disorientation and Reorientation," 188.

6. On nationalism, see Anderson, *Imagined Communities*. On the importance of landscape in national identity, see the essays in Hooson, *Geography and National Identity*; Herb and Kaplan, *Nested Identities*; Schama, *Landscape and Memory*.

7. A good starting point on placing U.S. history in a global context is Bender, *Rethinking American History in a Global Age*.

8. On the importance of the suburbs as a place in harmony with nature, see Jackson, *Crabgrass Frontier*, 12–19, 45–86; Fishman, *Bourgeois Utopias*, 4, 5, 15, 27, 47, 53, 71, 127–29, 135, 142, 146–48, 157, 160, 206–7; Stilgoe, *Borderland*, 22–25, 107–120; Whyte, *The Organization Man*. For quote, see Philip M. Klutznick, NT (October 1946), as quoted in Randall, *America's Original GI Town*, book epigraph.

9. On postwar nature television and film, see Mitman, *Reel Nature*, 109–56. On Sierra Club coffee table books, see Dunaway, *Natural Visions*, 117–47. On postwar nature recreation, see Rugh, *Are We There Yet?*; Pomeroy, *In Search of the Golden West*, 218–31; Nash, *Wilderness and the American Mind*, 263–73. On the notion that the masses were loving the wilderness to death, see, e.g., Pomeroy, *In Search of the Golden West*, 203–12; Nash, *Wilderness and the American Mind*, 316–41. On the suburban context for environmentalism, see Sellers, *Crabgrass Crucible*.

10. See, e.g., Jackson, *Crabgrass Frontier*; Fishman, *Bourgeois Utopias*: Stilgoe, *Borderland*. Also see Pomeroy, *In Search of the Golden West*; Nash, *Wilderness and the American Mind*.

11. On the social history of suburbs, see, e.g., Nicolaides, *My Blue Heaven*; Wiese, *Places of Their Own*. On nature recreation, see, e.g., Fisher, "African Americans, Outdoor Recreation, and the 1919 Chicago Race Riot"; Lipin, *Workers and the Wild*; Montrie, *Making a Living*, 13–34, 91–112; Chiang, "Imprisoned Nature"; Fisher, "Nature in the City"; Young, "'A Contradiction in Democratic Government'"; Kahrl, *The Land Was Ours*; McCammack, "Recovering Green in Bronzeville."

12. On creative misunderstanding and community formation, see White, *The Middle Ground*.

13. On contemporary migration to cities, see Nations Human Settlements Programme, *State of the World's Cities 2010–2011*; Davis, *Planet of Slums*. For population data, see United Nations, *World Urbanization* Prospects, 1–12.

# Bibliography

Archival Collections

*Chicago, Ill.*

Carter G. Woodson Regional Library, Vivian Harsh Collection
    Illinois Writers Project: The Negro in Illinois
Chicago Historical Society
    Bessie Louis Pierce Papers
    Chicago Area Project Papers
    Chicago Commons Settlement House Papers
    Claude A. Barnett Papers / Associated Negro Press
    George Patterson Papers
    John Fitzpatrick Papers
    Mary McDowell Papers
    Oral History Archives of Chicago Polonia
    United Charities Papers
    United Steelworkers of America Papers
    Welfare Council of Metropolitan Chicago Papers
Harold Washington Library, The Special Collections and Preservation
    Department
    Neighborhood History Research Collection: Back of the Yards
    Neighborhood History Research Collection: City Wide Community
    Collections
James P. Fitzgibbons Memorial Museum
    Southeast Historical Society Archives
Roosevelt University Library, Murray-Green Library, University Archives
    Roosevelt University Oral History Project in Labor History
Sultzer Library, Special Collections
    Neighborhood History Research Collection: Portage Park Community
    Collection
    Neighborhood History Research Collection: Ravenswood–Lake View
    Community Collection
University of Chicago Joseph Regenstein Library, Special Collections
    Research Center
    Chicago Foreign Language Press Survey
    Ernest W. Burgess Papers
    Robert Redfield Papers
University of Illinois at Chicago, Daley Library Special Collections
    Anthony Sorrentino Papers

Italian American Collection
Juvenile Protective Association
Near North West Side Community Council Papers
Stephen S. Bubacz Papers

*Washington, D.C.*

Library of Congress, Rare Books and Special Collections Reading Room
Frederick Law Olmsted Papers
Records of the National Association for the Advancement of
Colored People

## Newspapers and Newsletters

*Chicago Chronicle*
*Chicago Citizen*
*Chicago Daily News*
*Chicago Defender*
*Chicago Evening Post*
*Chicago Tribune*
*Chicago UE News*
*CIO News, PWOC Edition*
*Daily Evening Bulletin*
*Hull House Bulletin*
*Illinois Record*
*Journal of the Town of Lake*
*Milwaukee Journal*
*Steel Labor*
*Women in Steel*

## Primary Sources—Books and Articles

Abbott, Edith. *The Tenements of Chicago, 1908–1935.* Chicago: University of
Chicago Press, 1936.
"About the Illinois Turner Camp." In *Souvenir Program of the Dedication of the
New Home of the American Turners,* edited by American Turners Northwest
Chicago. Chicago: The Turners, 1960.
Addams, Jane. *The Spirit of Youth and the City Streets.* New York: Macmillan,
1909.
———. *Twenty Years at Hull-House with Autobiographical Notes.* New York:
Macmillan, 1910.
Ahern, M. L. *The Great Revolution: A History of the Rise and Progress of the People's
Party in the City of Chicago and County of Cook, with Sketches of the Elect in
Office.* Chicago: Lakeside, 1874.
Allen, Dora. "Saturday Afternoon Walks." *Playground* 5 (June 1911): 99–103.

Anderson, Arthur E. "Canoeing." In *Outdoors with the Prairie Club*, edited by
Emma Doeserich, Mary Sherburne, and Anna B. Wey, 194–96. Chicago:
Paqui, 1941.

Anderson, Nels. *The Hobo: The Sociology of the Homeless Man*. A Study
prepared for the Chicago Council of Social Agencies under the Direction
of the Committee on Homeless Men. Chicago: University of Chicago Press,
1923.

"Armour Camp at Round Lake," *The Nation's Health* 4 (May 1922): 313.

Attwell, Ernest T. "Recreation for Colored America." *American City Magazine* 35
(August 1926): 162–65.

Baur, Edward J. "Delinquency among Mexican Boys in South Chicago." Master's
thesis, University of Chicago, 1938.

Becker, Robert Henry. "Teaching Good Citizenship in Chicago's Parks and
Playgrounds." *Fort Dearborn Magazine* (September 1920): 19–20, 26.

Belknap, E. Clinton. "Summer Activities of Boys Back of the Yards in Chicago."
Master's thesis, University of Chicago, 1937.

Berger, Victor L. *Hearings before a Special Committee of the House*. Vol. 2.
Washington, D.C.: Government Printing Office, 1919.

Bond, Maxwell H. "The Chicago Board of Education, Playgrounds, and the
Colored Child." *Playground* 20 (July 1926): 211.

Bontemps, Arna, and Jack Conroy, *They Seek a City*. Garden City: Doubleday,
Doran, 1945.

Bossard, James H. S. "Nationality and Nativity as Factors in Marriage." *American
Sociological Review* 4 (December 1939): 792–98.

Bowen, Louise DeKoven. *The Colored People of Chicago: An Investigation Made
for the Juvenile Protective Association*. Chicago: Rogers and Hall, 1913.

Brown, Florence Warren, and Neva L. Boyd. *Old English and American Games for
School and Playground*. Chicago: Saul Brothers, 1915.

"Camp Yipsel Has a Very Successful Season," *Young Socialists' Magazine* 13
(October 1919).

Chebithes, V. I. *AHEPA and the Progress of Hellenism in America*. New York:
"Hermes" Chapter No. 186, 1935.

Chenery, William L. "Packington Steps Forward." *Survey* 40 (April 13, 1918):
35–38.

"Chicago Campers in Action," *Young Socialists' Magazine* 12 (September 1918).

Chicago Commission on Race Relations. *The Negro in Chicago*. Chicago:
University of Chicago Press, 1922.

Chicago Park District, *Annual Report*. Vol. 5. 1939.

"Chicago Playgrounds and Park Centers," *City Club Bulletin* 2 (March 4, 1908):
1–20.

"Chicago's Third Play Festival." *Survey* 23 (November 6, 1909): 195–200.

Cleveland, H. W. S. *The Public Grounds of Chicago: How to Give Them Character
and Expression*. Chicago: Charles D. Lakey, 1869.

Close, Kathryn. "Back of the Yards: Packingtown's Latest Drama; Civic Unity."
*Survey Graphic* (December 1940): 612–15.

De Groot, E. B. "Suggestions to Instructors in Municipal Playgrounds and Gymnasiums." In *American Playgrounds: Their Construction, Equipment, Maintenance and Utility*, edited by Everett B. Mero, 98–105. Boston: American Gymnasia, 1908.

Dean, Ruth. "A 'Swimming Hole' in Chicago," *National Municipal Review* 11 (May 1922): 138–40.

Doeserich, Emma. "Dunes Camp." In *Outdoors with the Prairie Club*, edited by Emma Doeserich, Mary Sherburne, and Anna B. Wey, 90. Chicago: Paqui, 1941.

Drake, St. Clair. *Churches and Voluntary Associations in the Chicago Negro Community*. Chicago: Works Progress Administration, 1940.

Drake, St. Clair, and Horace R. Cayton. *Black Metropolis: A Study of Negro Life in a Northern City*. New York: Harcourt, Brace, 1945.

Droba, Daniel D., ed. *Czech and Slovak Leaders in Metropolitan Chicago*. Chicago: Slavonic Club of the University of Chicago, 1934.

Du Bois, W. E. B. "Hopkinsville, Chicago, and Idlewild." *Crisis* 22, no. 4 (August 1921): 158–60.

———. "The Problem of Amusement." *Southern Workman* 27 (September 1897): 181–84.

Dubkin, Leonard. *Enchanted Streets: The Unlikely Adventures of an Urban Nature Lover*. Boston: Little, Brown, 1947.

———. *The Murmur of Wings*. New York: McGraw-Hill, 1944.

———. *My Secret Places: One Man's Love Affair with Nature in the City*. New York: McKay, 1972.

———. *The Natural History of a Yard*. Chicago: H. Regnery, 1955.

———. *The White Lady*. New York: Putnam, 1952.

———. *Wolf Point: An Adventure in History*. New York: Putnam, 1953.

Fan, Ting-Chui. "Chinese Residents in Chicago." Master's thesis, University of Chicago, 1926.

Farrell, James T. *Studs Lonigan: A Trilogy Comprising Young Lonigan, The Young Manhood of Studs Lonigan, and Judgment Day*. Urbana: University of Illinois Press, 1993.

Farwell, Charles B. "Chicago's Candidacy for the 1892 World's Fair." *Cosmopolitan* 8 (November 1889): 50–58.

*50th Anniversary of the Socialer Turnverein, Chicago, Ill., 1887–1937*. Chicago: Cosmopolitan, 1937.

Flinn, John Joseph, and John Elbert Wilkie. *History of the Chicago Police: From the Settlement of the Community to the Present Time, under Authority of the Mayor and Superintendent of the Force* (Chicago: Police Book Fund, 1887).

Forest Preserve District of Cook County in the State of Illinois. *The Forest Preserves of Cook County*. Chicago: Clohesey, 1918.

Frazier, Franklin. *Recreation and Amusement among American Negroes: A Research Memorandum*. Carnegie-Myrdal Study of the American Negro in America. New York, 1940.

Gary, Joseph E. *Law and Ordinances Governing the City of Chicago*. Chicago: E. B. Myers, 1866.

*Golden Jubilee of the Feast of Our Lady of Mt. Carmel, 1894–1944, Sunday July 16, 1944, Melrose Park, Illinois*. Melrose Park, Ill.: s.n., 1944.

Gompers, Samuel. *Seventy Years of Life and Labor*. New York: Dutton, 1923.

*The Great Depression: Mean Things Happening*. Part 5 of *The Great Depression*. VHS. Directed by Susan Bellows, Lynn Goldfarb, and John Else. Boston: Blackside, 1993.

Gulick, Luther Halsey. "Play and Democracy." *Charities and the Commons* 18 (August 3, 1907): 481–86.

Hall, G. Stanley. *Adolescence: Its Psychology and Its Relation to Physiology, Anthropology, Sociology, Sex, Crime, Religion, and Education*. Vol. 1. New York: D. Appleton, 1905.

———. "Recreation and Reversion," *Pedagogical Seminary* 22 (December 1915): 510–20.

Halsey, Elizabeth. *The Development of Public Recreation in Metropolitan Chicago*. Chicago: Chicago Recreation Commission, 1940.

Holman, Genevieve Turner. "What We Did on a Summer Playground in Chicago." *Playground* 14 (August 1920): 157–63, 245–50, 298–305.

Horak, Janus. "Assimilation of Czechs in Chicago." Ph.D. diss., University of Chicago, 1920.

Hughes, Langston. *Big Sea: An Autobiography*. New York: A. A. Knopf, 1940.

Jacobson, Jacob Zavel. *Thirty-five Saints and Emil Armin*. Chicago: L. M. Stein, 1929.

Jahelka, Joseph. "The Role of Chicago Czechs in the Struggle for Czechoslovak Independence." *Journal of the Illinois State Historical Society* 31 (December 1938): 381–410.

Jerome, Amalie Hofer. "The Significance of Recent National Festivals in Chicago." In *Proceedings of the Second Annual Playground Congress*, New York City, September 8–12, 1908, 75–86. New York: Playground Association of America, 1908.

Johnson, Charles S. *The Negro in American Civilization: A Study of Negro Life and Race Relations in the Light of Social Research*. New York: Henry Holt, 1930.

Johnson, Fenton. "Ethiopia." In *Visions of the Dusk*, ed. Fenton Johnson, 42–48. New York: F.J., 1915.

Jones, Anita. "Conditions Surrounding Mexicans in Chicago." Master's thesis, University of Chicago, 1928.

" 'The Jungle' and the Way Out." *Westminster Review* 166 (October 1906): 365.

"Keep off the Grass," *Current* 4 (July 18, 1885): 39.

Kerr, Rose Gough, ed. *The Story of a Million Girls: Guiding and Girl Scouting Round the World*. London: Girl Guides Association, 1937.

Kruse, William F. "The Flag of May Day." *Young Socialists' Magazine* 12 (May 1918): n.p.

Lebeson, Anita Libman. "Recall to Life." *Sentinel's History of Chicago Jewry, 1911–1961*, 7–46. Chicago: Sentinel, 1961.

Lee, Joseph. "Play as a School of the Citizen." *Charities and the Commons* 18 (August 3, 1907): 486–91.

Lewis, Lloyd, and Henry Justin Smith. *Chicago: The History of its Reputation.* New York: Harcourt, Brace, 1929.

Loomis, Frank D. *Americanization in Chicago: The Report of a Survey Made by Authority and Under Direction of the Chicago Community Trust.* Chicago: Chicago Community Trust, n.d.

Mann, James R. *Municipal Code of the South Park Commissioners.* Chicago: E. B. Myers, 1897.

Mather, Stephen T. "Report on the Proposed Sand Dunes National Park, Indiana." Washington, D.C.: Government Printing Office, 1917.

McDowell, Mary. "City Waste." In *Mary McDowell and Municipal Housekeeping,* compiled by Caroline Hill, 1–10. Chicago: Chicago Woman's Club, 1938.

———. "Easter Day after the Decision." *Survey* 40 (April 13, 1918): 38–46.

Meehan, K. E. "The World Brotherhood of Boys," *Boys Life* (November 1930): 58.

Melendy, Royal L. "The Saloon in Chicago." *American Journal of Sociology* 6 (November 1900): 303–5.

Millet, Philippe. "A Meeting and Mingling of Peoples." *Charities and the Commons* 20 (August 1, 1908): 548.

Monroe, Harriet. "Festivals—Masques—Pageants." In *Outdoors with the Prairie Club,* edited by Emma Doeserich, Mary Sherburne, and Anna B. Wey, 109. Chicago: Paqui, 1941.

Moses, John, and Joseph Kirkland, eds. *The History of Chicago, Illinois.* Chicago: Munsell, 1895.

Nestor, Mary. *Woman's Labor Leader: An Autobiography of Agnes Nestor.* Rockford, Ill.: Bellevue Books, 1954.

Olmsted, Frederick Law. "Memorandum as to What Is to Be Aimed at in the Planting of the Lagoon District of the Chicago Exposition, as proposed March 1891." Reprinted in *The American Florist* 11 (January 11, 1896): 602–4.

———. *Public Parks and the Enlargement of Towns.* Cambridge, Mass.: American Social Science Association, 1870.

Osborn, Marian. "The Development of Recreation in the South Park System of Chicago." Master's thesis, University of Chicago, 1928.

Park, Robert E. "The City: Suggestions for the Investigation of Human Behavior in the Urban Environment." In *The City,* edited by Robert E. Park, Ernest W. Burgess, and Roderick D. MacKenzie, 1–46. Chicago: University of Chicago Press, 1925.

Perkins, Dwight Heald. *Report of the Special Park Commission to the City Council of Chicago on the Subject of a Metropolitan Park System.* Chicago: W. J. Hartman, 1904.

Perkins, Eleanor Ellis. "Perkins of Chicago." 1966. Burnham Library, Art Institute of Chicago, Chicago, Ill. Manuscript.

Phillips, Herbert E. "Mary McDowell as We Knew Her in the Yards, Part 2." In *Mary McDowell and Municipal Housekeeping,* compiled by Caroline Hill, 120–26. Chicago: Chicago Woman's Club, 1938.

*Picturesque Chicago and Guide to the World's Fair.* Chicago: Lennox, 1893.

*Program and Chronological History: Souvenir of St. Augustine's Parish Golden Jubilee, 1880–1936.* Chicago: Saint Augustine, 1936.

Pullen, Clarence. "The Parks and Parkways of Chicago." *Harper's Weekly*, June 6, 1891.

Puzzo, Virgil Peter. "The Italians in Chicago, 1890–1930." Master's thesis, University of Chicago, 1937.

Rainwater, Clarence. *The Play Movement in the United States: A Study of Community Recreation.* Chicago: University of Chicago Press, 1922.

Rauch, John H. *Public Parks: Their Effects upon the Moral, Physical and Sanitary Condition of the Inhabitants of Large Cities: With Special Reference to Chicago.* Chicago: S. C. Griggs, 1869.

"Recreational Activities of Labor Organizations." *Monthly Labor Review* 26 (May 1928): 889–904.

Richards, John R. "Chicago's Recreation Problem as Related to a City-Wide Organization." *American City* 13 (December 1915): 468–85.

———. "Public Recreation." In *Human Welfare Work in Chicago*, edited by Harvey Clarence Carbaugh, 87–112. Chicago: A. C. McClurg, 1917.

Sandburg, Carl. "Happiness." In *Chicago Poems*, edited by Carl Sandburg, 20. New York: Henry Holt, 1916.

Sauers, Charles G. "A People's Paradise of Fifty-One Square Miles of Woodland." In *Chicago's Accomplishments and Leaders*, edited by Glenn A. Bishop. Chicago: Bishop, 1932.

Scheidlinger, Saul. "A Comparative Study of the Boy Scout Movement in Different National and Social Groups." *American Sociological Review* 13 (December 1948): 739–50.

Schwab, Michael. "Autobiography of Michael Schwab." In *The Autobiographies of the Haymarket Martrys*, ed. Philip S. Foner, 135–74. New York: Humanities Press, 1969.

Seeger, Eugen. *Chicago: The Wonder City.* Chicago: George Gregory, 1893.

Seman, Philip L. "Chicago's Program for Meeting Its Recreational Needs." In *The Proceedings of the National Conference of Social Work at the Annual Session in Chicago*, 52nd Annual Session, 493–509. Chicago: University of Chicago Press, 1925.

———. *Jewish Community Life: A Study in Social Adaptation.* Chicago: Observer, 1924.

Shaw, Clifford. *The Jack-Roller: A Delinquent Boy's Own Story.* Chicago: University of Chicago Press, 1930.

Sheridan, John. "Hiking in Chicago," *Recreation* 31 (November 1937): 477–78, 506.

Simon, Andreas, *Chicago, the Garden City: Its Magnificent Parks, Boulevards and Cemeteries; Together with Other Descriptive Views and Sketches.* Chicago: F. Gindele, 1893.

Sinclair, Upton. *The Jungle.* New York: Doubleday, Page, 1906.

*Social Service Directory.* Chicago: Council of Social Agencies, 1939.

Soong, Ruth Joan. "A Survey of the Education of Chinese Children in Chicago." Ph.D. diss., University of Chicago, 1931.

South Park Commissioners, *Annual Report*. 1908.

Special Park Commission. *Annual Report: Parks, Playgrounds and Bathing Beaches, Submitted to the City Council of Chicago, Feb. 1908*. W. J. Hartman: Chicago, 1908.

Steiner, J. F. "Recreation and Leisure Time Activities." In *Recent Social Trends in the United States: Report of the President's Research Committee on Social Trends*, edited by President's Research Committee on Social Trends, 2:912–57. New York: McGraw-Hill, 1934.

Strand, A. E. *History of the Norwegians of Illinois: A Concise Record of the Struggles and Achievements of the Early Settlers, Together with a Narrative of What Is Now Being Done by the Norwegian-Americans of Illinois in the Development of Their Adopted Country, with the Valuable Collaboration of Numerous Authors and Contributors*. Chicago: J. Anderson, 1905.

"Summer Camp for Yipsels Opened in Chicago," *The Young Socialists' Magazine* 11 (August 1917).

Taft, Lorado. "The Monuments of Chicago." In *Art and Archeology* 12 (September 1921): 120–27.

Tarbell, Ida. "An Old World Fete in Industrial America." *Charities and the Commons* 20 (August 1, 1908): 546–48.

Taylor, Graham Romeyn. "Chicago in the Nation's Race Strife." *Survey* 42 (August 9, 1919): 695–97.

———. "The Chicago Play Festival." *Charities and the Commons* 20 (August 1, 1908): 539–45.

———. "How They Played at Chicago." Paper presented at the Chicago Meeting of the Playground Association of America, June 1907.

———. "Recreation Developments in Chicago Parks." *Annals of the American Academy of Political and Social Science* 35 (March 1910): 88–105.

Thrasher, Frederic Milton. *The Gang: A Study of 1,313 Gangs in Chicago*. Chicago: University of Chicago Press, 1936.

Todd, Arthur J., William F. Byron, and Howard L. Vierow. *Private Recreation*. Vol. 3 of the *Chicago Recreation Survey*. Chicago: Chicago Recreation Commission and Northwestern University, 1938.

———. *Public Recreation*. Vol. 1 of the *Chicago Recreation Survey*. Chicago: Chicago Recreation Commission and Northwestern University, 1937.

Travis, Dempsey J. *An Autobiography of Black Chicago*. Chicago: Urban Research Press, 1981.

United Negro Improvement Association and George Alexander McGuire, *Universal Black Men Catechism*. New York: United Negro Improvement Association, 1921.

Vojan, J. E. S. *The Semi-Centennial Jubilee of the Bohemian National Cemetery Association, Chicago, Il*. Chicago: Bohemian National Cemetery Association, 1927.

Washington Intercollegiate Club of Chicago. *The Negro in Chicago, 1779–1929*. Chicago: Washington Intercollegiate Club, 1929.

Wassekigig (Thomas W. Allinson). "The Tribe of Ha Ha No Mak." In *Outdoors with the Prairie Club*, edited by Emma Doeserich, Mary Sherburne, and Anna B. Wey, 197. Chicago: Paqui, 1941.

Weller, Charles Frederick. "Recreation in Industries." *Playground* 11 (August 1917): 250–52.

Wells, H. G. *The Future in America: A Search after Realities*. New York: Harper & Brothers, 1906.

Wells, Ida B., Frederick Douglass, Irvine Garland Penn, and Ferdinand L. Barnett. *The Reason Why the Colored American Is Not in the World's Columbian Exposition*. 1893.

West Park Commission. *Second Annual Report of the West Chicago Park Commission*. 1871.

Whyte, William Hollingsworth. *The Organization Man*. New York: Simon and Schuster, 1956.

Williams, Fannie Barrier. "Social Bonds in the 'Black Belt' of Chicago: Negro Organizations and the New Spirit Pervading Them." *Charities* 15 (October 7, 1905): 40–44.

Woodson, Carter Goodwin. *African Myths and Proverbs*. Washington, D.C.: Associated Publishers, 1928.

———. *The Negro in Our History*. Washington, D.C.; Associated Publishers, 1922.

Woodson, Carter Goodwin, and Lois Mailou Jones. *African Heroes and Heroines*. Washington, D.C.: Associated Publishers 1939.

Wright, Richard. *Black Boy (American Hunger): A Record of Childhood and Youth*. New York: Perennial Classics, 1998.

———. *Native Son*. New York: Harper & Brothers, 1940.

Wright, R. R., Jr. "Social Work and Influence of the Negro Church." *Annals of the American Academy of Political and Social Science* 30 (November 1907): 81–93.

Yard, Robert Sterling. *Our Federal Lands: A Romance of American Development*. New York: Charles Scribner's Sons, 1928.

Zaloha, Ann. "A Study of Persistence of Italian Customs among 143 Families of Italian Descent, Members of Social Clubs at Chicago Commons." Master's thesis, Northwestern University, 1937.

Zglenicki, Leon Thaddeus. *Poles of Chicago, 1837–1937: A History of One Century of Polish Contribution to the City of Chicago, Illinois*. Chicago: Polish Pageant, 1937.

Zorbaugh, Harvey Warren. *The Gold Coast and the Slum: A Sociological Study of Chicago's Near North Side*. Chicago: University of Illinois Press, 1929.

Secondary Sources

Adams, Stephen B., and Orville R. Butler. *Manufacturing the Future: A History of Western Electric*. New York: Cambridge University Press, 1999.

Alston, Dana. "Moving Beyond the Barriers." In *The First National People of Color Environmental Leadership Summit, the Washington Court on Capitol Hill,*

*Washington, D.C., October 24–27, 1991*, edited by Charles Lee, 103–6. New York: United Church of Christ Commission for Racial Justice, 1992.

Altenbaugh, Richard J. *Education for Struggle: The American Labor Colleges of the 1920s and 1930s*. Labor and Social Change. Philadelphia: Temple University Press, 1990.

Anderson, Benedict. *Imagined Communities: Reflections on the Origin and Spread of Nationalism*. New York: Verso, 1983.

Aron, Cindy Sondik. *Working at Play: A History of Vacations in the United States*. New York: Oxford University Press, 1999.

Arredondo, Gabriela. *Mexican Chicago: Race, Identity, and Nation, 1916–39*. Statue of Liberty–Ellis Island Centennial Series. Urbana: University of Illinois Press, 2008.

Asbury, Herbert. "The Life, Times, and End of Dion O'Banion." In *This is Chicago: An Anthology*, edited by Albert Halper, 378–86. New York: Holt, 1952.

Avrich, Paul. *The Haymarket Tragedy*. Princeton, N.J.: Princeton University Press, 1984.

Bachin, Robin Faith. *Building the South Side: Urban Space and Civic Culture in Chicago, 1890–1919*. Historical Studies of Urban America. Chicago: University of Chicago Press, 2004.

Bachrach, Julia Sniderman. *The City in a Garden: A Photographic History of Chicago's Parks*. Santa Fe: Center for American Places, 2001.

Baldwin, Davarian L. *Chicago's New Negroes: Modernity, the Great Migration, and Black Urban Life*. Chapel Hill: University of North Carolina Press, 2007.

Bale, John. *Sports Geography*. London: E. & F. N. Spon, 1989.

Ballard, Barbara J. "A People without a Nation." *Chicago History* 28 (Summer 1999): 26–43.

Barker, Stan. "Paradises Lost." *Chicago History* 22 (March 1993): 26–49.

Barrell, John. *The Dark Side of the Landscape: The Rural Poor in English Painting, 1730–1840*. Cambridge: Cambridge University Press, 1980.

Barrett, James R. *The Irish Way: Becoming American in the Multiethnic City*. Penguin History of American Life. New York: Penguin Press, 2012.

———. *Work and Community in the Jungle: Chicago's Packinghouse Workers, 1894–1922*. Urbana: University of Illinois Press, 1987.

Barrett, James R., and David R. Roediger. "The Irish and the 'Americanization' of the 'New Immigrants' in the Streets and in the Churches of the Urban United States, 1900–1930." *Journal of American Ethnic History* 24 (Summer 2005): 4–33.

Beatley, Timothy. *Green Urbanism: Learning from European Cities*. Washington, D.C.: Island Press, 1999.

Bederman, Gail. *Manliness and Civilization: A Cultural History of Gender and Race in the United States, 1880–1917*. Chicago: University of Chicago Press, 1995.

Beijbom, Ulf. *Swedes in Chicago: A Demographic and Social Study of the 1846–1880 Immigration*. Stockholm: Läromedelsforlagen, 1971.

Belasco, Warren James. *Americans on the Road: From Autocamp to Motel, 1910–1945*. Cambridge: MIT Press, 1979.

Bender, Thomas. "The 'Rural' Cemetery Movement: Urban Travail and the Appeal of Nature." *New England Quarterly* 47 (June 1974): 196–211.

———. *Toward an Urban Vision: Ideas and Institutions in Nineteenth-Century America*. Lexington: University Press of Kentucky, 1975.

———, ed. *Rethinking American History in a Global Age*. Berkeley: University of California Press, 2002.

Benedict, Mark A., and Edward T. McMahon. *Green Infrastructure: Linking Landscapes and Communities*. Washington, D.C.: Island Press, 2006.

Bennett, Michael. "Anti-Pastoralism, Frederick Douglass, and the Nature of Slavery." In *Beyond Nature Writing: Expanding the Boundaries of Ecocriticism*, edited by Karla Armbruster and Kathleen R. Wallace, 195–210. Charlottesville: University of Virginia Press, 2008.

Bensman, David, and Roberta Lynch. *Rusted Dreams: Hard Times in a Steel Community*. New York: McGraw-Hill, 1987.

Benson, Harry. *Tivoli Gardens*. New York: Abrams, 2007.

Berkowitz, Michael. *Zionist Culture and West European Jewry before the First World War*. Cambridge: Cambridge University Press, 1993.

Bernstein, Irving. *The Turbulent Years: A History of the American Worker, 1933–1941*. Boston: Houghton Mifflin, 1970.

Beveridge, Charles E., ed. "The California Origins of Olmsted's Landscape Design Principles in the Semiarid American West." In *The California Frontier, 1863–1865*. Vol. 5 of *The Papers of Frederick Law Olmsted*, edited by Victoria Post Ranney, 449–73. Baltimore: Johns Hopkins University Press, 1990.

Beveridge, Charles, and Carolyn F. Hoffman, eds. *Writings on Public Parks, Parkways, and Park Systems*. Vol. 1 (Supplementary Series) of *The Papers of Frederick Law Olmsted*. Baltimore: Johns Hopkins University Press, 1997.

Blackmar, Elizabeth, and Roy Rosenzweig. "The Park and the People: Central Park and Its Public, 1850–1910." In *Budapest and New York: Studies in Metropolitan Transformation, 1870–1930*, edited by Thomas Bender and Carl E. Schorske, 108–34. New York: Russell Sage Foundation, 1994.

Bluestone, Daniel. *Constructing Chicago*. New Haven, Conn.: Yale University Press, 1991.

Bodnar, John. *The Transplanted: A History of Immigrants in Urban America*. Interdisciplinary Studies in History. Bloomington: Indiana University Press, 1987.

Bohlmann, Rachel E. "Sunday Closings." In *The Encyclopedia of Chicago*, edited by James R. Grossman et al., 804–5. Chicago: University of Chicago, 2004.

Bolund, Per, and Sven Hunhammar, "Ecosystem Services in Urban Areas." *Ecological Economics* (1999): 293–301.

Bone, Robert, and Richard A. Courage. *The Muse in Bronzeville: African American Creative Expression in Chicago, 1932–1950*. New Brunswick, N.J.: Rutgers University Press, 2011.

Botkin, Daniel. *Discordant Harmonies: A New Ecology for the Twenty-first Century*. New York: Oxford University Press, 1990.

Boyer, Paul S. *Urban Masses and Moral Order in America, 1820–1920*. Cambridge, Mass.: Harvard University Press, 1978.

Brandes, Stuart D. *American Welfare Capitalism, 1880–1940*. Chicago: University of Chicago Press, 1976.

Brody, David. *The Butcher Workmen: A Study of Unionization*. Cambridge, Mass.: Harvard University Press, 1964.

Brown, Dona. *Inventing New England: Regional Tourism in the Nineteenth Century*. Washington, D.C.: Smithsonian Institution Press, 1995.

Bunster-Ossa, Ignatio F. "The Importance of Landscaping in the Urban Environment." In *Cities and Nature: A Handbook for Renewal*, edited by Roger L. Kemp, 267–68. London: McFarland, 2005.

Cada, Joseph. "Czechs of Chicago." In *Panorama: A Historical Review of Czechs and Slovaks in the USA*, 30–34. Cicero, Ill.: Czechoslovak National Council of America, 1970.

Calmer, Alan. *Labor Agitator: The Story of Albert R. Parsons*. New York: International, 1937.

Cavallo, Dominick. *Muscles and Morals: Organized Playgrounds and Urban Reform, 1880–1920*. Philadelphia: University of Pennsylvania Press, 1981.

Chadwick, George F. *The Park and the Town: Public Landscape in the 19th and 20th Centuries*. New York: Frederick A. Praeger, 1966.

Chiang, Connie Y. "Imprisoned Nature: Toward an Environmental History of the World War II Japanese American Incarceration," *Environmental History* 15 (April 2010): 236–67.

———. *Shaping the Shoreline: Fisheries and Tourism on the Monterey Coast*. Seattle: University of Washington Press, 2008.

Christianson, J. R. "Danes." In *The Encyclopedia of Chicago*, edited by James R. Grossman et al., 229–30. Chicago: University of Chicago Press, 2004.

Christy, Steve. "Wide-Awake Dreaming: Creation of the Cook County Forest Preserve District." Brochure of the Open Lands Project. Chicago: Open Lands Project, 1982.

Chubat, Bev. "On the Stage at Camp Kinderland." *Chicago Jewish History* 23 (Summer 1999): 6–7, 14.

Clark, Paul, Peter Gottlieb, and Donald Kennedy. *Forging a Union of Steel: Philip Murray, SWOC, and the United Steelworkers*. Ithaca, N.Y.: ILR Press, 1987.

Cockrell, Ron. *A Signature of Time and Eternity: The Administrative History of Indiana Dunes National Lakeshore, Indiana*. Omaha: U.S. Department of the Interior, National Park Service, Midwest Regional Office, 1988.

Cohen, Lizabeth. *Making a New Deal: Industrial Workers in Chicago, 1919–1939*. New York: Cambridge University Press, 1990.

Cohen, Ronald D., and Stephen G. McShone, eds. *Moonlight in Duneland: The Illustrated Story of the Chicago South Shore and South Bend Railroad*. Bloomington: Indiana University Press, 1998.

Collier, Malcolm. "Jens Jensen and Columbus Park." *Chicago History* 4 (Winter 1975): 233–34.

Colten, Craig E. *An Unnatural Metropolis: Wresting New Orleans from Nature*. Baton Rouge: Louisiana State University Press, 2005.

Condit, Carl. *Chicago 1910–29: Building, Planning, and Urban Technology*. Chicago: University of Chicago Press, 1973.

Conzen, Kathleen Neils. "Ethnicity as Festive Culture: Nineteenth-Century German America on Parade." In *The Invention of Ethnicity*, edited by Werner Sollors, 44–76. New York: Oxford University Press, 1989.

Conzen, Kathleen Neils, David A. Gerber, Ewa Morawska, George E. Pozzetta, and Rudolph J. Vecoli. "The Invention of Ethnicity: A Perspective from the U.S.A." In *Journal of American Ethnic History* 12 (Fall 1992): 3–41.

Corbould, Clare. *Becoming African Americans: Black Public Life in Harlem, 1919–1939*. Cambridge, Mass.: Harvard University Press, 2009.

Cranz, Galen. "Models for Park Usage: Ideology and the Development of Chicago's Public Parks." Ph.D. diss., University of Chicago, 1971.

———. *The Politics of Park Design: A History of Urban Parks in America*. Cambridge: MIT Press, 1982.

Cronin, Mike. *Sport and Nationalism in Ireland: Gaelic Games, Soccer and Irish Identity since 1884*. Portland: Four Courts Press, 1999.

Cronon, William. "Kennecott Journey: The Paths Out of Town." In *Under an Open Sky: Rethinking America's Western Past*, edited by William Cronon, George Miles, and Jay Gitlin. New York: W. W. Norton, 1992.

———. "Modes of Prophecy and Production: Placing Nature in History." *Journal of American History* 76 (1990): 1122–31.

———. *Nature's Metropolis: Chicago and the Great West*. New York: W. W. Norton, 1991.

———. "The Trouble with Wilderness; or, Getting Back to the Wrong Nature." In *Uncommon Ground: Toward Reinventing Nature*, edited by William Cronon, 69–90. New York: W. W. Norton, 1995.

Cutler, Irving. "The Jews of Chicago: From Shtetl to Suburb." In *Ethnic Chicago: A Multicultural Portrait*, edited by Melvin G. Holli and Peter d'A. Jones, 122–72. 4th ed. Grand Rapids, Mich.: William B. Eerdmans, 1995.

———. *The Jews of Chicago: From Shtetl to Suburb*. Urbana: University of Illinois Press, 1996.

Dabrowski, Patrice M. *Commemorations and the Shaping of Modern Poland*. Bloomington: Indiana University Press, 2004.

Dagbovie, Pero Gaglo. *The Early Black History Movement, Carter G. Woodson, and Lorenzo Johnston Greene*. Urbana: University of Illinois Press, 2007.

Daniels, Roger. *The Work Ethic in Industrial America, 1850–1920*. Chicago: University Press, 1974.

Darby, Paul. "Emigrants at Play: Gaelic Games and the Irish Diaspora in Chicago, 1884– c.1900." *Sport in History* 26 (April 2006): 47–63.

Davis, Frank Marshall. *Black Moods: Collected Poems*, ed. John Edgar Tidwell. Urbana: University of Illinois Press, 2002.

Davis, Mike. *Ecology of Fear: Los Angeles and the Imagination of Disaster*. New York: Metropolitan Books, 1998.

———. *Planet of Slums.* New York: Verso, 2006.

Davis, Susan G. *Spectacular Nature: Corporate Culture and the Sea World Experience.* Berkeley: University of California Press, 1997.

Deloria, Philip Joseph. *Indians in Unexpected Places.* Lawrence: University Press of Kansas, 2004.

———. *Playing Indian.* New Haven, Conn.: Yale University Press, 1998.

Denker, Berit Elisabeth. "Popular Gymnastics and the Military Spirit in Germany, 1848–1871." *Central European History* 34 (2001): 503–30.

Denning, Michael. *The Cultural Front: The Laboring of American Culture in the Twentieth Century.* The Haymarket Series. New York: Verso, 1996.

Deutsch, Tracey. "Great Depression." In *The Encyclopedia of Chicago*, edited by James R. Grossman et al., 360–61. Chicago: University of Chicago Press, 2004.

de Wit, Wim, and William W. Tippens, "Prairie School in the Parks." In *Prairie in the City: Naturalism in Chicago's Parks, 1870–1940*, edited by Rosemary Adams and Claudia Lamm Wood, 33–41. Chicago: Chicago Historical Society, 1991.

Diamond, Andrew J. *Mean Streets: Chicago Youths and the Everyday Struggle for Empowerment in the Multiracial City, 1908–1969.* Berkeley: University of California Press, 2009.

Dilsaver, Lary M. *America's National Park System: The Critical Documents.* Lanham, Md.: Rowan & Littlefield, 1994.

Dippie, Brian. *The Vanishing American: White Attitudes and U.S. Indian Policy.* Lawrence: University Press of Kansas, 1982.

Doty, Carol. "Ecology, Community, and the Prairie Spirit." In *Prairie in the City: Naturalism in Chicago's Parks, 1870–1940*, edited by Rosemary Adams and Claudia Lamm Wood, 8–17. Chicago: Chicago Historical Society, 1991.

Draper, Joan. "The Art and Science of Park Planning in the United States: Chicago's Small Parks, 1902–1905." In *Planning the Twentieth-Century American City*, edited by Mary Corbin Sies and Christopher Silver, 100–119. Baltimore: Johns Hopkins Press, 1996.

Duis, Perry R. *Challenging Chicago: Coping with Everyday Life, 1837–1920.* Urbana: University of Illinois Press, 1998.

———. *The Saloon: Public Drinking in Chicago and Boston, 1880–1920.* Urbana: University of Illinois Press, 1983.

Dunaway, Finis. *Natural Visions: The Power of Images in American Environmental Reform.* Chicago: University of Chicago Press, 2005.

Eaton, Leonard K. *Landscape Artist in America: The Life and Work of Jens Jensen.* Chicago: University of Chicago Press, 1964.

Eichberg, Henning. "Body Culture and Democratic Nationalism: 'Popular Gymnastics' in Nineteenth-Century Denmark." *International Journal of the History of Sport* 12 (1995): 108–24.

———. "The Enclosure of the Body: The Historical Relativity of 'Health,' 'Nature' and the Environment of Sport." In *Body Cultures*, edited by Henning Eichberg, 47–66. London: Routledge, 1998.

Eichberg, Henning, and Gerlav Idraetshojskøle, "Race-Track and Labyrinth: The Space of Physical Culture in Berlin." *Journal of Sport History* 17 (Summer 1990): 245–52.

Engel, J. Ronald. *Sacred Sands: The Struggle for Community in the Indiana Dunes.* Middletown, Conn.: Wesleyan University Press, 1983.

Ensslen, Klauss. "German-American Working-Class Saloons." In *German Workers' Culture in the United States, 1850 to 1920*, edited by Hartmut Keil, 157–80. Washington, D.C.: Smithsonian Institution Press, 1988.

Enstad, Nan. "Popular Culture." In *A Companion to American Cultural History*, edited by Karen Halttunen, 356–70. Oxford, England: Blackwell, 2008.

Erb, Cynthia Marie. *Tracking King Kong: A Hollywood Icon in World Culture.* Detroit: Wayne State University Press, 2009.

Fanning, Charles, and Ellen Skerrett. "James T. Farrell and Washington Park: The Novel as Social History." *Chicago History* 8 (Summer 1979): 80–91.

Fanning, Charles, Ellen Skerret, and John Corrigan. *Nineteenth Century Chicago Irish: A Social and Political Portrait.* Urban Insights Series. Chicago: Center for Urban Policy, Loyola University Chicago, 1980.

Fass, Paula. *The Damned and the Beautiful: American Youth in the 1920s.* New York: Oxford University Press, 1977.

Fein, Albert, ed. *Landscape into Cityscape: Frederick Law Olmsted's Plans for a Greater New York City.* Ithaca: Cornell University Press, 1968.

Finfer, Lawrence. "Leisure as Social Work in the Urban Community: The Progressive Recreation Movement, 1890–1920." Ph.D. diss., Michigan State University, 1974.

Fisher, Colin. "African Americans, Outdoor Recreation, and the 1919 Chicago Race Riot." In *"To Love the Wind and the Rain": African Americans and Environmental History*, edited by Dianne Glave and Mark Stoll, 63–76. Pittsburgh: University of Pittsburgh Press, 2006.

———. "Nature in the City: Urban Environmental History and Central Park." *OAH Magazine of History* 25 (October 2011): 27–31.

Fishman, Robert. *Bourgeois Utopias: The Rise and Fall of Suburbia.* New York: Basic Books, 1989.

Flanagan, Kathleen M. "The History of the Development and Promotion of Irish Dancing in Chicago, 1893–1953." Ph.D. diss., Union Institute Graduate School, 1995.

Foner, Philip Sheldon. *American Labor Songs of the Nineteenth Century.* Music in American Life. Urbana: University of Illinois Press, 1975.

———. *History of the Labor Movement in the United States: Postwar Struggles, 1918–1920.* Vol. 8. New York: International, 1987.

Foner, Philip Sheldon, and David R. Roediger. *Our Own Time: A History of American Labor and the Working Day.* Contributions in Labor Studies. New York: Greenwood Press, 1989.

Ford, Liam T. A. *Soldier Field: A Stadium and Its City.* Chicago: University of Chicago Press, 2009.

Foster, Mark S. "In the Face of 'Jim Crow': Prosperous Blacks and Vacations, Travel, and Outdoor Leisure, 1890–1945." *Journal of Negro History* 84 (Spring 1999): 130–49.

Franklin, Jill. *The Liberty of the Park.* Vol. 3 in *Patriotism: The Making and Unmaking of British National Identity*, edited by Raphael Samule. London: Routledge, 1989.

Funchion, Michael F. "Irish Chicago: Church, Homeland, Politics, and Class: The Shaping of an Ethnic Group, 1870–1900." In *Ethnic Chicago: A Multicultural Portrait*, edited by Melvin G. Holli and Peter d'A. Jones, 57–92. 4th ed. Grand Rapids, Mich.: William B. Eerdmans, 1994.

Gabaccia, Donna. "Liberty, Coercion, and the Making of Immigration Historians." *Journal of American History* 84 (September 1997): 570–75.

Gaines, Kevin. *Uplifting the Race: Black Leadership, Politics, and Culture in the Twentieth Century*. Chapel Hill: University of North Carolina Press, 1996.

Gandy, Matthew. *Concrete and Clay: Reworking Nature in New York City*. Cambridge: MIT Press, 2002.

Ganz, Cheryl. *The 1933 Chicago World's Fair: Century of Progress*. Urbana: University of Illinois Press, 2008.

Gems, Gerald R. "The Neighborhood Athletic Club: An Ethnographic Study of a Working-Class Athletic Fraternity in Chicago, 1917–1984." *Colby Quarterly* 32 (March 1996): 36–44.

———. "Not Only a Game." *Chicago History* 18 (Summer 1989): 4–21.

———. "Sport and the Americanization of Ethnic Women in Chicago." In *Ethnicity and Sport in North American History and Culture*, edited by George Eisen and David Wiggins, 177–200. Westport, Conn.: Praeger, 1994.

———. "Sport and the Forging of a Jewish-American Culture." *American Jewish History* 83 (March 1995): 15–26.

———. "Sports and Culture Formation in Chicago, 1890–1940." Ph.D. diss., University of Maryland, 1989.

———. "Sports, Industrial League." In *The Encyclopedia of Chicago*, edited by James R. Grossman et al., 778–79. Chicago: University of Chicago, 2004.

———. "Welfare Capitalism and Blue-Collar Sport: The Legacy of Labour Unrest." *Rethinking History* 5 (March 2001): 43–58.

———. *The Windy City Wars: Labor, Leisure, and Sport in the Making of Chicago*. American Sports History Series. Lanham, Md.: Scarecrow Press, 1997.

Gerber, David A. "Forming a Transnational Narrative: New Perspectives on European Migrations to the United States." *History Teacher* 35 (November 2001): 61–78.

Gerdts, William H., ed. *The Lost Paintings of Tunis Ponsen (1891–1968)*. Muskegon, Mich.: Muskegan Museum of Art, 1994.

Glassberg, David. *American Historical Pageantry: The Uses of Tradition in the Early Twentieth Century*. Chapel Hill: University of North Carolina Press, 1990.

———. "Restoring a 'Forgotten Childhood': American Play and the Progressive Era's Elizabethan Past." *American Quarterly* 32 (Autumn 1980): 351–68.

Glave, Dianne D. *Rooted in the Earth: Reclaiming the African American Environmental Heritage.* Chicago: Chicago Review Press, 2010.

Goggin, Jacqueline Anne. *Carter G. Woodson: A Life in Black History.* Baton Rouge: Louisiana State University Press, 1997.

Goksøyr, Matti. "Phases and Functions of Nationalism: Norway's Utilization of International Sport in the Late Nineteenth and Early Twentieth Centuries." In *Tribal Identities: Nationalism, Europe, Sport,* edited by J. A. Mangan, 125–46. London: Frank Cass, 1996.

Goltermann, Svenja. "Exercise and Perfection: Embodying the Nation in Nineteenth-Century Germany." *European Review of History* 11 (Autumn 2004): 333–46.

Gonzales, Samuel L. "A Black Community in Wisconsin: A Historical Study of Lake Ivanhoe." Master's thesis, University of Wisconsin–Whitewater, 1972.

Goodman, Cary. *Choosing Sides: Playground and Street Life on the Lower East Side.* New York: Schocken Books, 1979.

Gori, Gigliola. *Italian Fascism and the Female Body: Sport, Submissive Women and Strong Mothers,* Sport in the Global Society. London: Routledge, 2004.

Gottlieb, Robert. *Forcing the Spring: The Transformation of the American Environmental Movement.* Washington, D.C.: Island Press, 1993.

Graf, John, and Steve Skarpad. *Chicago's Monuments, Markers, and Memorials.* Images of America. Charleston, S.C.: Arcadia, 2002.

Grant, Colin. *Negro with a Hat: The Rise and Fall of Marcus Garvey.* New York: Oxford University Press, 2010.

Green, James. *Death in the Haymarket: A Story of Chicago, the First Labor Movement and the Bombing that Divided Gilded Age America.* New York: Pantheon Books, 2006.

Greenberg, Dolores. "Reconstructing Race and Protest: Environmental Justice in New York City." *Environmental History* 5 (April 2000): 223–50.

Greenberg, Joel. "Leonard Dubkin." In *Of Prairie, Woods, and Water: Two Centuries of Chicago Nature Writing,* edited by Joel Greenberg (Chicago: University of Chicago Press, 2008), 287–88.

Grese, Robert E. *Jens Jensen: Maker of Natural Parks and Public Grounds.* Baltimore: Johns Hopkins University Press, 1992.

Griffin, Al. "The Ups and Downs of Riverview Park." *Chicago History* 4 (Spring 1975): 14–22.

Griffin, Farah Jasmine. *"Who Set You Flowin'?": The African American Migration Narrative.* New York: Oxford University Press, 1995.

Grossman, James R. *Land of Hope: Chicago, Black Southerners, and the Great Migration.* Chicago: University of Chicago Press, 1989.

Guglielmo, Thomas. *White on Arrival: Italians, Race, Color, and Power in Chicago, 1890–1945.* New York: Oxford University Press, 2003.

Guha, Ramachandra. "Radical American Environmentalism: A Third World Critique." *Environmental Ethics* 11 (Spring 1989): 71–83.

———. *The Unquiet Woods: Ecological Change and Peasant Resistance in the Himalaya.* Berkeley: University of California Press, 1989.

Gutman, Herbert G. "Work, Culture and Society in Industrializing America, 1815–1919." *American Historical Review* 78 (June 1973): 531–88.

Hagen, Joshua. *Preservation, Tourism and Nationalism: The Jewel of the German Past. Heritage, Culture, and Identity.* Burlington, Vt.: Ashgate, 2006.

Halpern, Rick. *Down on the Killing Floor: Black and White Workers in Chicago's Packinghouses, 1904–1954.* Urbana: University of Chicago Press, 1997.

Handlin, Oscar. *The Uprooted: The Epic Story of the Great Migrations That Made the American People.* New York: Grosset & Dunlap, 1951.

Haraway, Donna. "Teddy Bear Patriarchy: Taxidermy in the Garden of Eden, New York." In *Primate Visions: Gender, Race, and Nature in the World of Modern Science,* 26–58. New York: Routledge, 1989.

Hardy, Stephen. *How Boston Played: Sport, Recreation, and Community, 1865–1915.* Boston: Northeastern University Press, 1982.

Harzig, Christiane. "The Ethnic Female Public Sphere: German-American Women in Turn-of-the-Century Chicago." In *Midwestern Women: Work, Community, and Leadership at the Crossroads,* edited by Lucy Eldersveld Murphy and Wendy Hamand Venet, 141–57. Bloomington: Indiana University Press, 1998.

———. "German-American Women in Chicago." In *Peasant Maids, City Women: From the European Countryside to Chicago,* edited by Christiane Harzig, 185–222. Ithaca, N.Y.: Cornell University Press, 1997.

Haugh, Dolores. *Riverview Amusement Park.* Images of America. Charleston, S.C.: Arcadia, 2004.

Haverty-Stacke, Donna T. *America's Forgotten Holiday: May Day and Nationalism, 1867–1960,* American History and Culture. New York: New York University Press, 2008.

Hayes, William. "Development of Forest Preserve District of Cook Country, Illinois." Master's thesis, DePaul University, 1949.

Hays, Samuel P. *Conservation and the Gospel of Efficiency: The Progressive Conservation Movement, 1890–1920.* Cambridge, Mass.: Harvard University Press, 1959.

Heikkonen, Esko. *Reaping the Bounty: McCormick Harvesting Machine Company Turns Abroad, 1878–1902.* Helsinki: Finnish Historical Society, 1995.

Heineman, Elizabeth. "Gender Identity in the Wandervogel Movement." *German Studies Review* 12 (May 1989): 249–70.

Heiss, Christine. "Popular and Working-Class German Theatre in Chicago, 1870–1910." In *German Workers' Culture in the United States, 1850 to 1920,* edited by Hartmut Keil. Washington, D.C.: Smithsonian Institution Press, 1988.

Hellsmuth, Petra S. "Feis." In *Celtic Culture: A Historical Encyclopedia,* edited by John T. Koch, 737. Santa Barbara: ABC-CLIO, 2006.

Herb, Guntram Henrik, and David H. Kaplan, eds. *Nested Identities: Nationalism, Territory, and Scale.* Lanham, Md.: Rowman and Littlefield, 1999.

Higham, John. "The Reorientation of American Culture in the 1890s." In *Writing American History: Essays on Modern Scholarship,* edited by John Higham, 78–102. Bloomington: Indiana University Press, 1978.

Hilton, George W. *Eastland: Legacy of the Titanic.* Stanford, Calif.: Stanford University Press, 1995.

Hirsch, Arnold R. "E Pluribus Duo?: Thoughts on 'Whiteness' and Chicago's 'New' Immigration as a Transient Third Tier." *Journal of American Ethnic History* 23 (Summer 2004): 7–44.

Ho, Chuimei, and Chinese-American Museum of Chicago. *Chinese in Chicago, 1870–1945.* Images of America. Charleston, S.C.: Arcadia, 2005.

Hofmeister, Rudolf A. *The Germans of Chicago.* Champaign: Stipes, 1976.

Holt, Glen E. "Private Plans for Public Spaces: The Origins of Chicago's Park System, 1850–1875." *Chicago History* 8 (Fall 1979): 181–82.

Hooson, David, ed. *Geography and National Identity.* Oxford, England: Blackwell, 1994.

Horwitt, Sanford D. *Let Them Call Me Rebel: Saul Alinsky, His Life and Legacy.* New York: Alfred K. Knopf, 1989.

Hsu, Madeline. *Dreaming of Gold, Dreaming of Home: Transnationalism and Migration between the United States and South China.* Palo Alto, Calif.: Stanford University Press, 2000.

Hucke, Matt, and Ursula Bielski. *Graveyards of Chicago: The People, History, Art, and Lore of Cook County Cemeteries.* Chicago: Lake Claremont Press, 1999.

Hunt, John Dixon. *The Picturesque Garden in Europe.* New York: Thames & Hudson, 2002.

Hurley, Andrew. "Busby's Stink Boat and the Regulation of Nuisance Trades, 1865–1918." In *Common Fields: An Environmental History of St. Louis,* edited by Andrew Hurley, 145–162. St. Louis: Missouri Historical Society Press, 1997.

———. *Environmental Inequalities: Class, Race, and Industrial Pollution in Gary, Indiana, 1945–1980.* Chapel Hill: University of North Carolina Press, 1995.

———. "Fiasco at Wagner Electric: Environmental Justice and Urban Geography in St. Louis." *Environmental History* 2 (October 1997): 460–81.

———. "Floods, Rats, and Toxic Waste: Allocating Environmental Hazards since World War II." In *Common Fields: An Environmental History of St. Louis,* edited by Andrew Hurley, 242–61. St. Louis: Missouri Historical Society Press, 1997.

Huth, Hans. *Nature and the American: Three Centuries of Changing Attitudes.* Berkeley: University of California Press, 1957.

Hyde, Anne Farrar. *An American Vision: Far Western Landscape and National Culture, 1820–1920.* New York: New York University Press, 1990.

Innis-Jiménez, Michael D. "Organizing for Fun: Recreation and Community Formation in the Mexican Community of South Chicago in the 1920s and 1930s." *Journal of the Illinois State Historical Society* 98 (Autumn 2005): 144–61.

Irwin, William. *The New Niagara: Tourism, Technology, and the Landscape of Niagara Falls, 1776–1917.* University Park: Pennsylvania State University Press, 1996.

Isaacman, Daniel. "Development of Jewish Camping in the United States." *Gratz College Annual of Jewish Studies* 5 (1976): 111–20.

Jablonsky, Thomas J. *Pride in the Jungle: Community and Everyday Life in Back of the Yards Chicago.* Creating the North American Landscape. Baltimore: Johns Hopkins University Press, 1993.

Jackson, Kenneth T. *Crabgrass Frontier: The Suburbanization of the United States.* New York: Oxford University Press, 1987.

Jacobson, Matthew Frye. *Special Sorrows: The Diasporic Imagination of Irish, Polish, and Jewish Immigrants in the United States.* Cambridge, Mass.: Harvard University Press, 1995.

———. *Whiteness of a Different Color: European Immigrants and the Alchemy of Race.* Cambridge, Mass.: Harvard University Press, 1998.

Jacoby, Karl. *Crimes against Nature: Squatters, Poachers, Thieves, and the Hidden History of American Conservation.* Berkeley: University of California Press, 2001.

Jandásek, Ladislav. "The Sokol Movement in Czechoslovakia." *Slavonic and East European Review* 11 (July 1932): 65–80.

Jensen, Jens. "Natural Parks and Gardens." *Saturday Evening Post*, March 8, 1930, 18–19, 169–70.

Jentz, John B. "Turnvereins." In *The Encyclopedia of Chicago*, edited by James R. Grossman et al., 835–36. Chicago: University of Chicago, 2004.

Jentz, John B., and Richard Schneirov. *Chicago in the Age of Capital: Class, Politics, and Democracy during the Civil War and Reconstruction.* The Working Class in American History. Urbana: University of Illinois Press, 2012.

Johannesson, Eric. "The Flower King in the American Republic: The Linnaeus Statue in Chicago, 1891." In *Swedish-American Life in Chicago: Cultural Aspects and Urban Aspects of an Immigrant People, 1850–1930*, edited by Philip J. Anderson and Dag Blanck, 267–82. Urbana: University of Illinois Press, 1992.

Johnson, Benjamin Heber. "Conservation, Subsistence, and Class at the Birth of Superior National Forest." *Environmental History* 4 (January 1999): 80–99.

Jones, David R. "Forerunners of the Komsomol: Scouting in Imperial Russia." In *Reforming the Tsar's Army: Military Innovation in Imperial Russia from Peter the Great to the Revolution*, edited by David Schimmelpennick van der Oye and Bruce W. Menning, 56–81. Woodrow Wilson Center Series. New York: Cambridge University Press, 2004.

Kahrl, Andrew W. "The Black Metropolis at Work and Play outside the Metropolis." In *Escape from New York! The "Harlem Renaissance" Reconsidered*, edited by Davarian Baldwin and Minkah Makalani. Minneapolis: University of Minnesota Press, 2013.

———. *The Land Was Ours: African American Beaches from Jim Crow to the Sunbelt South.* Cambridge, Mass.: Harvard University Press, 2012.

Kaimakamis, Vasilios, Stella Duka, Dimitrios Kaimakamis, and Athanasios Anastasiou. "The Birth of the German Gymnastics System and Its Introduction in the Modern-Greek State." *Studies in Physical Culture and Tourism* 11 (2004): 43–51.

Kammen, Michael G. *The Mystic Chords of Memory: The Transformation of Tradition in American Culture.* New York: Vintage Book, 1993.

Kassen, John. *Amusing the Million: Coney Island at the Turn of the Century.* New York: Hill and Wang, 1978.

Kazin, Michael, and Steven J. Ross. "America's Labor Day: The Dilemma of a Workers' Celebration." *Journal of American History* 78 (March 1992): 1294–323.

Keating, Ann Durkin. *Chicagoland: City and Suburbs in the Railroad Age.* Historical Studies of Urban America. Chicago: University of Chicago Press, 2005.

Keil, Hartmut, and John B. Jentz, eds. *German Workers in Chicago: A Documentary History of Working-Class Culture from 1850 to World War I.* Urbana: University of Illinois Press, 1988.

———. "Picnics." In *German Workers in Chicago: A Documentary History of Working-Class Culture from 1850 to World War I,* edited by Hartmut Keil and John B. Jentz, 203–4. Urbana: University of Illinois Press, 1988.

Keiser, John Howard. "John Fitzpatrick and Progressive Unionism, 1915–1925." Ph.D. diss., Northwestern University, 1965.

Kellert, Stephen R., and Edward O. Wilson. *The Biophilia Hypothesis.* Washington, D.C.: Island Press, 1993.

Kennedy, David. *Over Here: The First World War and American Society.* New York: Oxford University Press, 2004.

Klingle, Matthew. *Emerald City: An Environmental History of Seattle.* New Haven, Conn.: Yale University Press, 2007.

Kolodny, Annette. *The Land before Her: Fantasy and Experience of the American Frontiers, 1630–1860.* Chapel Hill: University of North Carolina Press, 1984.

Koulouri, Christina. "Athleticism and Antiquity: Symbols and Revivals in Nineteenth-Century Greece." *International Journal of the History of Sport* 15 (December 1998): 142–49.

Krasner, David. *A Beautiful Pageant: African American Theatre, Drama, and Performance in the Harlem Renaissance, 1910–1927.* New York: Palgrave Macmillan, 2002.

Kraus, Bea. *A Time To Remember: A History of the Jewish Community in South Haven.* Allegan Forest, Mich.: Priscilla Press, 1999.

Kuropas, Myron Bohdon. "Ukrainian Chicago: The Making of a Nationality Group in Chicago." In *Ethnic Chicago: A Multicultural Portrait,* edited by Melvin G. Holli and Peter d'A. Jones, 199–228. 4th ed. Grand Rapids, Mich.: William B. Eerdmans, 1995.

Lace, Ed. "Native Americans in the Chicago Area." In *Native Chicago,* edited by Terry Straus. Chicago: Native Chicago, 2002.

Ladino, Jennifer K. *Reclaiming Nostalgia: Longing for Nature in American Literature.* Charlottesville: University of Virginia Press, 2012.

Laqueur, Walter. *A History of Zionism.* New York: Holt, Rinehart and Winston, 1972.

———. *Young Germany: A History of the German Youth Movement.* New Brunswick, N.J.: Transaction Books, 1962.

Lasdun, Susan. *The English Park: Royal, Private and Public.* London: Deutsch, 1991.

Leab, Daniel. "The Memorial Day Massacre." *Midcontinent American Studies Journal* 8 (Fall 1967): 3–17.

Leach, William R. *Land of Desire: Merchants, Power, and the Rise of a New American Culture.* New York: Vintage Books, 1993.

Lears, T. J. Jackson. *No Place of Grace: Antimodernism and the Transformation of American Culture, 1880–1920.* Chicago: University of Chicago Press, 1994.

Lekan, Thomas. "German Landscape: Local Promotion of the *Heimat* Abroad." In *The Heimat Abroad: The Boundaries of Germanness,* edited by Krista O'Donnell, Renate Bridenthal, and Nancy Reagin, 141–50. Ann Arbor: University of Michigan Press, 2005.

———. *Imagining the Nation in Nature: Landscape Preservation and Germany Identity, 1885–1945.* Cambridge, Mass.: Harvard University Press, 2004.

Lempa, Heikki E. *Beyond the Gymnasium: Educating the Middle-Class Bodies in Classical Germany.* Lanham, Md.: Lexington Books, 2007.

Lévi-Strauss, Claude. *Totemism.* Translated by Rodney Needham. Boston: Beacon Press, 1963.

Lewis, David Levering. *When Harlem Was in Vogue.* New York: Knopf, 1981.

Limerick, Patricia Nelson. "Disorientation and Reorientation: The American Landscape Discovered from the West." In *Something in the Soil: Legacies and Reckonings in the New West,* edited by Patricia Nelson Limerick, 186–90. New York: W .W. Norton, 2000.

Lindsey, Almont. *The Pullman Strike: The Story of a Unique Experiment and of a Great Labor Upheaval.* Chicago: University of Chicago Press, 1942.

Lipin, Lawrence M. *Workers and the Wild: Conservation, Consumerism, and Labor in Oregon, 1910–30.* Urbana: University of Illinois Press, 2007.

Liponski, Wojciech. "Still an Unknown European Tradition: Polish Sport in the European Cultural Heritage." *International Journal of the History of Sport* 13 (August 1996): 1–41.

Lipsitz, George. *Time Passages: Collective Memory and American Popular Culture.* Minneapolis: University of Minnesota Press, 1990.

Litwicki, Ellen M. "'Our Hearts Burn with Ardent Love for Two Countries': Ethnicity and Assimilation at Chicago Holiday Celebrations, 1876–1918." *Journal of American Ethnic History* 19 (Spring 2000): 3–34.

Lockwood, Allison. *Passionate Pilgrims: The American Traveler in Great Britain, 1800–1914.* New York: Cornwall Books, 1981.

Löfgren, Orvar. "Know Your Country: A Comparative Perspective on Tourism and Nation Building in Sweden." In *Being Elsewhere: Tourism, Consumer Culture, and Identity in Modern Europe and North America,* edited by Shelley Baranowski and Ellen Furlough, 137–54. Ann Arbor: University of Michigan Press, 2001.

———. "Materializing the Nation in Sweden and America." *Ethnos* 58 (1993): 161–96.

Logan, Gabe. "The Rise of Early Chicago Soccer." *Sports in Chicago,* edited by Elliot Gorn, 19–42. Urbana: University of Illinois Press, 2008.

———. "Soccer." In *The Encyclopedia of Chicago,* edited by James R. Grossman et al., 760–61. Chicago: University of Chicago Press, 2004.

Lovoll, Odd S. *A Century of Urban Life: The Norwegians in Chicago before 1930*. Northfield, Minn.: Norwegian American Historical Association, 1988.

———. *The Promise of America: A History of the Norwegian-American People*. Minneapolis: University of Minnesota Press, 1984.

MacCulloch, John Arnott. *The Religion of the Ancient Celts*. Edinburgh: T. & T. Clark, 1911.

MacNeill, Máire, and Irish Folklore Commission. *The Festival of Lughnasa: A Study of the Survival of the Celtic Festival of the Beginning of Harvest*. London: Oxford University Press, 1962.

Magida, Gil, and Esther Magida. "Memories of Camp Interlaken." *Chicago Jewish History* 23 (Summer 1999): 10–11.

Mandle, W. F. *The Gaelic Athletic Association and Irish Nationalist Politics, 1884–1924*. Dublin: Gill and Macmillan, 1987.

———. "The IRB and the Origins of the Gaelic Athletic Association." *Irish Historical Studies* 20 (September 1977): 418–38.

Martin, Andrew, Ivana Turčová, and Jan Neuman, "The Czech Outdoor Experience: Turistika and Connections to Friluftsliv." In *Nature First: Outdoor Life the Friluftsliv Way*, edited by Bob Henderson and Nils Vikander, 197–208. Toronto: Natural Heritage Books, 2007.

Martin, Tony. *Race First: The Ideological and Organizational Struggles of Marcus Garvey and the Universal Negro Improvement Association*. Dover, Mass: Majority Press, 1986.

Marx, Leo. *The Machine in the Garden: Technology and the Pastoral Ideal in America*. New York: Oxford University Press, 1964.

Massa, Ann. "Black Women in the 'White City.'" *Journal of American Studies* 8 (December 1974): 319–37.

Mathur, Nameeta. "Women and Physical Culture in Modern Poland." Ph.D. diss., West Virginia University, 2001.

Matusik, Przemyslaw. "Der polnische 'Sokół' zur Zeit der Teilungen und in der II. Polnischen Republic." In *Die slawische Sokolbewegung: Beiträge zur Geschichte von Sport und Nationalismus in Osteuropa*, edited by Diethelm Blecking, 104–35. Dortmund: Forschungsstelle Ostmitteleuropa, 1991.

McArthur, Benjamin. "The Chicago Playground Movement: A Neglected Feature of Social Justice." *Social Science Review* (September 1975): 377–82.

———. "Parks, Playgrounds, and Progressivism." In *A Breath of Fresh Air: Chicago's Neighborhood Parks of the Progressive Era, 1900–1925*, edited by Constance Gordon and Kathy Hussey-Arntson, 9–14. Chicago: Chicago Public Library and Chicago Park District, 1989.

McCammack, Brian James. "Recovering Green in Bronzeville: An Environmental and Cultural History of the African American Great Migration, 1915–1940." Ph.D. diss., Harvard University, 2012.

McCarthy, Eugene. "The Bohemians of Chicago and Their Benevolent Societies: 1875–1946." Master's thesis, University of Chicago, 1950.

McCarthy, Michael P. "Politics and the Parks: Chicago Businessmen and the Recreation Movement." *Journal of the Illinois State Historical Society* 65 (Summer 1972): 160–63.

McCrossen, Alexis. *Holy Day, Holiday: The American Sunday.* Ithaca, N.Y.: Cornell University Press, 2002.

McGurty, Eileen. *Transforming Environmentalism: Warren County, PCBs, and the Origins of Environmental Justice.* New Brunswick, N.J.: Rutgers University Press, 2009.

McKillen, Elizabeth. "Chicago Federation of Labor." In *Encyclopedia of U.S. Labor and Working-Class History*, edited by Eric Arnesen, 225–27. New York: Routledge, 2007.

———. *Chicago Labor and the Quest for a Democratic Diplomacy, 1914–1924.* Ithaca, N.Y.: Cornell University Press, 1995.

McMillan, Daniel Alexander. "Germany Incarnate: Politics, Gender, and Sociability in the Gymnastics Movement, 1811–1871." Ph.D. diss., Columbia University, 1997.

McNeill, J.R. "Observations on the Nature and Culture of Environmental History." *History and Theory* 42 (December 2003): 5–43.

Meis Knupfer, Anne. *The Chicago Black Renaissance and Women's Activism.* Urbana: University of Illinois Press, 2006.

Messer-Kruse, Timothy. *The Haymarket Conspiracy: Transatlantic Anarchist Networks.* Working Class in American History. Urbana: University of Illinois Press, 2012.

Meyerowitz, Joanne J. *Women Adrift: Independent Wage Earners in Chicago, 1880–1930.* Chicago: University of Chicago Press, 1991.

Miller, Perry. "Nature and the National Ego." In *Errand into the Wilderness*, edited by Perry Miller, 204–16. Cambridge, Mass.: Belknap Press of Harvard University Press, 1956.

———. *Nature's Nation.* Cambridge, Mass.: Belknap Press of Harvard University Press, 1967.

———, ed. *Errand into the Wilderness.* Cambridge, Mass.: Belknap Press of Harvard University Press, 1956.

Mishler, Paul C. *Raising Reds: The Young Pioneers, Radical Summer Camps, and Communist Political Culture in the United States.* New York: Columbia University Press, 1999.

Mitchell, Michele. *Righteous Propagation: African Americans and the Politics of Racial Uplift after Reconstruction.* Chapel Hill: University of North Carolina Press, 2004.

Mitman, Gregg. *Breathing Space: How Allergies Shape Our Lives and Landscapes.* New Haven, Conn.: Yale University Press, 2007.

———. *Reel Nature: America's Romance with Wildlife on Films.* Cambridge, Mass.: Harvard University Press, 1999.

Montgomery, David. *Beyond Equality: Labor and the Radical Republicans, 1862–1872.* New York: Knopf, 1967.

———. *The Fall of the House of Labor: The Workplace, the State, and American Labor Activism, 1865–1925.* New York: Cambridge University Press, 1987.

———. "The Farmer-Labor Party." In *Working for Democracy: American Workers from the Revolution to the Present*, edited by Paul Buhle and Alan Dawley, 73–82. Urbana: University of Illinois Press, 1985.

Montrie, Chad. *Making a Living: Work and Environment in the United States.* Chapel Hill: University of North Carolina Press, 2008.

Mosley, Stephen. "Common Ground: Integrating Social and Environmental History." *Journal of Social History* 39 (Spring 2006): 915–33.

Mosse, George L. *The Nationalization of the Masses: Political Symbolism and Mass Movements in Germany from the Napoleonic Wars through the Third Reich.* Ithaca, N.Y.: Cornell University Press, 1975.

Moy, Susan Lee. "The Chinese in Chicago: The First One Hundred Years." In *Ethnic Chicago: A Multicultural Portrait*, edited by Melvin G. Holli and Peter d'A. Jones, 378–408. 4th ed. Grand Rapids, Mich.: William B. Eerdmans, 1995.

Moynihan, Paul. *An Official History of Scouting.* London: Hamlyn, 2006.

Mrozek, Donald. "The Natural Limits of Unstructured Play, 1880–1914." In *Hard at Play: Leisure in America, 1840–1940*, edited by Kathryn Grover, 210–26. Amherst: University of Massachusetts Press, 1992.

———. *Sports and American Mentality, 1880–1910.* Knoxville: University of Tennessee, 1983.

Mumford, Kevin. *Interzones: Black-White Sex Districts in Chicago and New York in the Early Twentieth Century.* New York: Columbia University Press, 1997.

Nasaw, David. *Going Out: The Rise and Fall of Public Amusements.* New York: Basic Books, 1993.

Nash, Roderick. "John Muir, William Kent, and the Conservative Schism." *Pacific Historical Review* 36 (November 1967): 423–33.

———. *Wilderness and the American Mind.* New Haven, Conn.: Yale University Press, 1967.

Nations Human Settlements Programme. *State of the World's Cities 2010–2011: Bridging the Urban Divide.* London: Earthscan, 2010.

Nelli, Humbert S. "The Role of the 'Colonial' Press in the Italian-American Community of Chicago, 1886–1921." Ph.D. diss, University of Chicago, 1965.

Nelson, Bruce. *Beyond the Martyrs: A Social History of Chicago's Anarchists, 1870–1900.* New Brunswick, N.J.: Rutgers University Press, 1988.

Nemecek, Paul. "The Pilsen Brewery and Pilsen Park in Chicago History." *Kořeny (Roots): Journal of the Czech and Slovak American Genealogical Society of Illinois* 2 (Spring 1998): 1, 12.

Newell, Barbara. *Chicago and the Labor Movement: Metropolitan Unionism in the 1930s.* Urbana: University of Illinois Press, 1961.

Nicolaides, Becky M. *My Blue Heaven: Life and Politics in the Working-Class Suburbs of Los Angeles, 1920–1965.* Chicago: University of Chicago Press, 2002.

Nolin, Catharina. "Stockholm's Urban Parks: Meeting Places and Social Contexts from 1860–1930." In *The European City and Green Space: London,*

*Stockholm, Helsinki and St. Petersburg, 1850–2000*, edited by Peter Clark, 111–26. Aldershot, England: Ashgate, 2006.

Nolte, Claire E. "All for One! One for All! The Federation of Slavic Sokols and the Failure of Neo-Slavism." In *Constructing Nationalities in East Central Europe*, edited by Pieter M. Judson and Marsha L. Rozenblit, 126–40. New York: Berghahn Books, 2005.

———. "'Every Czech a Sokol!': Feminism and Nationalism in the Czech Sokol Movement." *Austrian History Yearbook* 24, no. 1 (1993): 265–88.

———. "Our Brothers across the Ocean: The Czech Sokol in America to 1914." *Czechoslovak and Central European Journal* 11 (1993): 15–37.

———. *The Sokol in Czech Lands to 1914: Training the Nation*. New York: Palgrave Macmillan, 2002.

Nur, Ofer. "Hashomer Hatzair Youth Movement 1918–1924 from Eastern Galicia and Vienna to Palestine: A Cultural History." Ph.D. diss., University of California–Los Angeles, 2004.

O'Rourke, Kevin H. "The European Grain Invasion, 1870–1913." *Journal of Economic History* 57 (December 1997): 775–801.

Odem, Mary E. *Delinquent Daughters: Protecting and Policing Adolescent Female Sexuality in the United States*. Charlotte: University of North Carolina Press, 1995.

Olwig, Kenneth. "Reinventing Common Nature: Yosemite and Mount Rushmore—A Meandering Tale of a Double Nature." In *Uncommon Ground: Toward Reinventing Nature*, edited by William Cronon, 379–408. New York: W. W. Norton, 1995.

Orsi, Robert A. *The Madonna of 115th Street: Faith and Community in Italian Harlem, 1880–1950*. New Haven, Conn.: Yale University Press, 1985.

Ottley, Roi. *The Lonely Warrior: The Life and Times of Robert S. Abbott*. Chicago: H. Regnery, 1955.

Outka, Paul. *Race and Nature from Transcendentalism to the Harlem Renaissance*. New York: Palgrave Macmillan, 2008.

Øverland, Orm. *Immigrant Minds, American Identities: Making the United States Home, 1870–1930*. Urbana: University of Illinois Press, 2000.

Ozanne, Robert W. *A Century of Labor-Management Relations at McCormick and International Harvester*. Madison: University of Wisconsin Press, 1967.

Pacyga, Dominic A. *Chicago: A Biography*. Chicago: University of Chicago Press, 2009.

———. "Chicago's Ethnic Neighborhoods: The Myth of Stability and the Reality of Change." In *Ethnic Chicago: A Multicultural Portrait*, edited by Melvin G. Holli and Peter d'A. Jones, 604–17. 4th ed. Grand Rapids, Mich.: William B. Eerdmans, 1995.

———. "Chicago's 1919 Race Riot: Ethnicity, Class and Urban Violence." In *The Making of Urban America*, edited by Raymond Mohl, 187–207. Wilmington, Del.: Scholarly Resources, 1997.

———. "Chicago's Pilsen Park and the Struggle for Czechoslovak Independence during World War One." In *Essays in Russian and East European History:*

*Festssschrift in Honor of Edward C. Thaden,* edited by Leo Schelbert and Nick Ceh, 117–29. Boulder, Colo.: East European Monographs, 1995.

———. "Parks for the People." In *A Breath of Fresh Air: Chicago's Neighborhood Parks of the Progressive Era, 1900–1925,* edited by Constance Gordon and Kathy Hussey-Arntson, 15–19. Chicago: Chicago Public Library and Chicago Park District, 1989.

———. "The Russell Square Community Committee: An Ethnic Response to Urban Problems." *Journal of Urban History* 15 (February 1989): 159–84.

Pacyga, Dominic A., and Ellen Skerrett. *Chicago: City of Neighborhoods.* Chicago: Loyola University Press, 1986.

Paddon, Anna R., and Sally Turner, "African Americans and the World's Columbian Exposition." *Illinois Historical Journal* 88 (Spring 1995): 19–36.

Peiss, Kathy. *Cheap Amusements: Working Women and Leisure in Turn-of-the-Century New York.* Philadelphia: Temple University Press, 1986.

Pellow, David N. *Garbage Wars: The Struggle for Environmental Justice in Chicago.* Cambridge: MIT Press, 2002.

Pesavento, Wilma J. "Sport and Recreation in the Pullman Experiment, 1880–1900." *Journal of Sport History* 9 (Summer 1982): 38–62.

Phillips, Denise. "Friends of Nature: Urban Sociability and Regional Natural History in Dresden, 1800–1850." *Osiris* 18 (2003): 43–59.

Philpott, Thomas Lee. *The Slum and the Ghetto: Neighborhood Deterioration and Middle-Class Reform, Chicago, 1880–1930.* New York: Oxford University Press, 1978.

Pienkos, Donald E. *One Hundred Years Young: A History of the Polish Falcons of America, 1887–1987.* Boulder, Colo.: East European Monographs, 1987.

Pierce, Bessie. *From Town to City, 1848–1871.* Vol. 2 of *A History of Chicago.* New York: Knopf, 1937.

Platt, Harold L. *Shock Cities: The Environmental Transformation and Reform of Manchester and Chicago.* Chicago: University of Chicago Press, 2005.

Pomeroy, Earl S. *In Search of the Golden West: The Tourist in Western America.* New York: Knopf, 1957.

Pouyat, Richard V., Ian D. Yesilonis, and David J. Nowak. "Carbon Storage by Urban Soils in the United States." *Journal of Environmental Quality* 35 (2006): 1566–75.

Presner, Todd Samuel. *Muscular Judaism: The Jewish Body and the Politics of Regeneration.* Routledge Jewish Studies Series. London: Routledge, 2007.

Price, Jennifer. *Flight Maps: Adventures with Nature in Modern America.* New York: Basic Books, 1999.

Pulido, Laura. *Environmentalism and Economic Justice: Two Chicano Struggles in the Southwest.* Tucson: University of Arizona Press, 1996.

Puskar, Samira. *Bosnian Americans of Chicagoland.* Images of America. Charlestown, S.C.: Arcadia, 2007.

Quirke, Carol. "Reframing Chicago's Memorial Day Massacre, May 30, 1937." *American Quarterly* 60 (March 2008): 129–55.

Rabinovitz, Lauren. *For the Love of Pleasure: Women, Movies, and Culture in Turn-of-the-Century Chicago*. New Brunswick, N.J.: Rutgers University Press, 1998.

Rainey, Reuben M. "William Le Baron Jenney and Chicago's West Parks." In *Midwestern Landscape Architecture*, edited by William H. Tishler. Urbana: University of Illinois Press, 2000.

Randall, Gregory C. *America's Original GI Town: Park Forest, Illinois*. Baltimore: Johns Hopkins Press, 2000.

Ranney, Victoria Post. *Olmsted in Chicago*. Chicago: Open Lands Project, 1972.

———, ed. *The California Frontier, 1863–1865*. Vol. 5 of *The Papers of Frederick Law Olmsted*. Baltimore: Johns Hopkins University Press, 1990.

Rawick, George P. *From Sundown to Sunup: The Making of the Black Community*. Westport, Conn.: Greenwood, 1972.

Rawson, Michael. *Eden on the Charles: The Making of Boston*. Cambridge, Mass: Harvard University Press, 2010.

Redlich, Shimon. *Together and Apart in Brzezany: Poles, Jews, and Ukrainians, 1919–1945*. Bloomington: Indiana University Press, 2002.

Reed, Christopher Robert. *"All the World Is Here!": The Black Presence at White City*. Bloomington: Indiana University Press, 2000.

———. *Black Chicago's First Century*. Columbia: University of Missouri Press, 2005.

———. *The Rise of Chicago's Black Metropolis, 1920–1929*. Urbana: University of Illinois Press, 2011.

Renner, Richard Wilson. "In a Perfect Ferment: Chicago, the Know-Nothings, and the Riot for Lager Beer." *Chicago History* 5 (Fall 1976): 161–70.

Retzlaff, Rebecca C. "The Illinois Forest Preserve District Act of 1913 and the Emergence of Metropolitan Park System Planning in the USA." *Planning Perspectives* 25 (October 2010): 433–55.

Riess, Steven A. *City Games: The Evolution of American Urban Society and the Rise of Sports*. Urbana: University of Illinois Press, 1989.

———. "Ethnic Sports." In *Ethnic Chicago: A Multicultural Portrait*, edited by Melvin G. Holli and Peter d'A. Jones, 530–56. 4th ed. Grand Rapids, Mich.: William B. Eerdmans, 1995.

———. "Introduction: The History of Sports in Chicago." In *The Chicago Sports Reader: 100 Years of Sports in the Windy City*, edited by Steven A. Riess and Gerald R. Gems, 1–58. Urbana: University of Illinois Press, 2009.

———. "Sports and the American Jew: An Introduction." In *Sports and the American Jew*, edited by Steven A. Riess, 1–59. Syracuse: Syracuse University Press, 1998.

Roberts, Andrew Lawrence. *From Good King Wenceslas to the Good Soldier Svejk: A Dictionary of Czech Popular Culture*. New York: Central European University Press, 2005.

Roediger, David. *The Wages of Whiteness: Race and the Making of the American Working Class*. London: Verso, 1991.

Rogers, Daniel. *The Work Ethic in Industrial America, 1850–1920*. Chicago: University of Chicago Press, 1978.

Rollins, William H. *A Greener Vision of Home: Cultural Politics and Environmental Reform in the German Heimatschutz Movement, 1904–1918*. Ann Arbor: University of Michigan Press, 1997.

Rome, Adam. "Nature Wars, Culture Wars: Immigration and Environmental Reform in the Progressive Era." *Environmental History* 13 (July 2008): 432–53.

Rosenzweig, Roy. *Eight Hours for What We Will: Workers and Leisure in an Industrial City, 1870–1920*. Cambridge: Cambridge University Press, 1983.

Rosenzweig, Roy, and Elizabeth Blackmar. *The Park and the People: A History of Central Park*. Ithaca, N.Y.: Cornell University Press, 1992.

Ross, Dorothy. *G. Stanley Hall: The Psychologist as Prophet*. Chicago: University of Chicago Press, 1972.

Rudwick, Elliot M., and August Meier. "Black Man in the 'White City': Negroes and the Columbian Exposition." *Phylon* 26 (Winter 1965): 354–61.

Rugh, Susan Sessions. *Are We There Yet?: The Golden Age of American Family Vacations*. Culture America. Lawrence: University Press of Kansas, 2008.

Runte, Alfred. *National Parks: The American Experience*. Lincoln: University of Nebraska Press, 1984.

Rutkoff, Peter M., and William B. Scott. "Pinkster in Chicago: Bud Billiken and the Mayor of Bronzeville, 1930–1945." *Journal of African American History* 89 (Autumn 2004): 316–30.

Rydell, Robert W. "Editor's Introduction" In *The Reason Why the Colored American Is Not in the World's Columbian Exposition*, by Ida B. Wells, Frederick Douglass, Irvine Garland Penn, and Ferdinand L. Barnett, xi–xlviii. Edited by Robert W. Rydell. Urbana: University of Illinois Press, 1999.

———. *World of Fairs: The Century-of-Progress Expositions*. Chicago: University of Chicago Press, 1993.

Sachs, Aaron. *Arcadian America: The Death and Life of an Environmental Tradition*. New Haven: Yale University Press, 2013.

Sanchez, George J. *Becoming Mexican American: Ethnicity, Culture, and Identity in Chicano Los Angeles, 1900–1945*. New York: Oxford University Press, 1993.

Sarna, Jonathan. "The Crucial Decade in Jewish Camping." In *A Place of Our Own: The Rise of Reform Jewish Camping*, edited by Michael M. Lorge and Gary P. Zola, 27–51. Judaic Studies Series. Tuscaloosa: University of Alabama Press, 2006.

Sawislak, Karen. *Smoldering City: Chicagoans and the Great Fire, 1871–1874*. Historical Studies of Urban America. Chicago: University of Chicago Press, 1995.

Sayer, Derek. *The Coasts of Bohemia: A Czech History*. Princeton, N.J.: Princeton University Press, 1998.

Schama, Simon. *Landscape and Memory*. New York: A. A. Knopf, 1995.

Schlossman, Steven, and Michael Sedlak. *The Chicago Area Project Revisited*. Santa Monica, Calif.: Rand Corporation, 1983.

Schmitt, Peter J. *Back to Nature: The Arcadian Myth in Urban America*. The Urban Life in America Series. New York: Oxford University Press, 1969.

Schneirov, Richard. *Labor and Urban Politics: Class Conflict and the Origins of Modern Liberalism in Chicago, 1864–1897.* The Working Class in American History. Urbana: University of Illinois Press, 1998.

Schrepfer, Susan R. *Nature's Altars: Mountains, Gender, and American Environmentalism.* Lawrence: University Press of Kansas, 2005.

Schultz, April R. *Ethnicity on Parade: Inventing the Norwegian-American through Celebration.* Amherst: University of Massachusetts Press, 1994.

Schuyler, David. *The New Urban Landscape: The Redefinition of City Form in Nineteenth-Century America.* New Studies in American Intellectual and Cultural History. Baltimore: Johns Hopkins University Press, 1986.

Schuyler, David, and Jane Turner Censer, eds. *The Years of Olmsted, Vaux, & Company, 1865–1874.* Vol. 6 of *The Papers of Frederick Law Olmsted.* Baltimore: Johns Hopkins University Press, 1992.

Sclair, Helen A. "Ethnic Cemeteries: Underground Rites." In *Ethnic Chicago: A Multicultural Portrait,* edited by Melvin G. Holli and Peter d'A. Jones, 618–39. 4th ed. Grand Rapids, Mich.: William B. Eerdmans, 1995.

Scott, Franklin D. *Sweden: The Nation's History.* Carbondale: Southern Illinois University Press, 1988.

Sears, John F. *Sacred Places: American Tourist Attractions in the Nineteenth Century.* New York: Oxford University Press, 1989.

Sellars, Richard West. *Preserving Nature in the National Parks: A History.* New Haven, Conn.: Yale University Press, 1997.

Sellers, Christopher C. *Crabgrass Crucible: Suburban Nature and the Rise of Environmentalism in Twentieth-Century America.* Chapel Hill: University of North Carolina Press, 2012.

Shabowski, Annette. "Camp Sokol." *Kořeny (Roots): Journal of the Czech and Slovak American Genealogical Society of Illinois* 6 (Winter 2002): 18.

Shaffer, Marguerite S. *See America First: Tourism and National Identity, 1880–1940.* Washington: Smithsonian Institution Press, 2001.

Shaw, Clifford R. *Delinquency Areas: A Study of the Geographic Distribution of School Truants, Juvenile Delinquents, and Adult Offenders in Chicago.* University of Chicago Press, 1929.

Shiffman, Daniel. "Ethnic Competitors in Studs Lonigan." *MELUS* 24 (Autumn 1999): 67–79.

Shpak-Lissak, Rivkah. *Pluralism and Progressives: Hull House and the New Immigrants, 1890–1919.* Chicago: University of Chicago Press, 1989.

Sisson, Elaine. *Pearse's Patriots: St Enda's.* Cork, Ireland: Cork University Press, 2004.

Skilnik, Bob. *The History of Beer and Brewing in Chicago, 1833–1978.* Saint Paul, Minn.: Pogo Press, 1999.

Slayton, Robert A. *Back of the Yards: The Making of a Local Democracy.* Chicago: University of Chicago Press, 1986.

Smith, Carl. *Urban Disorder and the Shape of Belief: The Great Chicago Fire, the Haymarket Bomb, and the Model Town of Pullman.* Chicago: University of Chicago Press, 1995.

Smith, Henry Nash. *Virgin Land: The American West as Symbol and Myth.*
Cambridge, Mass.: Harvard University Press, 1950.

Smith, Kimberly K. *African American Environmental Thought: Foundations.*
Lawrence: University Press of Kansas, 2007.

Sniderman, Julia. "Bringing the Prairie Vision into Focus." In *Prairie in
the City: Naturalism in Chicago's Parks, 1870–1940*, edited by Rosemary
Adams and Claudia Lamm Wood, 19–31. Chicago: Chicago Historical
Society, 1991.

Sofchalk, Donald. "The Memorial Day Incident: An Episode of Mass Action."
*Labor History* 6 (Winter 1965): 3–43.

Sollors, Werner. "Introduction: The Invention of Ethnicity." In *The Invention of
Ethnicity*, edited by Werner Sollors, ix–xx. New York: Oxford University
Press, 1989.

Sørlin, Sverker. "Nature, Skiing and Swedish Nationalism." *International Journal
of the History of Sport* 12, no. 2 (1995): 147–63.

Spear, Allan H. *Black Chicago: The Making of a Negro Ghetto, 1890–1920.* Chicago:
University of Chicago Press, 1967.

Spears, Timothy B. *Chicago Dreaming: Midwesterners and the City, 1871–1919.*
Chicago: University of Chicago Press, 2005.

Spence, Mark David. *Dispossessing the Wilderness: Indian Removal and the Making of
the National Parks.* New York: Oxford University Press, 1999.

Stilgoe, John R. *Borderland: Origins of the American Suburb, 1820–1939.* New
Haven, Conn.: Yale University Press, 1988.

Stovall, Mary E. "The *Chicago Defender* in the Progressive Era." *Illinois Historical
Journal* 83 (Autumn 1990): 159–72.

Stroud, Ellen. "Troubled Waters in Ecotopia: Environmental Racism in
Portland, Oregon." *Radical History Review* 74 (Spring 1999): 65–95.

Strout, Cushing. *The American Image of the Old World.* New York: Harper & Row,
1963.

Subtelny, Orest. *Ukraine: A History*, 3rd ed. Toronto: University of Toronto Press,
2000.

Sutter, Paul S. "When Environmental Traditions Collide: Ramachandra Guha's
*The Unquiet Woods* and U.S. Environmental History." *Environmental History* 14
(July 2009): 543–50.

Suttles, Gerald D. *The Social Order of the Slum: Ethnicity and Territory in the Inner
City.* Chicago: University of Chicago Press, 1970.

Sutton, Silvia Barry, ed. *Civilizing American Cities: Writings on City Landscapes.*
New York: Da Capo Press, 1997.

Sze, Julie. *Noxious New York: The Racial Politics of Urban Health and Environmental
Justice.* Cambridge: MIT Press, 2007.

Taylor, Alan. "Unnatural Inequalities: Social and Environmental Histories."
*Environmental History* 1 (October 1996): 6–19.

Teja, Angela, and Marco Impiglia. "Italy." In *European Cultures in Sport:
Examining the Nations and Regions*, edited by James Riordan and Arnd Krüger,
139–141. Bristol: Intellect Books, 2003.

Thomopoulos, Elaine Cotsirilos. *Resorts of Berrien County, Michigan*. Images of America. Charleston, S.C.: Arcadia, 2005.

——. *St. Joseph and Benton Harbor*. Images of America Series. Charleston, S.C.: Arcadia, 2003.

——. "Summer Memories: The Greeks Who Vacationed in Southwestern Michigan." Unpublished Paper. 2003.

Thompson, E. P. *The Making of the English Working Class*. London: Victor Gollancz, 1963.

Tippens, William W., and Julia Sniderman. "The Planning and Design of Chicago's Neighborhood Parks." In *A Breath of Fresh Air: Chicago's Neighborhood Parks of the Progressive Era, 1900–1925*, edited by Constance Gordon and Kathy Hussey-Arntson, 21–28. Chicago: Chicago Public Library and Chicago Park District, 1989.

Tracy, Steven C. *Writers of the Black Chicago Renaissance*. Urbana: University of Illinois Press, 2011.

Turak, Theodore. *William Le Baron Jenney: A Pioneer of Modern Architecture*. 1967. Reprint Ann Arbor: UMI Research Press, 1986.

Turner, Frederick W. *John Muir: Rediscovering America*. Cambridge, Mass.: Perseus, 2000.

Tuttle, William M. *Race Riot: Chicago in the Red Summer of 1919*. New York: Atheneum, 1984.

Tyrell, Ian. "American Exceptionalism in an Age of International History." *American Historical Review* 96 (October 1991): 1031–55.

Ueberhorst, Hoorst. *Friedrich Ludwig Jahn and His Time, 1778–1852*. Translated by Timothy Neville. Munich: Moos, 1978.

United Nations. *World Urbanization Prospects: The 2007 Revision*. New York: United Nations, 2007.

Vaillant, Derek. *Sounds of Reform: Progressivism and Music in Chicago, 1873–1935*. Chapel Hill: University of North Carolina Press, 2003.

Van Bottenburg, Maarten. *Global Games*. Translated by Beverly Jackson. Urbana: University of Illinois Press, 2001.

Van Dalen, Deobold B., and Bruce L. Bennett. *A World History of Physical Education: Cultural, Philosophical, Comparative*. 2nd ed. Englewood Cliffs, N.J.: Prentice Hall, 1971.

Vari, Alexander. "From Friends of Nature to Tourist-Soldiers: Nation Building and Tourism in Hungary, 1873–1914." In *Turizm: The Russian and East European Tourist under Capitalism and Socialism*, edited by Anne E. Gorsuch and Diane P. Koekner, 72–81. Ithaca, N.Y.: Cornell University Press, 2006.

Vecoli, Rudolph. "Chicago's Italians Prior to World War I." Ph.D. diss., University of Wisconsin, 1963.

——. "Contadini in Chicago: A Critique of the Uprooted." *Journal of American History* 5 (December 1964): 404–17.

——. "Cult and Occult in Italian American Culture: The Persistence of a Religious Heritage." In *Immigrants and Religion in Urban America*, edited by

Randall M. Miller and Thomas D. Marzik, 25–47. Philadelphia: Temple University Press, 1977.

———. "Prelates and Peasants: Italian Immigrants and the Catholic Church." *Journal of Social History* 2 (Spring 1968): 229–35.

Wachholz, Ted. *The Eastland Disaster*. Images of America. Charleston, S.C.: Arcadia, 2005.

Wagner, Ralf. "Turner Societies and the Socialist Tradition." In *German Workers' Culture in the United States, 1850 to 1920*, ed. Hartmut Keil, 221–39. Washington, D.C.: Smithsonian Institution Press, 1988.

Warren, Louis S. *The Hunter's Game: Poachers and Conservationists in Twentieth-Century America*. New Haven, Conn.: Yale University Press, 1997.

Washington, Sylvia Hood. *Packing Them In: An Archaeology of Environmental Racism in Chicago, 1865–1954*. Lanham, Md.: Lexington Books, 2005.

Weber, Eugen. "Gymnastics and Sports in Fin-de-Siècle France: Opium of the Classes?" *The American Historical Review* 76 (February 1971): 70–98.

Weir, Robert E. *Beyond Labor's Veil: The Culture of the Knights of Labor*. University Park: Pennsylvania State University Press, 1996.

White, Evelyn. "Black Women and the Wilderness." In *The Stories that Shape Us: Contemporary Women Write about the West*, edited by Teresa Jordan and James Hepworth, 376–383. New York: W.W. Norton, 1995.

White, Richard. "Are You an Environmentalist or Do You Work for a Living?" In *Uncommon Ground: Toward Reinventing Nature*, edited by William Cronon, 171–85. New York: W. W. Norton, 1995.

———. *The Middle Ground: Indians, Empires, and Republics in the Great Lakes Region, 1650–1815*. New York: Cambridge University Press, 1991.

———. *The Organic Machine: The Remaking of the Columbia River*. New York: Hill and Wang, 1995.

———. *Remembering Ahanagran: A History of Stories*. Seattle: University of Washington Press, 2004.

Wiese, Andrew. *Places of Their Own: African American Suburbanization in the Twentieth Century*. Chicago: University of Chicago Press, 2009.

Wille, Lois. *Forever Open, Clear, and Free: The Struggle for Chicago's Lakefront*. Chicago: Regnery, 1972.

Williams, John Alexander. *Turning to Nature in Germany: Hiking, Nudism, and Conservation, 1900–1940*. Stanford, Calif.: Stanford University Press, 2007.

Williams, Raymond. *The Country and the City*. London: Chatto and Windus, 1973.

Wilson, Benjamin C., and Lewis Walker. *Black Eden: The Idlewild Community*. East Lansing: Michigan State University Press, 2002.

Wilson, Edward O. *Biophilia*. Cambridge, Mass.: Harvard University Press, 1984.

Wiltse, Jeff. *Contested Waters: A Social History of Swimming Pools in America*. Chapel Hill: University of North Carolina Press, 2007.

Wolf, Kathleen. "Metro Nature: Its Functions, Benefits, and Values." In *Growing Greener Cities: Urban Sustainability in the Twenty-First Century*, edited by Eugenie Ladner Birch and Susan M. Wachter, 259–78. City in the Twenty-First Century Book Series. Philadelphia: University of Pennsylvania Press, 2008.

Wolfe, Linnie Marsh. *Son of the Wilderness: The Life of John Muir*. New York: Alfred A. Knopf, 1945.

Wyman, Mark. *Round-Trip to America: The Immigrant Return to Europe*. Ithaca, N.Y.: Cornell University Press, 1993.

Yearwood, Pauline Dubkin. "Family Memoir: The Urban Nature Lover." *Chicago Jewish History* 29 (Fall 2005): 4–5.

Yeracaris, Constantine A. "A Study of the Voluntary Associations of the Greek Immigrants of Chicago from 1890 to 1948 with Special Emphasis on World War II and Post War Period." Master's thesis, University of Chicago, 1950.

Young, Terence. "'A Contradiction in Democratic Government': W.J. Trent, Jr. and the Struggle for Non-Segregated National Park Campgrounds" *Environmental History* 14 (October 2009): 651–682.

———. *Building San Francisco's Parks, 1850–1930*. Baltimore: Johns Hopkins Press, 2004.

Zaborniak, Stanisław. "An Outline of Development of Tourism in the Activity of Ukrainian Organizations of Physical Culture in Galicia and in the South-East Borderland of Poland (1894–1939)." *Studies in Physical Culture and Tourism* 13 (2006): 61–74.

Zachariasiewicz, Walter. "Organizational Structure of Polonia." *Poles in America: Bicentennial Essays*, edited by Frank Mocha, 627–70. Stevens Point, Wisc.: Worzalla, 1978.

Zivich, Edward Andrew. "Fighting Union: The CIO at Inland Steel, 1936–1942." Master's thesis, University of Wisconsin, Milwaukee, 1972.

Zola, Gary P. "Jewish Camping and Its Relationship to the Organized Camping Movement in America." In *A Place of Our Own: The Rise of Reform Jewish Camping*, edited by Michael M. Lorge and Gary P. Zola, 1–26. Judaic Studies Series. Tuscaloosa: University of Alabama Press, 2006.

# Index

Wabash YMCA, 107
Walden Pond, 148
*Wandervogel*, 72, 73
Washington, Booker T., 110
Washington Park, 20, 64, 80, 84, 87, 93, 94, 96, 103, 104, 112; blacks in, 95, 97, 110–11; building, 14; canal connecting, 16; commission for, 14; football at, 85; Lonigan and, 65, 66; nostalgia for, 65; plan for, 15; social control and, 23; work on, 10
Washington Square, 45
WCFL (radio station), 130
Weber, Max, 25
Weinberg, S. Kirson, 77–78
Welfare, 133, 134, 137
Wells, H. G., 41
Wells, Ida B., 93, 100, 103
West, Mollie, 135
Western Electric, 127, 128, 130
West Michigan Resort, 100
West Parks District, 16, 28
West Side, 10, 13, 14, 128, 139
White City, 16, 23, 105
Whyte, William, 147
Wicker Memorial, 135
Wigwams (gang), 84
Wilderness, 2, 17–22, 22–29, 40, 63, 71, 145; immigrants and, 48; indigenous, 10; leisure in, 18, 27; loving, 148; middle-class tourists and, 3; national park, 52; privilege and, 3; working-class, 126–32
Wilderness camps, 136, 142, 150
Wilderness parks, 26, 80, 128; nature in, 6; racial politics and, 22
Williams, Eugene, 97, 98–99
Williams, Raymond, 12
Williams, Wilberforce, 89
Wilson, Woodrow, 133

Wisconsin Lake Country, 50
Wizard Arrows Social Athletic Club, 84
Wolf Point, 34, 36
Women's Trade Union League (WTUL), 130
Wooded Island, 16
Woodson, Carter, 107–8
Woodstreeters, The, 82
Working class, 8, 120, 122; green spaces and, 113
Works Progress Administration, 103
World's Fair (1893), 16, 23, 105
World's Fair (1933), 34, 111
World War I, 59, 83, 90, 91, 95, 99, 100, 110, 128, 132
Wright, Frank Lloyd, 17, 28
Wright, Richard, 108, 113
Wright's Grove, 31, 58
Württemberg, King of, 55

Yellowstone National Park, 3, 7, 36, 109, 145
YMCA. *See* Young Men's Christian Association
Yosemite National Park, 3, 10, 21
Young Men's Christian Association (YMCA), 70, 94, 95, 107; blacks and, 96, 101, 102
Young People's Labor Club, 130
Young Peoples Socialist League (YIPSEL), 130
Young Women's Christian Association (YWCA), blacks and, 96, 101
YWCA. *See* Young Women's Christian Association, blacks and

Zionism, 72, 83
Zionist camps, 77
*Zoo Parade*, 148
Zorbaugh, Harvey Warren, 84